The Man With The Key Has Gone!

Dr Ian Clarke

New Wine Press

New Wine Press
PO Box 17
Chichester
West Sussex PO20 6YB
England

ISBN: 1 874367 23 X

Typeset by CRB (Drayton) Typesetting Services, Norwich
Printed in England by Clays Ltd, St Ives plc.

Acknowledgements

This book has come about as the result of our experiences in Uganda since 1987. It has been our privilege to work in that country which has become our second home. Uganda has gone through some trying times in the past, but as the infrastructures are being rebuilt and the country now has good leadership, the future looks brighter than it has been for many years.

The richest resource which Uganda has is its own people. It has been our privilege to work among them and get to know them. The story in this book would not have been possible without many dedicated people, some of whom literally laid down their lives for the hospital. All of them have made a deep impression on me.

Mere words are inadequate to express my gratitude to all the friends who have worked with me over the years, but more than that, they have loved me and accepted me, warts and all. I am proud that even though I am Irish, I have a very special Ugandan family. I hope this story pays tribute in some small way to the community at Kiwoko hospital whom God has used to bring hope to so many. May you always be a bright shining light in Uganda.

I would also like to pay tribute to the many people outside Uganda who have supported the hospital over the years through their prayers, love and finances.

I want to thank Leslie Stewart who spent many hours typing up the manuscript and my wife Robbie who has carried out the proof reading.

Our grateful thanks go to Michael Timmis, Cornerstone Developments, Uganda for the cover photograph.

Finally I would like to thank my children, Sean, Michael and Lauren who have moved half way across the world, changed schools and homes numerous times, usually not knowing what the future held for them, and still shown amazing flexibility and good humour in all these situations.

Note: Some names have been changed for the protection of patients and their families.

To
Robbie, my wife
and my best friend

Contents

Foreword

When Roy was having chemotherapy we allowed a TV crew to film what he was going through. The very day the programme was screened Ian was just starting chemotherapy himself and watched it on television from his hospital bed. Roy's experience was one of the things which helped to carry Ian through a very difficult period. We subsequently did a book review together and it was shortly after that Roy's cancer recurred. Over the past year Roy and I have had to live with the possibility of death, placing our lives in God's hands and taking each day at a time. During this time we have discovered the reality of our faith to carry us through. When Roy died we did not regard it as an awful event which we could not face, because we had a faith which did not just encompass life here, but also death and with it the resurrection.

Ian and his family have lived in Uganda over the past six years in the aftermath of civil war and in the epicentre of the AIDS epidemic. For them death has also been a daily reality in a way with which we are not familiar in this country. Finally Ian himself had to face death, as he was diagnosed with advanced cancer. This book is not a book about death, it is bursting with life, but it is written with the consciousness that life is in the midst of death and though we cannot explain every aspect of suffering and death we can look death in the eye and work out our faith in meeting the needs of those who suffer.

The book is not just another 'missionary story'. The Clarkes were involved in a situation where they were dealing on a daily basis with poverty, deprivation and sickness. In the midst of this one can see the hope and faith which carried them through. The Irish sense of humour in dealing with the frustrations of life while taking a wry perspective on Ian's own short-comings also comes through. You will find yourself alternately laughing and crying at many of the situations.

In the security of our western developed civilisation it is easy to assume that life will go on in the routine to which we have become accustomed and in which we find security. For some of us that assumption is rudely shattered by sickness or the death of a loved one. As Roy and I have gone through the last two years we have savoured the richness and fullness of life. When you read the stories of the people in Uganda who are dealing with AIDS as a part of life, you will find a richness and intensity of life and relationships which we can easily miss because we make too many assumptions. You will find this a book which you cannot put down but I hope that your heart will also be touched.

Fiona Castle

Chapter 1

'God, Is This It?'

I struggled to keep control of my emotions as I stood on the roof of that derelict house. I was thousands of miles from home, in the heart of the Ugandan bush, surveying the devastation of a war which was barely over and feeling that my destiny was deeply linked with this place.

Little did I know then, just how deeply. If I had been able to gaze over the vista of the next six years of my life as I gazed over the Ugandan bush, I would have been crushed. If I had been able to see the dimensions of human suffering, disease and death which we would face in the future, if I had known that sickness and death would touch our dearest friends and that finally I would not be immune myself, I would have wanted to turn back there and then. However that day I was spared the knowledge of what lay ahead and my thoughts were preoccupied with the question – 'God, is this it? Is this the place to which we should come?'

The place was the middle of the Luweero triangle or the so-called killing fields of Africa, where thousands of ordinary people had died in the preceding four years. I had driven into the area and had witnessed hundreds of skulls and bones piled by the sides of the road – evidence of what had really happened as, until the war was over in 1986, not even the people in Kampala had known what was going on. Official estimates were that 250,000 people died in what was often senseless slaughter as the Government troops tried to wipe out the insurgents and the rebels retaliated in kind.

The carnage had just ceased the previous year when Government troops had started fighting among themselves and Yoweri Museveni with his fledgling army of 2,000, including many 'boy' soldiers, marched into Kampala and took control.

I wanted to pinch myself to see if I was awake; perhaps this was all a bad dream and it wasn't actually happening. I would wake up and find myself back in Northern Ireland, back in the real world of normality, where every day I dropped the kids at school, did my day job as a doctor and had dinner in the evening with my family. Surely all this evidence of killing and destruction couldn't be part of the real world.

Being there, in the Luweero triangle was, in fact, the culmination of a process which had begun several years before. My wife Robbie and I had been faithful church members, our life was full of work, family and church activities, but there was a growing dissatisfaction with our lifestyle. We didn't seem to touch anyone or make an impact outside of our own circle of friends. I was working very hard, but it all appeared to be only for the benefit of myself and my own family.

We asked ourselves where we were going in life. We were committed Christians and wanted to serve God meaningfully but how were our lives different from any-one around us? Many years ago as students we had felt we should go abroad as missionaries, but now we had three children, we were committed to career, lifestyle and schools in Northern Ireland and the opportunity seemed to have passed us by.

Then one evening we spent hours talking to friends who had just returned from Africa, and over the next few days and weeks the conviction grew that someday our family would be there.

During the next year we found out about different African countries. We were interested in Zambia but nothing opened up there. Mozambique was in a state of ferment and the reports from Uganda were not encouraging either. Ideally I wanted some place where my medical skills would be needed, but which would also provide a safe stable environment for the family.

Uganda definitely wasn't first on our list of preferences. There were lots of places to choose from which were far more stable and suitable for missionary activity. Maybe now with hindsight it does seem a bit strange that someone born in Northern Ireland with its history of civil unrest and terrorist activity should worry about political stability, but from my middle class lifestyle in Ulster, Uganda didn't seem to be a haven of peace and tranquillity even for a Northern Irish man.

At first Uganda was one African country we didn't really want to go to. However more and more information was reaching us about Uganda and we were becoming drawn to the country despite our reservations. Thus when Dr John Kelly, the pastor of our church announced that he would be visiting Uganda with a group of church leaders led by Barney Coombs, I decided to tag along. At least I would have the opportunity to see the place for myself and make my own assessment.

Now here I was in the heart of the most notorious area in Uganda, surveying the landscape from the top of a derelict farmhouse. Not one house in the area had been left unscathed. The place we were visiting had, at one time, been a grand two storey farmhouse, headquarters of a ranch with 2,000 head of cattle. In its former glory, it had a bathroom, running water and electricity. It was now a barren concrete shell and not a single cow was left on the ranch. The old grandmother of the family was living in a room downstairs, with the gaping holes in the walls barricaded by iron sheets. The rats had arrived in force and could be seen crawling everywhere. As I stood mesmerised by the scene, the smooth talking Ugandan businessman, a member of the clan from that area who had brought me to the place, was apparently making some kind of offer – my family and I could live in the upstairs floor of this house, if we did the minor repairs necessary to make it habitable. Minor repairs! – it would be easier to take a bulldozer to it and start again. Not one door, one window, one piece of plumbing or electrics remained. The concrete roof leaked like a sieve. If someone didn't do major repairs soon, the house would fall down – and yet I was seriously considering this character's offer.

I decided to take stock of my situation again.

I was a (not yet) middle aged, but definitely middle class General Practitioner from Northern Ireland suburbia.

I had flown half way around the world to get to a country which wasn't exactly rated highly in the tourist brochure.

I had rattled and bumped over terrible roads in a Suzuki jeep designed for midgets, but which gave ordinary people concussion as heads ricocheted off the roof every time it hit a bump.

I had finally reached the destination, remote even by Ugandan standards, where virtually everything had been destroyed in the recent war. I was now viewing a piece of real estate which currently housed rats, goats and one old lady, the kind of property estate agents would have described as 'has potential, needs some repair, quiet outlook'.

Was I seriously considering bringing my family here?

Ten days previously I had arrived in Uganda for a two week trip not really knowing what I was going to do, but having the feeling I would find out as I went along. I had taken the local transport to see the sights. These were vehicles called matatus – various shapes and sizes of mini-buses which appeared to have elastic sides and could cope with at least 30% more people than they were ever designed for.

Kampala was a seething mass of people and a completely disorderly mass of traffic. In the words of the Old Testament, 'every man did that which was right in his own eyes', or at least in this case, every driver. For example, I had personally witnessed three ways to get round a round-about, depending on how busy it was or if there was a traffic jam. You could go the right way round it – left, the wrong way round it – right, or straight across!

Kampala had a buzz, the people were irrepressible. Even though they had gone through so much, their spirits seemed to be undaunted.

During the previous regime it was unsafe to travel at night, but under Museveni's rule, freedom had returned to the streets. Night time markets had sprung up and people were seen to be moving freely all around Kampala. Gun-fire was still commonplace at night, but that didn't stop the night life.

However, I felt it was a bit too close for comfort when it was directed at the car I was travelling in. One evening we had been invited to dine with the Bishop of Namirembe; so after a delightful and very satisfying meal we were making our way down Namirembe hill. We had become used to hearing sporadic gunfire in the distance – 'guards letting off a few shots to scare off thieves,' we were told, but we had not yet experienced it at close quarters. Sud-denly a volley of shots was released in the vicinity of our car. We didn't see anyone in the darkness, so I put my foot down and we sped on, ploughing over the potholes and bad roads at great speed. As we all slunk down in our seats and raced to escape, Una, the wife of Irish doctor, Donald Brownlee, quickly rolled up her window, presumably to keep the bullets out – well, perhaps none of us were thinking quite rationally then!

Within a few days I had found a Ugandan Doctor, Stephen Watiti, who took me under his wing so that I could experience hospital life in Kampala. The reality was grim, at least for someone who was used to modern west-ern medicine with its emphasis on sterility, clean white sheets, the most modern treatments and equipment, and a huge Health Service budget. Getting through the out-patients waiting area was like pushing through a football crowd at a Liverpool match on a Saturday afternoon –

hoards of people all waiting hopefully. I saw diseases I had never even heard of before, treated with the most basic of resources. Stephen would spend almost as long trying to get into the resterilised, badly stuck rubber gloves as he would doing the minor surgical procedures. They weren't designed to be resterilised, but here they had to make the best use of their limited supplies. Sometimes the smells were overpowering – the combinations of overcrowding, poor ventilation and every sort of body smell. Everything seemed bigger, more advanced and more virulent as far as medicine was concerned – the abscesses were bigger, the pneumonias were more severe. As a GP I was used to dealing with more minor complaints. Suddenly the medical conditions I was seeing were fulminant and there weren't enough doctors to deal with them. Maybe it was because of this, maybe it was something in the people's faces, but I felt as if they were saying 'You're a doctor – come and help us'.

I spent a week working with Stephen in the hospital in Kampala. Everything was strange, the very numbers of people waiting to be seen was 'mind boggling' for me, people blocking the corridors waiting patiently, people in beds pushed into every nook and cranny. The wards dealt with every conceivable illness or injury. The patients were put wherever there was space, the only strict division being between male and female.

I watched with admiration as Stephen diagnosed and treated his patients. There was tremendous pressure to get through the work, yet he had time to be compassionate, to reach out to the patient, to have a word of encouragement or even a joke. Some of the old men could not pass urine and were in incredible pain from a bladder distended two or three times its normal size. If the normal passage was completely blocked Stephen used a piece of drip tubing introduced directly into the bladder to the immense relief of the patients. People with TB, diabetes, AIDS, cancer, pneumonia, peritonitis, hernias, gun-shot injury, typhoid, malaria, gastro-enteritis, all appeared in the out-patients department or were admitted to a ward.

By the end of the week I knew I was needed in Uganda as a doctor, but I still wasn't sure where. Then came the offer to visit the Luweero triangle.

As I stood that day in Luweero I questioned if this was the place where I should come and put to use my medical skills. I had felt a cry in my heart for months now, 'Lord let my life be useful to people, let me serve where people will really need me.' Now I was in a place where there could be no doubt this was the case. There were no missionaries in the Luweero triangle. The country had a general shortage of doctors, and of those Ugandan doctors who were available none wanted to come to such a barren place. It was no coincidence that I had ended up here.

However the country frightened me. I didn't know if I could cope, I didn't know if Robbie and the children could cope. What was I going to say to them when I got back? Should I tell them how bad some of it was or should I paint a rosy and more positive picture? Anyway how would we find sponsorship to be missionaries in Uganda? Would we just roll up to a Missionary Society and say 'Excuse me, but we would like you to send us to Uganda; in fact we have picked out the exact spot that we would like to go to. It is a place called the Luweero Triangle where a programme of genocide has just finished. No, we don't have any previous missionary experience, but I have a strong feeling that we should go there anyway.'

I could just imagine the blank looks I would get from any Mission Board. Apart from that we weren't even in any 'mainstream' denomination which had an established Missionary Society which we could go to.

At the end of the trip when my wife Robbie met me at the airport I was a bundle of mixed emotions. She was eager to know my impressions of Uganda.

How could I explain it? I was emotionally drained. I had seen the dead and dying. I had seen devastation and destruction, I had seen hopelessness, but I had also sensed that these people were not altogether hopeless. They were trying against all the odds to rebuild their lives and rebuild

14

their country. I wanted to run away, to get home to security and stability. Yet I was drawn back. Part of me wanted to turn my back on the unpleasantness. I wanted to be insulated again in my familiar and comfortable environment, where the hungry and poor could only stare out at me from the confines of the television screen. I feared to live among them, to touch them, to smell them, to be affected by their physical presence. But I knew that if I were to run away my life would be an empty shell.

The emotion all flooded out when I was safe at home again. I held my wife in my arms and wept. I wept for the poor and sick that I had seen. I wept for those who had seen their husbands, wives and children slaughtered. I wept for those who looked at me to see if I would offer them some hope.

'We are definitely going back,' I said.

Chapter 2

Preparing

As I tried to settle back into life in Northern Ireland, Uganda seemed a distant place, which became even more distant each time I sat down and thought of the obstacles which had to be overcome if we were to return.

Firstly, there was our children's education. Our oldest boy was approaching Secondary School age, which was not a good time to pull him out of the system. The children had always been able to attend good local schools, and we had no idea of what educational facilities were available in Africa and what might lie ahead for them. We were not sure what we might be exposing our children to, in terms of education.

Secondly, there was my partnership in the medical practice. This was not a big problem in itself. I could simply give notice and resign, but I had never been in the position of not having a secure income before and I was fearful of the unknown.

Thirdly, there was my involvement in business which was an added complication. About 10 years earlier I had started a retail business. While I could resign from the practice, I could not resign from the business. It would have to be sold or I would have to find someone else to run it on my behalf.

Fourthly, there was the question of our financial support abroad. Who would sponsor us to go? We would need money for living expenses, travel etc. Without financial support we could go nowhere.

There certainly were plenty of good reasons why I couldn't go back to Uganda and drag my family along with me, but as I tried to settle back into the work again, my heart was not in it and so much of what I was doing now seemed irrelevant.

Robbie and I talked late into the night. We had ideas of how the business would finance us. We could go for a relatively short time and still keep tabs on things at home. Robbie wasn't very enthusiastic about the idea of 'home schooling' but if no schools existed she would try it; after all she was a teacher. However she would have preferred not to teach her own children and to stick to the role of being 'mother' only.

We kept coming back to finances and sponsorship. Without proper financial backing we couldn't go. Without either selling the business or having it on some sort of sound management footing, we could not go. We realised how much we were limited by pure financial necessity. It was alright to have ideas of 'saving the world', but who was going to pay for it?

Then one night it hit me. If I was a real Christian why was I not trusting in God to provide the means to do what we believed He was calling us to? I was obviously trying to work things out myself. Where did faith come into all this? Did I believe that God was big enough to take care of our needs? Was the answer to our financial problems staring me in the face – were we to take a step of faith and trust God to meet the needs? The question was, could God be trusted? Or put the other way round were we prepared to trust Him in this very practical area of our lives?

As I pondered the issue, revelation dawned and faith began to strengthen my resolve. I should let go trying to control everything myself and allow God to work things out. It was a tremendous release to me. I didn't know how things would be worked out but I knew I was to stop worrying about it and stop trying to make things happen myself. I had been used to providing for my own family and to trust someone else to do it for me, even if it was

God, made me feel peculiarly vulnerable. I was used to giving, not receiving and I didn't know how this new role was going to suit me. Yet I also knew that I suddenly had a lightness of spirit about the financial issue.

I didn't have to wait long to see things happen. The next day I bumped into my brother Ken. Ken opened the conversation by enquiring how things had been on the trip to Uganda. I told him of my experiences and how they had affected me, that now we were making definite plans to go there as missionaries.

'What will you do with the business?' he enquired.

I started to explain to him my thoughts on how we could put in a Manager because I anticipated a buyer would be hard to find. 'After all,' I said, 'who would want to buy a business in Belfast, especially in "bomb alley"?' as the street where the business was located was sometimes called, because of the number of IRA bombs which had been planted on that street.

'I would,' he replied.

There was no hassle, no trouble, everything was very straightforward. This was the problem I had thought would be most difficult to solve and it had been solved in a sentence. It seemed supernatural confirmation of our plans to go to Africa.

The next problem was our own support. Would we be able to find an organisation to sponsor us to go to Uganda? Our church was supportive but they didn't have sufficient finances to send a family to Africa. We would need to look around elsewhere.

While in Uganda I had met some missionaries who worked with the Church Missionary Society. This was an Anglican mission which had a long and honourable tradition of missionary activity in Uganda. It was through CMS that the church of Uganda had come into being over 100 years ago, and one of their early pioneers, Sir Albert Cook, founded the first mission hospital in Kampala – Mengo Hospital on Namirembe Hill. Why not try CMS? I hesitated, mainly because I was not from an Anglican background. I had hailed from staunch Presbyterian roots, but had later defected to a non-denominational Church which was associated with the Fellowship Church movement. Some of the more traditional members of the Anglican church viewed such movements as interlopers and I wasn't sure what kind of reception we would receive at CMS.

So very tentatively I phoned up their office in Belfast. I spoke to the Irish General Secretary, the Rev Cecil Wilson. As I explained that I had visited Uganda and wished to go back to work in the Luweero triangle, he said,

'In that case, you had better come in for an interview.'

When I put the phone down I thought, 'he doesn't sound too bad, he sounds like the sort of guy I could talk to.'

As I understood it, missionary societies liked to select their own candidates and then send them to the destination they chose for them. I had not heard of missionaries selecting their own destination, and then asking the Society to send them there, which was precisely what I was doing. If there was a system or a stereotype for CMS, it looked as if we were not going to fit into it. However it would do no harm to talk to them.

My initial interview was encouraging. They were very open minded and were prepared to take non-Anglican applicants. Not only so, they were actively involved in work in Uganda, and were prepared to consider sending me to the Luweero triangle. However, the process for selection was not in the hands of the staff. We would have to go forward to a Selection Committee, which was not due to meet until September. This all seemed very encouraging, if somewhat indefinite. I had now sold the business, and there was a realistic hope that CMS would sponsor us, despite the fact that we didn't fit into the usual Anglican mould, and were asking them to send us to the destination of our choice.

In the meantime while we awaited the Selection Committee meeting, I wondered if there was anything we could do to prepare ourselves for life in Uganda. Robbie made enquiries about courses which she could use for 'home school' and I made enquiries about courses in Tropical Medicine. The possibilities for a tropical medicine course narrowed down to one in Liverpool for three months, starting in September. However I would have to enrol before we had the Selection Board or miss it. So it was a question of another step of faith or else playing it safe and waiting until we were sure that someone would sponsor us. I decided to press on and enrol but I asked myself if this was faith ... was this faith that God was leading us in the right direction and that things would work out, or was this simple foolhardiness?

In September we set out for Liverpool laden down with, if not all our worldly possessions, a considerable number of them – pots and pans, bedding, bicycles, books, even our TV – all got packed into or onto the car. There was barely enough room for Sean, Michael and Lauren to squeeze in on top of the huge pile of blankets, duvets etc on the back seat. There was just enough room, as an afterthought, to store Michael's skateboard below the seat.

We had made contact with a Church of England Vicar in Liverpool, who had arranged for us to stay in a little cottage on the outskirts of Liverpool. I had visions of a little cottage with roses round the door in a rural English village. The reality was somewhat different from my idealised perception.

The cottage was a former stables which had now been converted into a garage and spray shop for car body repairs, with the residential accommodation tucked in above and beside. That was where we were to stay. The edge of Liverpool was the edge of Toxteth in the inner city, an area of Liverpool which was infamous for its riots some years ago, and now looked like a post-war bombed out city because of the great tracks of land cleared for redevelopment. The people of the area were uncommunicative. This was a great shock to us coming from

Ireland where two strangers could always find an inconsequential topic to open a conversation, usually revolving around the weather. The people of Toxteth just seemed to want to hurry about their business, keep themselves to themselves and not speak to anyone. If our children picked up a magazine in a shop, they would immediately be evicted by the owner, as he was accustomed to child thieves. However, this behaviour of shop owners came as a great shock to the kids who were used to browsing about their local corner shop in Northern Ireland without being summarily ejected.

The downstairs room of the cottage smelt so strongly of damp and decay that the carpet had to be disposed of and replaced by linoleum. This proved to be a good move as it enabled me to easily find and remove the social gathering of slugs and snails which congregated each morning in the kitchen. The upstairs rooms were habitable – that is until the car spraying began next door. Then they had to be evacuated or one would get high on the fumes. These rooms were definitely out of bounds to the children while car spraying was going on as we didn't want them to become glue sniffers.

Through these experiences I had begun to learn something about myself. I was an optimist. I also began to learn something about my wife. She was a pessimist, or at least she regularly felt compelled to balance my optimism.

I said, 'It's not too bad.'

She said, 'It's worse.'

I suppose it's all relative to what you are comparing it to. Unfortunately we had just left a spacious five-bedroomed, two-bathroomed home overlooking the ocean. We were now in a cramped foul-smelling, one time stables overlooking a brick wall.

We had hoped to find a suitable school for the children in Liverpool but none was suitable for a short period in the area we were living, so Robbie had to start home school. My heart went out to her. To be confined in a small damp room trying to teach three children below the age of 11, looking out on a brick wall day in and day out, was soul destroying. The only ray of hope in the situation was that it wasn't going to last too long. However this was preparation for things to come.

As the edge of Toxteth was not far from the University I was able to cycle to lectures. However I discovered that the streets of Toxteth were often strewn with broken glass to which my bicycle tyres were not very resistant. When the taxi driver began to think that my punctured bicycle and I were a regular fare, I decided it was time to give up, in fact I didn't seem to have the talent for mending punctures. My repairs constantly went flat and it seemed that the only thing which blew quicker than my puncture repairs was my temper! I didn't realise it then, but punctures were something which I was to continue to struggle with in Uganda. Perhaps there was some lesson which I wasn't learning.

Half way through the course, the school of Tropical Medicine decided it would be a good experience for the students to visit a centre of alternative technology. So we set out one Sunday for a location in the heart of Wales. However we discovered, on arrival, that the main interest of this centre was in composting. Now composting is probably something most people have not given much thought to. It concerns re-cycling waste. You save it, mix it and eventually use it to grow vegetables. Actually when I reached the Third World, I discovered that the problem was not one of saving it, rather one of teaching people to dispose of it properly!

After this informative if somewhat irrelevant trip to Wales we returned to find that our house had been burgled. My camera was gone, along with some pieces of Robbie's jewellery, nothing valuable but a few things of real sentimental value. Again we were to discover that this seemed to be something of a preparation for life in Africa where burglary was commonplace, especially in the big cities. However, in this case we were told the thieves were probably drug addicts who would steal anything to support their habit. In Africa the thieves were often poor people who were stealing as a way of life to support their families.

Three weeks after I had begun the course we travelled back to Ireland for our CMS Selection Board. They had now decided we would meet the committee over a weekend. The process consisted of a series of interviews, together and separately. Robbie and I checked, did our stories match? Would we tell them the same thing? It was certainly a good way to check if a husband and wife were united. At least Robbie and I were sure that we both had a sense of calling to Uganda. I knew that if Robbie and I had not been united in this, at the outset, we could never have started the process.

The questions ranged far and wide and by the end of the day we were both exhausted and apprehensive. No one was giving anything away in the course of the day. We had no indication if we would be accepted or not. Finally we were called in for the result.

It was the unanimous decision of the committee that we were suitable candidates for CMS. We were being sent to Luweero in Uganda. We breathed a sigh of relief and allowed ourselves to relax.

The subject of our non-Anglican background had come up during the weekend. The next day when we all attended communion together at the local Parish Church, one of the committee members, knowing I was rather green on the format and liturgy of the service, leaned over and whispered, 'Did you not take your shoes off as you came in?'

Possibly this was 'holy ground' but I knew that although I might get mixed up in when to stand up, sit down or kneel in different parts of the service, I could still keep my shoes on.

Before the weekend concluded Rev Declan Smith, the overseas secretary for CMS produced a cheque for the fees for the Tropical Medicine Course. These had been paid by APSO – Agency for Personal Service Overseas – an Irish Government Agency. We were truly seeing God take care of our needs in ways we had not expected. In fact APSO co-funded us with CMS for the rest of our stay in Africa.

The course in Liverpool prepared me medically for life in Uganda and the living conditions prepared Robbie, at least to some extent, for what was to come.

Chapter 3

Arrival

The culture shock on reaching Kampala wasn't so great. I had already visited Uganda and Robbie found Kampala quite pleasant, after having lived in Toxteth Park in Liverpool. Kampala still had some of the amenities and services of a big city, even if they often were broken down and erratic. There were office buildings and hotels, there was electricity – on and off – there was running water in certain parts of the city, there were telephones which sometimes worked. All the services were unreliable, but Kampala still had that 'big city' feel to it. There were still lots of things about it that someone from a western culture could identify with. This could not be said of rural Uganda where we were about to make our home.

Our first trip to Luweero was memorable. We set out in a car borrowed from CMS. Since the Clarkes do not travel light the car was again loaded up with all our worldly possessions. Half way to Luweero we got a flat tyre. We unpacked our things at the side of the road and found the spare wheel but no wheel brace. As Robbie prayed fervently, I tried to flag down the few passing cars on that stretch of the road. The first one didn't stop, the next one did. It was a dilapidated taxi and it didn't have a wheel brace either. Another one stopped, his wheel brace didn't fit. Robbie's prayers became even more fervent.

It was getting towards evening and she didn't like camping, especially with no tent! Finally we found a motorist whose wheel brace fitted. The wheel was changed and we were finally on our way. Oddly enough a few days later when we were going through the car, now empty, we found the wheel brace under the driver's seat! We'd just learned our first lesson about travelling in Africa – find out where the wheel brace is before you leave – it can save a lot of hassle.

As the broken tarmac road changed to a dirt road and the dirt road became a dirt track, my family wondered where I was bringing them. The elephant grass got higher and overhung the road. The view was of fifteen foot elephant grass, banana trees and mud huts. Eventually as twilight approached we reached our destination.

The two storey house still looked fairly derelict but I knew that doors and windows had been fitted, the roof no longer leaked and a toilet had been installed. Not bad I thought, really quite habitable. This was where my optimism was again contrary to Robbie's realism. As I looked at her face, I could see clearly the question, 'What have you brought us to, Ian?'

I saw the repairs which had been done since I last visited. Robbie saw the rats peering at us through the ventilator shafts. It was true that the colony of rats didn't seem to have moved out yet, but they would go in time. I saw a toilet had been installed; she saw there was no water. I saw the roof didn't leak; she saw that the rain came straight in through the windows, which didn't yet have any glass.

The place hadn't been painted yet and I did have to admit that it was a bit rough, but this is often where a husband's and wife's position differs in moving house. I saw there were some problems which would have to be overcome. Robbie's opinion of her new home could be summed up in one word – '*awful*'!

Our first few months in our new house seemed to involve an on-going battle with the previous residents of the house – that is the rats! I suppose they were not happy about us invading their territory. They may have made a

26

tactical retreat but they were only regrouping to advance at opportune moments. Although I had been brought up on a farm where rats in the outhouses were not uncommon, I was definitely not comfortable with them living in our home. This attitude was in stark contrast to that of most Ugandans in the village who became used to rats as a routine part of life. Rats are very clever, well adapted little creatures, who can quietly chew the thick skin of the underside of a sleeper's foot, without even waking him up.

A few nights after we arrived Sean crept into our bedroom.

'Dad, there's a rat in our bedroom.'

I went to investigate and found a large rat running up and down the bunk-bed rails. There followed an uncomfortable night when mum and dad moved over and all three children moved into mum and dad's bed. They slept well while their parents spent the night clinging tenaciously to the edge of the bed.

Then there was the rat who liked swimming and spent the whole night splashing around in the toilet! Or the rat who hid in the roller blind to make a surprise appearance when it was unrolled!

One day Robbie was cooking; she was finishing a batch of home made cakes in the oven and the delicious smell of fresh baking was emanating from the kitchen when she said to me: 'Ian, why do you think the cooker is making funny scratchy noises?'

When I went to investigate I had no sooner tilted the cooker on its side when a rat came bouncing out. It had made its home in the lining of the cooker, but had become rather uncomfortable when the oven was switched on. This rat was taking seriously the proverb – 'if you can't stand the heat, get out of the kitchen' – or in this case the cooker!

We then discovered that the kitchen was about the worst place to corner a rat. It had too many hiding places, from the cooker to under the fridge, back to the cupboard, up over the sink, back to the fridge etc. In the confined space with brush-handles, staves and mops flying, we were more in danger of doing ourselves an injury than the rat.

'There it goes – *wham*, *bam* – missed – now it's gone behind the cupboard, move the cupboards out from the wall.'

'There it is – thump, whack – sorry did I hit you with my stick?'

The rat still enjoys its freedom, now it's under the fridge.

'Just a minute, I will poke it out. There must be an easier way than this. Here it comes – this rat is so fast – there it goes, on top of the cupboard. It's coming, I've got it!'

A heavy boot on the tail and the poor creature is pinned down and finished off by a cudgel.

The Ugandans just stare at us in consternation.

'All that fuss over one little rat, surely they don't do anybody any harm?'

As we settled into the house the first thing to do was to make ourselves some furniture. There were various bits and pieces of wood around and some self-assembly furniture had been sent over from Northern Ireland, so for a few days there was hammering and banging about the house as we tried to establish some order. Our furniture was of the variety that could be described as inexpensive but robust. A large packing case became a dressing table. A wardrobe had been made locally, but we discovered it was too narrow to hang our clothes in. The size of the wardrobe was obviously dependent on the width of the pieces of wood to hand, more than the width of a clothes hanger. Bunk-beds were assembled from an assortment of odds and ends.

The local people were somewhat concerned with this carpentry activity. They had been told they were getting a doctor but it appeared they had been sent a carpenter instead. The Ugandans didn't understand why the doctor would be hammering in nails. Another thing which concerned them was that I was seen on occasion to be washing dishes. That was what house girls and wives were for –

'What was the doctor doing washing dishes?' The Elder of the community tactfully suggested that when I was washing dishes I should pull the curtains as it was rather embarrassing for them all to witness me performing this menial act.

Despite the initial reservations of the local people about my true profession, patients began to arrive in greater and greater numbers. Every few moments a message would come, 'The doctor is needed downstairs.'

Many of the patients didn't have a lot wrong with them but, they wanted to get a look at the new doctor. I was finding the interruptions to my serious carpentry activities rather frustrating. So we decided we had better arrange a formal clinic where I could see everyone together.

'Tell everyone to come tomorrow afternoon,' I explained and 'I will see everyone then.'

By 2.00 pm a large crowd had assembled outside our house. I had some medicines with me and I had my doctor's bag with all the usual instruments. Robbie was delegated to give out the pills that I would prescribe and the local chief was to act as translator. What more could one ask for in a health team? A doctor, a teacher acting as a pharmacist and a village chief as a nurse complete with wellington boots!

The clinic was held under a tree and the people lined up in an orderly fashion. All went well until the skies darkened and large drops of rain began to fall. The venue was then abruptly moved to the bottom floor of the house (which was still in a derelict state) and continued with hardly a pause.

When I thought I had reached the end, my translator presented himself for my attention.

'I too am sick', he said, and listed his complaints.

I was learning that people thought that if a doctor was available one had better have one's symptoms or potential symptoms ready for the occasion, as the opportunity to see a doctor did not present itself every day. After all prevention is better than cure.

We had just done our first clinic in the bush in true missionary style, under a tree, but it was obvious that some more permanent arrangement would have to be made.

At the beginning of our stay in the bush we were joined by some people – Paul and Jodene Kessels who helped to fix up our house, and later, for a few months, by Elizabeth, a nurse from YWAM who helped with the medical work.

As I was putting furniture together and treating patients, Robbie was trying to get 'home school' organised for the kids. This was not an easy task because the children regarded school as an unwelcome interruption to the exciting adventure of living in Africa.

The routine of school was rudely interrupted one morning by cries of 'Snake, snake!'

A black mamba had been found in a pit latrine and all the local boys rushed with long sticks to kill it. Being from North Dakota and being familiar with hunting, Paul decided to teach Sean and Michael how to skin snakes, so life in the classroom hardly seemed as exciting as life in the bush with opportunities for skinning black mambas! Actually the procedure for skinning a snake is a rather messy, time-consuming activity. The skin is split and the fleshy parts of the snake removed. The skin is then stretched on a board to dry and all the remaining fleshy bits adhering to the skin can be removed with a blunt edge.

Sean had been engaged in this procedure on the front verandah of the house. Unfortunately he had chosen his location outside the room of Elizabeth, our nurse. Elizabeth had been having rather a trying time. She had a very small cramped room which opened directly onto the verandah and the patients who arrived very early in the morning tended to congregate directly outside her door. At least I was protected a little by living on the first floor. Added to that was the fact that the village livestock also tended to congregate on the verandah. It was not unknown for the collections of pigs, chickens and goats to assemble outside Elizabeth's room leaving their trade mark behind them!

I really felt sorry for Elizabeth. She would step out of her room in the morning to use the pit latrine, shoo away the chickens and fight her way through the patients, meantime being careful where she put her feet. She'd come to Africa prepared to make sacrifices but she hadn't quite imagined this is how it would be.

So when Sean decided to skin his snake outside her door and absentmindedly forgot to remove the fleshy bits, it was hardly surprising that Elizabeth could be heard all around the house loudly demanding that the culprit, who had left the pieces of dead snake at her door, be brought to justice.

Purely by coincidence Sean decided that he needed to stay indoors and concentrate on his school work that day and was seen to keep a low profile for several days afterwards.

Michael, our nine year old middle child, got on particularly well with the local people. They enjoyed his outgoing personality and he enjoyed making new friends. One morning we wondered why a noisy crowd had gathered outside the house. The mystery was solved when we discovered Michael standing on the flat roof distributing clothes to the enthusiastic crowd below. Fortunately the clothes were second-hand clothes which had been earmarked for distribution and not our own personal garments. The clothes had become a bit damp and had been left on the roof to dry. Michael simply decided to take the programme of distribution into his own hands!

'What size are you?' he was yelling down from the roof to the hopefuls below.

'Size 15,' and a size 15 shirt would come fluttering down.

'Michael, I need large trousers,' and trousers would be supplied.

'Michael, give me a dress,' and a dress would waft down.

It wasn't surprising Michael was popular.

Michael discovered a little boy from a hut nearby who wore only a very dirty ragged vest, so he found him a new T shirt and shorts and proudly dressed him in his new clothes. They fitted perfectly and both Michael and the boy were delighted with the result. The next day the boy appeared in his ragged vest again. When the boy's elder sister was questioned as to why her little brother wasn't wearing his new clothes she looked surprised.

Surely everyone knew that good clothes were only supposed to be worn on Sundays!

For the children, life in Luweero was definitely a contrast to life in Northern Ireland. They had already discovered how to kill rats and skin snakes. They now found another little creature that was even harder to deal with. It was the jigger flea. These were little fleas which lived in dust or sawdust. However they were most comfortable when they could burrow into the soft fleshy parts of the toes. They then proceeded to produce eggs and enlarge enormously until they produced a painful and itchy pustule filled with something that looked like pus.

It did not seem to matter if one wore shoes or open sandals. The fleas were able to find a way in. There was a knack of removing them with a pin but if parts were left behind they became infected and painful. The children kept picking up these fleas and many evenings were spent in 'jigger flea surgery'! There was definitely an on-going battle between the missionaries and the jigger fleas with the fleas usually getting the upper hand. The highest score was obtained against Michael. He declared one evening that he had removed a total of 27 jiggers!

As the children battled with the jigger flea, Robbie battled with the dust which seemed to be present everywhere. It was the dry season and clouds of red dust hung in the atmosphere. Brushing the floors resulted in raising small clouds of dust which then settled back on all the surfaces. The cement was unsealed, so repeated brushing or washing didn't deal with the problem. There was little cupboard space and as the children tended to 'hang up' their clothes on the floor, when they had finished with them, there seemed to be a constant pile of washing. Eventually we hit upon the idea of painting the floors. The paint would seal the cement and at least prevent the clothes from being coated in dust if they touched the floor. So one evening I began the task. The next day we were going out so I painted all the floor except a path which was to act as our 'escape route'. As I left I painted in the path behind us and locked the door. When we returned we had beautifully painted floors and we felt our home was beginning to take shape.

This could not be said of the stairway leading up to our flat. At the bottom of the stairs there was an assortment of debris, bits of old iron, pieces of wood etc, an assortment of odds and ends which had been there before we arrived. In the midst of this collection, a hen had started to roost. However as time went on a vile smelly odour began to ascend. Eventually I decided I needed to do something about it. As I dislodged the hen and the contents of the stair well, I discovered the problem. The eggs were rotting. The chicken was most upset when I removed the rotting eggs and continued to cluck around looking for her eggs. I suppose chickens must not have a well developed sense of smell and something had certainly gone wrong with this chicken's biological clock.

Gradually out of the chaos order began to arise and a reasonably comfortable little home was created in the midst of Luweero. We now felt we had a base from which to operate and it was also a place where we could take refuge and be refreshed.

Chapter 4

First Patients

From the day on which we arrived in Luweero patients streamed to our house, so I decided I should try and arrange some regular clinics and train local people as health care workers. There were no other doctors and no hospital in the area. The only building which was suitable for a clinic was the Church at Kiwoko, the Parish Centre about three miles away, it being the only large building which had remained with a roof after the war. During the war Government soldiers had been billeted in the church and, as with the other buildings in the area, they had intended to strip off the corrugated iron sheets and sell them when they left. However, as they left rather hurriedly, being chased away in the end, they had no time to carry out their plan. Indeed according to the locals, misfortune had seemed to dog them when they made an attempt to remove the sheets, the soldier assigned to the task having fallen off the roof and broken his arm.

Kiwoko was literally a 'fork in the road' with a few market stalls. There was evidence of previous development, as the signs for two petrol stations still remained. However apart from the signs there was little else to show of the petrol stations. The forecourts were overgrown with the inevitable elephant grass and somewhere among the grass stood the skeletal remains of the petrol pumps.

Parts of what had once been large buildings stood engulfed again by the dense undergrowth. One of the local people estimated that seven to eight hundred people were killed in Kiwoko itself during the war. The killings were usually through anarchy and ill discipline of Government troops. If a soldier wanted the wife of a villager, the husband could be summarily shot if he did not give way. If rebels were suspected to be in the area and the villagers couldn't lead the soldiers to them, they could be shot as collaborators. A favourite form of torture used by the soldiers was to heat up plastic jerry cans and let the hot plastic drip onto the victims.

Villagers left their homes and fled into the bush, but if they were then caught hiding in the bush by the soldiers, they were automatically treated as rebels and either tortured or killed. The evidence of the killing was still all around us. Parish headquarters, now a building with no roof or windows, had several hundred skulls laid out on the floor. It was a macabre sight. At least we were spared the horrors of the first days after liberation where the sight of putrefying corpses was commonplace. Nakaseke, a town about 15 miles south of Kiwoko, saw some of the worst atrocities. The town had a four storey hotel with a flat roof. The soldiers favoured throwing people off the roof as a means of killing them. Few corpses were buried properly and many were stacked in a corrugated iron store. A colleague of mine visited the place after the war and found it full of stinking corpses. A few hundred shillings, just a few pence, could have meant the difference between life and death. A soldier could stop anyone and demand money. If the person produced money they could pass, if they didn't, the soldier, especially if drunk, could vent his frustration by shooting them.

Fortunately when we arrived there was peace, but there were still a few incidents of retribution killings. One young man returned to his village near Kiwoko after the war to be accused of being a member of the Youth Wingers. The Youth Wingers were a youth group which had collaborated with the previous regime, albeit sometimes through coercion and pressure. A village 'kangaroo court' was set up and the young man was beaten to death. The body was then left unburied, thrown on the road as a warning to anyone else. As I drove past, the sickening sweet smell of decay rose up to meet me and the corpse buzzed with flies.

The people of Kiwoko had been through a lot, but they were now intent on rebuilding their lives. They had no medical care and they wanted a clinic, in fact they had started to make bricks for a dispensary beside the church. So with the help and encouragement of the people there, I decided to establish Kiwoko as the main centre for our medical activity.

In that area the church was the largest community organisation with a surviving infrastructure, and the church people were very keen to be involved in a health programme. Soon I had 15 willing volunteers from surrounding villages with the most enthusiastic being the pastor of the Kiwoko church. My task was to train these local people in the basics of health care so they, in turn, could begin to address the problems of their own communities. They would also help me to carry out medical clinics and vaccination clinics in the area.

Our first clinics at Kiwoko were carried out on the steps of the church. The vestry, a small room which had no door and stank of bats, was my consulting room. The pastor provided a rickety folding chair and small table for me, but the examination couch was a mat on the floor. The patients lined up along the side of the church and if the queue was long enough it stretched right around to meet at the other side. The health workers dispensed the medicines and did the dressings. When we were particularly busy we separated the line into two groups. Those who had straightforward problems, such as worms or backache, were seen and treated by our best health workers, and the rest were seen by me. Often many of the conditions were trivial but the people wanted to see the new doctor, so when the little old ladies with backache were put in the line to see the health worker they would surreptitiously slip across to the other line to see the 'real doctor'. Our health workers didn't receive any pay and worked long hours enthusiastically. As time went on I was to get more help in the form of trained nurses, both expatriot and Ugandan, but these local people formed the backbone of the development of the work at Kiwoko.

Even though there was a national programme of immunization in Uganda the Luweero district had fallen far behind due to the war and many children were not vaccinated. We therefore had a higher incidence of preventable diseases such as measles and tuberculosis. The need to expand the programme of immunization was urgent. We had been provided with a little Suzuki jeep through the Irish Government, so we established a programme of vaccination clinics in the surrounding villages and set out with our team of health workers. Those who could fit into the Suzuki came with us, the rest went on bicycles. It always surprised me how many people could fit into a car in Uganda. The official capacity of the Suzuki was 5 people; however, if we put 3 in the front, 5 in the back and 3 more behind the back seat we could fit 11! I always found it difficult to explain to my Ugandan colleagues the concept of over-loading. It seemed logical to them that if any space remained in the vehicle, even if it was on someone's knee, it was for sitting on. However there are two advantages of carrying a lot of people over potholed bad roads:

Number one was that when one hit the potholes, people were so tightly wedged in, they didn't bang around the car and injure themselves.

The second advantage was that there were many more people to push the car out of the mud when it got stuck!

I discovered the importance of preparation in running an efficient vaccination clinic. How did one get through a clinic of 500 children in a morning? By having all the syringes loaded and prepared, lining the children up in four or five rows and getting the teachers to issue the vaccination cards. Then the trained health workers were free to do 'production line' vaccination! Hold arm, swab, inject, new needle, hold arm, swab, inject. It amazed me

38

how many vaccinations could be carried out with the proper organisation.

Sometimes the pastor arranged to combine his functions as Anglican priest and health worker. He was certainly looking after the 'whole' man, seeing to the spiritual and physical needs of his flock. However he did sometimes omit to tell me what he had organised. At some clinics I was caught 'off guard' when Livingstone whipped out his white surplus from a concealed bag, donned his clerical garb and proceeded to gather the people together for a service. Despite my surprise the young mothers present didn't bat an eyelid, they seemed to take this all as a matter of course. In fact not only did they line up and get their infants baptized and vaccinated, they immediately presented themselves for my attention for a quick check-up. Imagine the money and resources which the National Health Service could save if they combined forces with the Church. Baptisms, vaccinations and health checks could be offered under one roof.

Livingstone's parish was spread 10 miles in one direction and 30 miles in another. He had 25 outlying congregations and we sometimes went with him to preach at one of the churches. On one occasion he had asked us to go with him to a new congregation at the very end of the parish 30 miles north. Unfortunately there was no good road running directly there and we had to detour for several hours to reach the place. When we arrived we found the people still preparing the church. It was made of poles and branches with leaves stretched over it to form a canopy. The ladies had cut fresh grass and were spreading it over the floor to form a carpet. Then they produced spotless cotton cloths to cover the seats for the VIPs, the lectern and the communion table, so that by the time they had completed the task they had made a very comfortable and picturesque little church. After the inevitable baptism of 15 infants and the usual race through the liturgy Livingstone preached. Then I preached and Livingstone interpreted. These people were certainly getting value for money. After the traditional luncheon of matoke – steamed bananas – and stewed meat, the congregation presented my wife with a chicken and Livingstone with a young gazelle.

'Funny,' I thought, 'I did the preaching, she got the chicken,' but perhaps that was a reflection of what the villagers thought of my preaching!

With all the members of the congregation out to wave us 'Good-bye', we were on our way again.

On the return journey we decided to try the direct route. Livingstone conceded that it wasn't a good road, but we did have a four wheel drive vehicle so he felt it would be the quickest route home. By this time we had a capacity load again, with our own family, Livingstone and several members of his family, and some members of the congregation who wanted to travel to Kiwoko. Among them was an enormously fat lady who took up most of the back seat. Livingstone was quite a small man and as I looked around I could see him flattened between the fat lady and the window. I wondered if he would survive the journey or if we would find him slumped in the back, crushed like a rag doll by journey's end. Of course we had to find room for our livestock after that.

None of these animals were house trained and Livingstone's children were not used to travelling in a car. As we bumped along, the cry suddenly went out from the back, 'stop the car, he's going to be sick!'

Too late! As I jammed on the brakes and lunged to open the back door the child let fly all over the inside of the door. I noticed the child wasn't the only one who had made a mess. The chicken obviously wasn't used to vehicular transport.

The road at first was a track but this deteriorated quickly and disappeared altogether. We were then following directions such as – 'turn left at that banana tree, right at the next bush' etc. Somehow Livingstone was seeing a road which I wasn't aware of. At one point we appeared to be in a middle of a swamp.

'Don't worry,' said Livingstone, and led us across an unseen causeway. The short cut proved to be considerably longer than the detour and as we struggled on for hours on end Livingstone remarked, 'the road seems to have deteriorated since I last came.'

'What did you come in?' I asked.

'A bicycle' he admitted.

This wasn't a road we were on at all. It was a meandering bicycle track! No vehicle had ever gone before us.

Darkness had set in before we made it home.

'Please Ian, next time, don't let us take any more short-cuts,' my wife pleaded when we finally arrived home. I had to admit I did think she had a point.

Holding clinics at Kiwoko still didn't deter patients from coming to our home for treatment. One patient who turned up at our house was a boy who had been badly burned. He appeared one morning with horribly infected burns on his arms and knees. He was burning off dry grass and had become surrounded by the flames. I enlisted Sean's help to hold the plastic bag in which I was disposing of the dirty dressings. Sean valiantly stood his ground for a few minutes, then asked weakly, 'Dad, could you get someone else to do this?'

As I looked at the colour of Sean's face, I realised I would soon have two patients if Sean didn't lie down quickly. He staggered into the house, where his face had now become a pale shade of green, and collapsed on the settee.

The verandah didn't afford any opportunity for privacy when treating patients. The private consultation with one's doctor didn't exist. There were often nasty abscesses in embarrassing parts of the anatomy which required drainage. It was a question of doing the best we could, chasing away the spectators while we drained the abscesses or carried out the necessary procedures as privately as the circumstances allowed. Sometimes at clinics I would wonder why I would see a whole batch of patients with the same complaint. As there was little privacy and the patients waiting could listen to the complaints of the preceding patient, it appeared there was something of a domino effect with each patient being affected by the complaint of the previous person.

I couldn't help thinking of my General Practice back home, where every patient had their private consultation with the doctor. The idea of having the patients in the waiting room listen in to the previous person's complaints didn't exactly fit in with the concept of the confidential relationship between doctor and patient.

Although we were tackling some of the basic health needs of the area, as time went on we became increasingly aware that there were many conditions we were not able to deal with due to lack of facilities and basic equipment.

One Sunday morning we heard singing at a distance. The singing became louder and appeared to be accompanied by rattles and bangs. As we gazed out of the window wondering what was going on, an ancient pickup rounded the corner with what seemed to be at least 30 people hanging onto the sides having a party. As the pickup stopped at our front door I went down to enquire what was going on. As I approached, the crowd parted, revealing a young woman lying semi-conscious in the back among sacks of potatoes and bundles of belongings. One look revealed that the girl was near to death. She had been bleeding after childbirth and had obviously lost an enormous quantity of blood. Although I didn't have much medical equipment at the house I had enough to put up a drip. However, she needed an urgent blood transfusion and a curettage, and for that one needed a theatre and a laboratory with facilities to cross match and screen blood.

The driver of the vehicle felt he had now done his duty and was intent on leaving the lady with the doctor so that they could continue with their festivities.

'This lady needs to go to hospital urgently,' I protested.

'But I am not going anywhere near a hospital,' argued the driver 'and anyway I have no petrol.'

After some time and some strenuous negotiations, with

the inducement of free petrol from me, the driver agreed to take the patient on to hospital where she could have a blood transfusion. So the singing crowd set off again this time holding the intravenous fluids bottle as the vital fluids dripped in and kept the patient from going into further shock. I was left with nagging doubts: would they take her to a hospital, and if they reached one would she get the necessary treatment? Some of the Government hospitals were woefully lacking in supplies and facilities and there were no mission hospitals at all in our district. We had given some help to spare the girl's life for the present but would it be enough?

Five days later I returned home to find a lady sitting under the tree. When she saw me she approached and handed me an empty intravenous fluids bottle.

'This isn't the lady whom I last saw almost dead in the back of the pickup,' I gasped. But it was. She had been taken to a hospital and had got a blood transfusion. She had returned to say thank-you and return the empty fluids bottle. Now she was standing in front of me smiling and shaking my hand. I was filled with gratitude. Even though our resources were meagre this woman had survived.

I knew the services we were offering were very limited but for the present it was the best we could do.

Chapter 5

Bush Medicine

It was 7 o'clock on a Saturday morning, definitely the time to turn over and experience the honey-heavy dew of slumber, but Michael was trying to communicate some urgent information.

'Daddy you must come, you're needed downstairs, there are patients there'.

'Tell them to go away. It's only 7 am, this is ridiculous, I want to sleep'.

'But Daddy, a woman is having a baby'.

That brought me round to a sufficient level of consciousness to scramble into my trousers and shirt and bolt downstairs.

Our front porch looked like an Airport Departure Lounge. People were milling around all over the place, coming and going. In my hazy state I wondered what they were doing and then realised that these people were all patients waiting to see me. It is at times like this that a GP is programmed to say:

'This is a private residence. You should all phone up and make an appointment at the proper time.'

Then I realised that I was still in the bush and there were no phones and no appointments. I had better see what I could do. Now what was it Michael had been communicating to me? Something about a lady having a baby. Where was she? I looked around hastily. There she was right at my front door squatting.

'We had better get you inside quickly Mama. You look like you're about to deliver.'

At this precise moment, wandering down the dirt road towards the front of the house, was a young man absolutely covered in blood. The scalp looked as if someone had taken a tin opener to it. But what amazed me was his nonchalant attitude. Then I realised that although it was only 7 am he was completely inebriated and was feeling no pain whatsoever. The unfortunate fellow had been celebrating, happily riding on top of the cab of a truck when he was swept from his perch by an overhanging branch. Though he landed on his head, the alcohol anaesthesia seemed to preserve him from much pain or concern and he staggered happily down the road to present himself at our door for suturing.

The lady in labour delivered successfully to be followed later by another lady in labour who arrived on the back of a bicycle.

Now folks, this is going a bit far. This is not a maternity centre, this is my house. I am not equipped for this!

But surely by this stage I was realising that there was little that I could consider private and I reminded myself that I was the only doctor in the area. So I found a vacant room and looked around for something to spread on the floor. We had no beds or sheets, but we did have something which resembled a sheet. An aid organisation had made a donation of shrouds to the country and we had acquired some of them. It's not that we felt we would have a lot of dead bodies to deal with, although that would come later, but I was always of the opinion that one should refuse nothing. You never know when it might come in useful. I am one of those people who never throws anything out, but hoards it all in the garden shed. However, this was the very occasion to bring our shrouds out. The shroud looked like a sheet and the mother could lie on it and have her baby.

By that evening this patient still hadn't delivered. She was obviously in obstructed labour. As I had no instruments available to me, there was nothing I could do on the

46

spot. So I would have to take the patient the long journey to Kampala. By this stage it was getting late and it was not regarded as safe to travel at night, so my wife volunteered to come along riding as 'shotgun', along with our Ugandan house-girl who would act as translator. We set out. Several miles along the dirt road our patient indicated that she needed to use the toilet. For me as a doctor this meant that she might be feeling like pushing, that is, the baby might be coming. The Suzuki was rather small to deliver the baby, so I got her out by the side of the road. Fortunately I had had the foresight to bring along the shroud. The sheet was spread out and the patient took her place, but examination showed she was still not ready to deliver, so off we set again. A few more miles and there was another stop. Another false alarm! Despite the bumpy road, the lady didn't deliver and we went all the way to a Kampala hospital where she finally had a caesarian section.

As we were returning from Kampala about 1 am, we felt somewhat unsafe driving so late and were speeding along to get home as quickly as possible when we spied a body on the road. Fortunately the body was on the opposite side or we would have run over it. Instinctively I jammed on the brakes and went back to have a look. By this time Robbie was warning me:

'Be careful Ian, this could be a "set-up".'

Although I was unaware of it at the time, it was a fairly common hijack technique, used in some African countries, for thieves to lure a driver to stop by pretending to be injured. I approached the body which looked very dead and shone my torch in his eyes to see if the pupils reacted to light. They were constricted. They should be dilated if he were dead! Then I looked carefully and found the corpse was breathing. I took a deep breath and sniffed; the odour of 'waragi' – the equivalent of Irish poteen, filled the air. The man was dead – dead drunk. At least it was not a set-up. We heaved the body off the road out of danger and set out again. As we took off we looked around to see him stagger to his feet. It was one of those situations where I didn't know if I was being a 'Good Samaritan' or just a foolish 'do-gooder', putting myself and those travelling with me in danger. It would have been safer to drive on. Conversely a truck could have come along after us and run over our drunk friend and I would have been responsible. It made me think a lot about the story of the Good Samaritan in the Bible. I must confess I felt slightly virtuous and self-righteous that I had stopped and done the right thing; that is, until I heard the story of another missionary couple who stopped in a similar situation. This time it was a set-up. The end of that story was that the wife was murdered and the husband was left unconscious. It left me feeling that maybe I wasn't so virtuous after all, maybe I was just somewhat naive and foolish.

By this time we were used to patients gathering around our door early in the mornings. We would be wakened by the general hubbub of voices below our bedroom window. But it wasn't usual for patients to arrive in the middle of the night as people still didn't like to travel at night after the war. However, one night I heard voices outside. It was pitch black and I confess I didn't want to go outside to investigate. Then I heard a conversation going on and realised that Benon, one of the local family members was having a discussion with some strangers. 'He will sort it out, he will call me if I am needed,' I thought, and turned over and went back to sleep.

Early the next morning I was summoned. It had been patients who had come during the night but Benon, trying to protect the doctor, had sent them away. They had returned again at first light. 'My wife is delivering and the baby is stuck' was the message. Hurriedly I grabbed a pair of gloves and set out to find the man's wife. She was about two miles away, lying by the side of the road. She had delivered a breech baby and the head was stuck. Fortunately with the right technique the head was not too difficult to dislodge. However by this stage the baby was dead.

I had mixed feelings about the incident. If I had gone to investigate earlier in the night I might have saved the baby. As it was, the mother was OK, but she had begun delivering a baby in the middle of the night by the side of the road with no help, and it had died. The family were so grateful for my help, but what had I done? I had come too late. I marvelled at these people. They had so little. A few bundles of clothes, a few saucepans, nothing that we would consider of any value. I had let them down because I hadn't got there on time to deliver the baby. Yet they had a graciousness of spirit and a sense of thankfulness which touched my heart and made me feel small.

This was one of the many incidents where I felt I could have done more. Yet on the other hand sometimes I was so frustrated with myself because I was impatient with people who kept coming to my door at all hours of the day.

'Why can't they come at the proper time? Can't they see that sometimes I also need peace and quiet?'

However I realised that I had come to Uganda with the motive of serving people, yet I often found myself being irritable with the very people I had come to serve. I'm sure it had a lot to do with the constant demands. Patients would come to our doors at all hours.

Even though we had started the weekly clinic at Kiwoko, the word had gone out, 'the doctor goes out during the day, so if you want to see him, be there before he leaves, or when he gets back.'

I was not always kind and charitable when I had a crowd of patients on my front doorstep every morning. If I felt they were trivial or non-urgent cases, I would send them away to come to the clinic at Kiwoko at the proper time. However, the thing which I found most difficult, was not being able to distinguish between those demands which were serious and needed my immediate attention, and those which could legitimately wait for a formal clinic.

One morning I was asked to see a patient who was paralysed. At the same time a message came that a mother who had just delivered was bleeding. I had committed myself to visiting the man who was paralysed, so I sent one of the health workers off to see the other lady, with instructions to give her an injection of ergometrine to stop the bleeding. I found my patient to be in a completely non-communicative state. He didn't talk, he didn't eat. When I questioned the relatives I found that the condition had occurred in the past and resolved spontaneously after a week. I could find no objective physical abnormality and had to conclude that his condition was more mental than physical. The other possibility was that he was showing symptoms of cerebral AIDS. Either way there was little I could do to help.

When I returned, the health worker reported that his patient was not bad and the bleeding was controlled. However, either the patient was worse than he reported, or her condition deteriorated subsequently, as the next day word came that the lady had died during the night. 'If only,' I thought, 'if only I had gone to see her instead of the man.' There were so many 'if onlys'. So many times I reflected if only I had taken another course of action, given another form of treatment, if I had seen the person earlier, it could have been different. I usually consoled myself, 'well, I did my best,' but often I had a nagging feeling my best wasn't good enough because I was not a good enough expert in that field or I had very little experience in treating that condition.

It was true I was only a GP turned Bush Doctor. I was not an experienced gynaecologist or surgeon, but the experienced people were not there. I was the one who was on the spot. Sometimes I was filled with a sense of 'What good am I doing here?' So much seemed beyond my control, or even if I could have done something I lacked the facilities to do it.

One morning a neighbour came to ask me to see his wife. They lived less than a mile from my house but his wife had been sick for a week before he called me. Perhaps in this case he didn't want to disturb me, or perhaps he had consulted the witch doctor first and spent all his money. Whatever the reason for the delay, by the time I arrived at their mud hut his wife was unconscious. It appeared that she had meningitis and she had now been unconscious for two days. I decided to start treatment immediately as well as taking her to a hospital in Kampala. Her condition was critical. Two hours later we reached the hospital but we knew it was a futile journey. By this stage her breathing was laboured and it was obvious she was dying. She died within an hour. She had just lived round the corner from me but no one came for me in time and she still died. If I had been called two days earlier she would have lived.

It was partly these feelings of inadequacy and sometimes frustration that made me want to do more for the people. People had heard there was a doctor in the area and they just kept coming. They had faith that we could do something but I, at least, knew my limitations. Sometimes these were limitations of skill and experience but often they were due to the complete lack of facilities. I was prepared to do my best with what was available but how long could I go on delivering babies in our own house, suturing people on the doorstep and flying off to Kampala at all hours with seriously ill patients? There were also issues of ignorance and superstition among the villagers which the community health workers needed to address.

The progress in building the dispensary at Kiwoko was slow and there was little money to complete it. I decided to appeal to my church back home for a few hundred pounds to finish the dispensary. This they gave willingly. The dispensary would provide a room where we could do our clinics, but no facilities for deliveries or inpatient beds. There were so many other needs to be met which would require a larger clinic. At the time we had no idea that within a short period the needs would begin to be met in a most remarkable way, but in a way that would cause us deep pain and much personal sorrow.

Chapter 6

Barbara

We had known John and Barbara since University days. John was a leader of the University Christian Union prayer group which Robbie and I attended. It was this prayer group which was the seed from which our church later developed. John was a highly intense single-minded individual whose dedication to the Lord was a challenge to us all. We used to meet at 6.30 am every morning so that we could pray together before lectures started. At that time the troubles in Northern Ireland were at their height and John was appalled at the apathetic spirit which many Christians displayed towards the current political events. While he was not a political activist he felt that Christians in Northern Ireland needed to unite and pray and call out to God for his healing for the land.

> *'If my people, who are called by my name will humble themselves and pray and seek my face and turn from their wicked ways, then will I hear from heaven and will forgive their sin and will heal their land.'*
>
> (2 Chronicles 7:14)

John was so committed to prayer that he didn't have time for a social calendar, not surprisingly. As well as studying medicine he was spending every free moment attending prayer meetings. However perhaps he did have a small distraction on his mind at that time in the form of a young language student by the name of Barbara, who was also attending these prayer meetings. I always felt that there must have been some surreptitious sign language going on between the two of them during some of the prayers because, relatively quickly, they announced their engagement. The whole getting to know each other and courting process had taken place in 'prayer meetings'!

One of Barbara's interests at University had been the Friendship Society where students from Northern Ireland had the opportunity to get to know and befriend foreign students. At that time many of the foreign students came from Uganda and Barbara developed a particular interest in this country and friendships with a number of Ugandan students.

It appeared that life for John and Barbara was never to be smooth. Just before they were to be married Barbara developed some gastro-intestinal symptoms. An investigation showed she had progressive liver cirrhosis. Worse still, the back pressure on the blood vessels due to the cirrhosis was liable to cause a fatal haemorrhage. An urgent operation was necessary. Barbara's health looked precarious and John was advised to call off the wedding. It was a confusing time for both, but it only served to strengthen their faith and draw them closer together.

The operation was successful and the wedding went ahead. For some time after that they didn't know how long they would have together, as Barbara's liver cirrhosis appeared to progress more rapidly and her symptoms became worse. There was no cure for this type of disease and John and Barbara lived with the knowledge that their time together could be short. They learned to live as if each day could be their last together. Above all they trusted God and sought for His will in their lives.

John was convinced that he should leave medicine and go into full-time Christian work. By this time he had qualified as a doctor and the prospect of a rewarding and lucrative career was beckoning him. Few people were in favour of his decision to quit medicine and more than a few eyebrows were raised and criticisms vented. He abandoned a secure future in medicine believing the calling of God on his life was to devote himself to prayer and the word of God. In taking this step he was open to misunderstanding and ridicule. Most people could not understand what he was doing or why he was doing it. How would he get financial support? He had given up a career in which he could do a lot of good. However despite what other people felt, John felt a clear calling on his life, and knew he must devote himself to that, even if it meant giving up a secure future.

As time passed Barbara's liver disease appeared to be more under control, and they thought of starting a family. Again there was disappointment. They were told that Barbara could not bear children because of her liver complaint. Various eminent medical specialists in that field were consulted and the opinions were always the same – it was highly unlikely that Barbara could get pregnant, and if she did it would be very dangerous in view of her liver condition. Years passed and Barbara's condition seemed stable. By this time John had established a church and they had adopted a little girl. John's gift as a Bible teacher and his integrity as a Christian leader were well recognised. But the Christian work he was leading had just been through a particularly rough year. However, one amazing event had happened, Barbara had become pregnant. The joy of knowing they were soon to have a child, carried them through what would have been a difficult time. Barbara's health was excellent during the pregnancy, but the doctor in charge decided to admit her to hospital when she was five months pregnant to do some routine tests on her liver condition. Then the unthinkable happened. She went into premature labour and delivered a stillborn infant. Barbara had conceived and borne a child, but the child was too small to survive. Humanly speaking, their one ray of light, in what was a dark year, had been snuffed out.

Somehow through all these experiences Barbara maintained a quiet faith which could not be shaken. She had a relationship of confidence in God as her Father, and adversity only drove her more deeply into that relationship.

Some time later Barbara had another brush with death. She had been admitted to hospital again for what she was told was a fairly minor investigation. A liver biopsy was to be carried out. To prepare her for the biopsy she was given some plasma and fluids. The procedure was carried out and the medical staff departed, apart from one nurse who was tidying up. Quite suddenly Barbara became short of breath, and her lungs began to fill with fluids. She was having an allergic reaction to the plasma. The doctors were hurriedly summoned back, and as the doctors worked with her she began to lose consciousness and drift. She could hear and see, but not communicate. She knew that if the process wasn't arrested she was going to die.

She said later, 'I was aware that I was dying and remember thinking that if this is death then there is just nothing to fear in it. The Lord was so real to me and I was so peaceful that I just felt that if one is dying with the Lord there is no big deal to it.'

Her only concern was for John and their adopted daughter Sarah. She thought 'if it is your will Lord, I am ready, if it is not your will, please prompt someone to pray for me.'

Finally the doctors were successful in reversing the allergic affects and Barbara recovered. She later found that two friends from the church had been praying for her at that precise moment. Barbara later said, 'The experience encouraged me so much to know that when the time comes for any of us to go with Him, He will be there with us and we will not have to go through something that will make us afraid.'

Over the years Robbie and I had been close friends with John and Barbara. Their faith in God through all their trials had been a tremendous example to us. It seemed that in so many ways they were called to suffer, but their trust in God was deepened through every experience and redeemed their suffering. It was a process of death and resurrection. Barbara became more radiant as time went on, and Robbie drew on Barbara's strength as a close friend and confidante.

When we set out for Uganda it was with the firm assurance that John and Barbara would be among the first people to visit us. Barbara confided to Robbie that she couldn't wait. She had always had a special place in her heart for Uganda since her student days and our going there as missionaries was at last giving her an opportunity to visit Uganda.

As our first few months in Uganda were especially difficult for Robbie, she looked forward immensely to seeing her friend Barbara and unburdening her heart. Through those first few months we struggled, we prayed, we committed the situation in trust to God and we looked forward to seeing our friends John and Barbara. We wanted to tell them all about it, perhaps to 'cry on their shoulder', but we just wanted to be with them.

The visit, when it came, fulfilled all our expectations. While John and I went off to do clinics, Robbie and Barbara talked and talked. It was just what Robbie needed. She and Barbara had never been closer. Barbara loved Uganda. She walked around the village and talked to the local people. People told her of their experiences during the war. How they had hidden from the soldiers in the bush. One man described how he pretended to be dead and the soldiers had walked over him. Another showed her the plants that he had been forced to eat while fleeing in the bush.

During that time we talked to John and Barbara about the frustration of our work, how so many people were dying of TB and many mothers and babies were dying because there was no clinic to go to for delivery.

Behind the church where I was treating patients, I had discovered some old foundations which had been laid during the time of Idi Amin. They had been put down for a school, but this idea had been abandoned and the church had no use for them. The foundations were almost completely hidden by elephant grass. We all went to see these foundations. We stood up on the highest part to see how far they extended through the elephant grass. We talked about how these old foundations could be used for a clinic with a laboratory and maternity centre.

Of course we didn't have any money to do it, but it was good to share ideas, even if they were only ideas.

Finally we all went on Safari to see the Big Game in Kenya. It was our first time away from the work and we were like children being let out of school. We laughed and giggled together and generally had a wonderful time. When we parted in Nairobi they flew on to Germany, en route home, and while we were still in Nairobi they phoned us.

Barbara said that she just wanted to say what a great time she had had, she had enjoyed the whole trip, she liked seeing things in Kenya, but her heart was with Uganda. She loved Luweero, she loved the people.

That was the last time that we were to hear Barbara's gentle voice. A week later she was dead.

The shock for us was terrible. I had been in Kampala picking up supplies when a telex message came through. I couldn't believe it. I didn't want to believe it, but there it was written down in black and white. She had suddenly collapsed and died in John's arms. It was evening when I had to make the two hour trip back to Luweero, and my heart was heavy. How could it have happened? We had just seen her. She had been in wonderful health. How was I going to tell Robbie?

There was no easy way. I got home and just blurted it out. All of us sat on the settee and hugged each other and wept. We felt so cut off, so isolated, we couldn't lift a phone and talk to John, we couldn't be with our friends, we couldn't grieve with them. All we could do was weep. Never before had we felt so cut off. Never before did we feel so much on the edge of blackness and despair.

The next day we drove into Kampala again to try and make contact with John by phone. We eventually got through and found that he was calm and at peace. He wanted to tell us that he had decided to start a Memorial Fund for Barbara to build a clinic in Luweero. What could be a more fitting way to remember Barbara, than for a clinic to be built in a land where the people had touched her heart so deeply? As we had driven into Kampala I had had the same thought and had determined to speak to John about my idea. Before I could say anything John had pre-empted me.

Barbara's passing left a tremendous gap in our lives but some of the pain was lessened by knowing that she had lived her life on an eternal dimension and was totally prepared for death. For her, death was simply passing over to be with the one whom she had loved and served all her life. Now as her life had meant so much to many people, her death was going to be the source of life and hope to many others, through the clinic to be built in her memory. As in Barbara's life she had gone through the process of death and resurrection many times through what she had suffered, so her death was going to be the means of resurrection for many in Luweero. A people who had known war, destruction and hopelessness were to see a place of healing and hope grow up in their midst. As a result of Barbara's death there would come life for many others.

Chapter 7

Building

So through Barbara's death we had funds to build a clinic. When Barbara was alive, we had stood on the old foundations of the school, and reflected that these foundations could be put to good use. Now we had the money to do something.

I went back to those foundations – so overgrown with elephant grass that I couldn't see the other end – and wondered how I would go about building the clinic. I sat down and reviewed my resources. I had money and motivation but that was about all. I had very little knowledge of building. It wasn't something I had covered in my medical curriculum. I didn't know if any local building skills were available, and I didn't know where to procure the building supplies, or how to transport the building materials. The more I pondered, the more I realised that there were immense difficulties to be overcome. I also realised that if I just kept thinking about the problems I would never do anything. The thing to do was to make a start. As the saying goes 'fools rush in where angels fear to tread'. I initiated a building project, which was to continue for the next five years, and result in a medical facility which was far more extensive than I had ever dreamed of.

The first thing we needed were building materials – concrete blocks, sand and cement. Where could we get concrete blocks? Our friend the Rev Livingstone, who was totally involved in the project, came to the rescue. He knew of many houses which had been destroyed during the war. We could get the blocks from the rubble. We would be building the clinic from second-hand blocks. However, most of these destroyed houses were deep in the villages, and had now been virtually overrun by the bush again. How could we transport the blocks back to Kiwoko?

The answer lay in the form of a very old Land Rover, which had been sent out from Northern Ireland, and a very small trailer. The Land Rover had seen better days, but worked. Its biggest disadvantage was that it consumed vast amounts of fuel. It used so much petrol that we thought at first it must have a leak in the tank. Unfortunately it didn't, and there was no simple way to remedy the problem. However it was all that was available, and we were grateful.

Having solved the problem of where to get cement blocks, we turned our attention to the problem of where to get sand. I had never thought of these types of difficulties in construction before. At home I would simply have phoned up the local Builders' Suppliers. But no such service existed here. However the problem was easily solved when I spoke to the local villagers. Lots of areas had very sandy soil and if one dug below the surface, in the right location, sand was available in plentiful supply.

That is how I found myself one morning, waiting for my friend Henry to load up the small trailer with sand from his farm. It was wet and miserable and I was asking myself what I was doing here in Africa, fixing broken down Land Rovers, fetching sand, getting soaked? I used to have a prestigious job as a GP in Northern Ireland.

My troubles that morning were not over, as the Land Rover got stuck in the swamp, and all the sand had to be unloaded again. By the end of the morning I was thoroughly wet and bedraggled. However, I was now certainly getting involved in a wide variety of activities and expanding my field of expertise, even if it was only learning how to shovel sand. Between clinics I would dash off in the

Land Rover and get a load of sand or blocks so that the brick-layers would not be idle.

It proved to be fairly easy to find brick-layers locally. David, our first builder, was a stocky man, 5ft 3ins in height, who was distinguished most by his colourful hats, made from an assortment of rags sewn together, and the fact that his trousers were always just on the point of falling down. David was very consistent in coming on time, even though he had to cycle, or walk, 10 miles to get to work and he always wanted to work the public holidays for extra pay as he was chronically in debt. Possibly because David had a plausible personality, people seemed to lend him money, or advance him money to do work for them, which of course, he never had time to do. Throughout David's career as a builder, I became accustomed to various individuals coming to me, complaining that he owed them money. I was constantly amazed that someone, who was relatively well paid by local standards, could be in debt to so many different people. Perhaps he had a number of girls or many children to support. Unfortunately David was not averse to solving his debt problems through a bit of private enterprise on the side, selling cement – the clinic's cement! It was a very good business venture for him, since it was all clear profit. Unfortunately for him, he was eventually caught and went to prison.

Theft of cement was endemic on many building projects, often only discovered when the floors or walls of the buildings would start to crumble. An investigation would show that the mortar was made with virtually pure sand with only a hint of cement added, the rest of the cement having 'got lost' between the store and the cement mixer! We therefore had to watch carefully that cement given out from our stores was actually mixed with the sand before our very eyes.

I did admire the Ugandan brick-layers or 'fundies', as they are called. They didn't seem to have any requirement for universally uniform blocks or bricks. They could build with bricks of any shape or size. The second-hand blocks which we procured from the bush were certainly not regular in size. Some had bits of plaster attached, almost all had the corners knocked off, some were large and some were small, but they used them all. When I looked at the moss covered, round edged, irregular concrete blocks, I wondered how anyone could build anything with them. But these were the blocks that built our clinic.

When we finally cleared the elephant grass from the foundations, we discovered they measured 170ft by 28ft, enough for a substantial building. To say that they were 'old and crumbling' was an under-statement. They had been built during the time of Idi Amin, and had been deteriorating ever since. I thought, at times, we might be better starting from scratch. However the builders knocked down the worst bits and used the better parts, and soon a building was arising.

The fact that the clinic was built on the site of old defunct foundations, using blocks from the rubble of houses destroyed in the war, said a lot in itself about what we were doing. The symbolism of what was happening was powerful. Literally out of the ashes of a war was arising a building which would bring life to the community. Stones which had been left as rubble after the war were being incorporated into a building where life would be restored.

As I was the only driver at the time, I made many excursions into the bush to bring back blocks. By loading the back of the Land Rover, and filling the small trailer, we could carry a substantial load. The old six cylinder engine coughed, spluttered, complained, and used even more fuel, but usually got us to journey's end. On some occasions the tyres, which were somewhat worn, gave out under the weight of the blocks. The first time I was ill prepared. The wheel wrench slipped off the nuts and the jack wouldn't elevate. However, I was rescued by the crowd of bystanders, who would inevitably appear in any situation of crisis in Uganda. The blocks were unloaded and the Land Rover levered up onto a block, as the wheel was changed. But I forgot to check that the nuts had been tightened. It was only when somebody noticed on the next load that the wheel was wobbling badly that I discovered my mistake. I obviously wasn't a very good mechanic, and the sooner I got a competent driver the better.

Sometimes we had to cut a trail through the bush to get near the site of the blocks, and then carry them down a track to the Land Rover. If the blocks themselves were in poor condition, we might arrive back at journey's end to find they had disintegrated going over the potholes on the way.

Another problem I had was that the fuel gauge didn't work. On one occasion we were about to load, when the Land Rover spluttered and I realised that we were probably very low on fuel. I estimated that if I put the Land Rover in high gear, and kept going at a steady speed, I might just reach the next village where fuel was available. However, the road we had to take was basically a bicycle track through banana trees and coffee plantations, which twisted and turned and was pitted with potholes. Batte, the new foreman was with me. I got the Land Rover into top gear and kept going. The speed was moderate for a good road, but our track wasn't in that category. So we were moving fairly fast for the conditions. Batte bounced and rolled round the back, but we made it to the next village and the supply of petrol. As he picked himself up and climbed out he asked, 'Did you ever think of taking up rally driving Doctor?'

With the roads in the condition they were in, driving around Kiwoko was like doing a permanent autocross.

Wood was another building material which was necessary for this construction. Again Livingstone was the man who knew where to find it. On this occasion we borrowed a truck from Mengo Hospital, the big Protestant hospital in Kampala, and set off. Mengo Hospital was very helpful to us in getting things going at this early stage. Most of our drugs were supplied through them and if they could help with equipment or transport they did so. I had no idea how wood was prepared in Uganda. I imagined that some sort of sawmill was used. When the truck finally drew to a halt, I couldn't hear any sounds of wood cutting machinery, or see anything resembling a saw mill. We set off on foot. About a quarter of a mile along a track, a large muvuli tree, a Ugandan hardwood tree, had been cut down and was partially sawn into planks. There was no sign of a mechanical saw anywhere, but a group of men was standing around, with a long two-handled saw. I realised that everything had been done by hand. Some of the planks had been cut into widths of 15 inches by 1 inch and they were cut as straight as a die. I thought of my own attempts to keep the saw straight when I was cutting a small piece of wood – not very impressive. These men had cut 14 feet lengths out of a tree with a consistent 1 inch or 2 inch thickness.

The wood had now to be carried back to the truck. Everyone broke off some banana leaves and rolled them into a little crown to serve as a cushion for the head. The wood was then hoisted up and carried on the top of their heads back to the truck. I lent a hand, or in this case, a head, and it caused great amusement among the locals, seeing the doctor carrying wood on his head through the forest. Perhaps they felt my head was a bit soft for that kind of work.

Another building material which we used was fired mud bricks. These were shaped in moulds and then fired in the kiln. Sometimes when we collected these bricks we formed a chain and passed them from hand to hand. Rev Livingstone and I would be sweating side by side. It caused more than a few raised eyebrows that the Doctor and the Rev were doing physical work. Livingstone was one of our most able health workers, and he managed to fit in these activities alongside his duties as a pastor. If anyone criticised him for being too involved in the health work, he defended himself by saying that he had been called to look after the whole needs of his parishioners. If they were sick, it was his duty to do what he could to help them, and anyway if the doctor could carry wood and blocks, he would work for the sick in whatever way was most useful.

It was true that professionals in Uganda did have a sense of status and prestige. A cleric always wore his dog collar and received the appropriate recognition. It was unusual to find a doctor doing manual work. The sight of Livingstone and me working side by side did show an example to the local community which was more useful than many words spoken...

Chapter 8

Personalities

The building gradually took shape, despite the second-hand blocks and the irregular shapes. As soon as one section was finished, we decided to use that part as a maternity ward. The need for a maternity ward was urgent, as we did not have a place to do the deliveries, but mothers kept coming to the dispensary. One morning I was opening up the dispensary, when I noticed a lady kneeling by the window. 'What is she doing there?' I thought. Then the lady, as if reading my thoughts, addressed me in English, 'Doctor, I want to have a baby.'

I felt that that wasn't such an uncommon sentiment among many of the village women, but then I realised that this lady was not making a wish, but stating a fact. She not only wanted to have a baby, she was about to have it right outside the window.

The dispensary only contained one room and one examination couch. I soon had her on the couch and did a quick examination to see what was going on. The baby wasn't far away from the outside world and within an hour he was squealing lustily. During all this time the mother had not uttered a sound. This was fairly typical of many villagers. They suffered the labour pains silently. When the baby was born she collected her things and walked home. It all seemed to be part of a day's work for her. However, it was probably just as well she left, as three more women promptly arrived in labour. Late that evening, we were still delivering babies in our small one room dispensary. As the night wore on, everyone who was available to help became involved, even the watchman complete with his bow and arrows.

Keni, the watchman, was definitely the right man for the job. One look at Keni on a dark night would have frightened most people. It wasn't that he was so ugly, but his front teeth were missing and when he smiled his canines tended to protrude in the manner of Dracula. On a dark night all one could see of him was the whites of his eyes and the teeth. The fact that he was friendly and smiling didn't help, because he didn't understand English, so he just said 'Aai', as a form of greeting. The other unfortunate habit which Keni had, was to stand too close to people. He would arrive behind someone with his bow and arrow, and stand there silently waiting. If the person then inadvertently turned around, they were immediately faced with two eyes, two teeth and a bow and arrows, and further frightened out of their wits by Keni's friendly greeting 'Aai'.

Because of the number of deliveries, we decided that it was absolute priority to have a proper maternity ward and delivery room. So these were the first rooms to be functioning when the main clinic building was partway completed. The women still had to climb over piles of building materials and concrete blocks to get to it, but it was better than nothing and the mothers could at least rest for a day after delivery, before tackling life in the bush again. We had real hospital beds with mattresses. One local man looked at the comfortable beds and commented, 'Our wives won't want to leave.' Most people only had a mat in their mud huts.

Now, no mother delivering a baby in a hospital in Africa, waits around for long after delivery, but she will usually stay at least 12 to 24 hours for some monitoring. If there are any signs of complications, she will stay longer. Before this we knew that people were actually dying, because we did not have the basic facilities to admit and treat them. We had been working flat out to meet the need. Some of that work involved delivering babies in rather basic circumstances or treating patients where there was a complete lack of privacy. However, they still kept coming in droves. Some of that work involved delivering loads of sand and bricks. Everyone was under pressure, yet during this period of this development there was no alternative. We couldn't turn patients away. We were not in control of what was happening. Many times we felt like putting up a sign 'The Clinic is not ready yet, please wait until it is finished'. We may have felt like that, but we knew that people couldn't time their illnesses to meet our opening date, so we did our best. Sometimes we were able to help with what we had, sometimes we were not.

There were other pressures on the staff which made life a little difficult, or in some cases at least, rather inconvenient. We had now been joined by a nurse from Germany, Gudrun, who was living in a house without a toilet, so she used the pit latrine of the local school. However, like everything else in the area, the pit latrine was partially destroyed. In this case the walls stopped half-way up. Some thoughtful person had erected a temporary papyrus wall to screen the latrine, in the interests of modesty, but one day in a storm Gudrun found herself somewhat exposed to the outside world when the papyrus blew away. At the time I was doing a crash course in the construction of septic tanks, so that I could alleviate the problem. I had learned something of the theory of septic tanks while doing the tropical medicine course, but had not paid enough attention to the practical details, not realising then I would have to build my own in the future. Now the problem became acute, as Gudrun was finding she could only visit the pit latrine under cover of darkness, in the interests of modesty. After finally figuring out the technicality of inlet pipes, outlet pipes, soakaways and ventilation pipes, the septic tank was constructed, you might say to everyone's relief!

It wasn't easy to get qualified Ugandan nursing and

medical staff to come to work in the Bush. I soon realised that it was at least as big a step for a Ugandan nurse to leave the bright lights of Kampala and move to village life in Luweero, as for an Irish doctor to leave the bright lights of Belfast, and move to Luweero. In fact, at first, it was easier to get ex-patriot staff than Ugandan professionals. We had been joined by Gudrun from Germany and Elizabeth, a nurse from Washington, and later Karen from California, a bacteriologist. The first Ugandan nurse to join us was Grace, a registered nurse from Kampala. Add to this our locally trained health workers, and we had our team. It was definitely a cosmopolitan group, an Irish doctor, a German 'high-tech' burns unit nurse, an American community health nurse, an American laboratory specialist and a Ugandan nurse and our 15 local health workers. We all blended in together or bounced off each other, depending on the occasion, but in everything we did manage to maintain our sense of humour. Actually without a sense of humour we would have been crushed by the evidence of suffering we saw round us every day.

Our humorous perspective on life was also much enhanced by Heather. Heather was sent out by CMS Ireland, just after the beginning of our second year in Uganda. She had just finished a Degree in Sociology and wanted to work with children. I saw the deplorable needs among children in the local primary schools and felt that perhaps Heather could help there. Most of the teachers were either untrained or only partially trained and had not really a grasp of what they were supposed to be teaching. Their teaching technique also consisted of them learning by rote method, 'Children repeat after me.' Heather was to distribute textbooks which we had received as a donation and help the teachers with more constructive teaching methods. However, she also got involved in the medical work, even if it was only holding a lamp, while someone delivered a baby.

One could say that Heather had a rather loose job description and in the early days she sometimes struggled with exactly what she should be doing. Everyone else seemed to have a well-defined role, they were either a nurse, working in the dispensary, a laboratory specialist setting up a lab, a community health nurse training health workers or a doctor – that was me – doing some building work. Well perhaps my job description was not very well defined either!

In most circumstances it was not advisable to have someone working in Africa without a well-defined job description. However, in Heather's case it gave her time to get to know the local situation and see where she could best help. It also gave her time to establish good relationships with the people so that when she left two years later she had more friends in the community than any other expatriate working there.

Some of the most amusing episodes in which Heather was involved, arose from the differences in the usage of language. Our local village health workers were very keen to improve their English, so all our conversations with them took place in English. Sometimes the confusion arose over names. Heather once gave a lift on her motor cycle to a local man who said he was on his way to visit 'God'. She thought that he must be going to the church, and this was just his way of expressing himself. However, during the course of the conversation the person showed himself to be on most intimate terms with God, referring to Him constantly and the fact that he was going to visit 'His place'. One is not too surprised with such religious talk as there are many very devout people in Uganda but Heather was severely disillusioned in this case. The person refused to be left at the church and insisted on being dropped further on, to Heather's confusion. All was revealed when he said that he had now arrived. He was now at **God**frey's house!

As we were living and working in close proximity everyone's personality traits were highlighted. During this period I was constantly rushing around between medical work and building work. I would see some patients, make

71

sure everything was under control, and go off to get cement, or wood, or bricks. Sometimes the nurses would need me and would find me standing on top of a wall, haranguing the builders because it was not built straight. The Ugandan builders were very philosophical about my temperament. They said I sometimes got very hot about things but I cooled down quickly; in other words they didn't take my reprimands too seriously.

Karen, our American laboratory specialist, liked to discuss developments for the laboratory with me and I was very happy to be involved. It was just that I usually had other pressing things to think about also and was often pre-occupied. I was giving half my attention, and trying to solve some problem with the other half of my mind. Finally Karen got frustrated with my habit of getting up and leaving in the middle of the conversation. I hadn't realised I was doing it, but something else which needed urgent attention would suddenly occur to me and I would leave to deal with it. Finally after this had happened on a number of occasions and I rose to leave again, Karen's voice suddenly changed to one of authority, and I froze.

'Sit down!' she commanded, 'or I'll nail your foot to the floor!'

Now this was a side of Karen's personality that I had not seen. Maybe it was not a good sentiment for a good Christian girl but it was effective. She got my undivided attention after that.

Grace, our Ugandan nurse, was the opposite. She wouldn't say anything, even when subjected to extreme discomfort. On one notable occasion, we were returning from a vaccination clinic, all crammed into the little Suzuki jeep. To accommodate our excess passengers, several people sat on small 3-legged stools placed on the floor of the jeep. We had to negotiate a very swampy, very potholed part of the road. We bumped and jostled each other and when I had covered the worst stretch of the road and looked around to see that everyone was alright, Grace was sitting with the most pained expression on her face.

When I looked at her foot I could see the reason. One leg of the stool was resting on her foot! The occupant of the stool, a fairly 'chubby' individual was totally unaware of the fact. Grace was enduring in silence, too polite to ask the person to move.

Gudrun was Germanic in temperament. She expressed exactly how she felt with no hidden nuances. This was of course the very opposite to the usual Ugandan temperament. Gudrun was completely open and direct, as the Irish say, 'she called a spade a spade'! It is not that Ugandans could not be direct, but one could say they generally didn't like to be confrontational or negative. In their culture it was not polite. Gudrun had no such inhibitions, greatly to the surprise, at first, of her colleagues. However gradually they all got used to the peculiar mannerisms of these foreigners and accepted us as part of their community, despite our idiosyncrasies.

Edward Sosi was a person of small stature but large ideas, usually expressed in the most complicated and colourful language he could think of. As English was Edward's second language, his expressions were not always entirely appropriate to what he was describing, in the normal usage of the English vernacular, but they were always so descriptive of the circumstances that he never had any trouble in getting his meaning across. His words were usually accompanied by movements and gestures with his hands, so that he looked as though he were conducting an orchestra in a complicated piece of music. To add to his many talents and occupations, Edward was the lay reader for the main Kiwoko congregation, as well as being one of the trainers of village health workers. When he came to the house with a message he would stand to attention at the door, draw himself up to his full height of 5ft 1in, take a deep breath and make his pronouncement in the most flowery language possible. Meanwhile his hands would automatically begin to move and gesture with the words, as if he were conducting the theme to music, while his face broke into a beaming smile.

It was indeed an experience to be the receiver of Edward's messages or announcements. However, sometimes the general manner and gestures and facial expression was somewhat at odds with the content of the message. Added to this was the fact that Edward, in common with many Ugandan speakers, had been taught at the local schools by rote and by question and answer. The teacher would say 'Johnny went to market with a pig,' now class 'Johnny went to market with a what?' To which the class would chorus the answer 'a pig'. Indeed even preachers would sometimes use the same method to see if their congregation was still with them. Edward used the same strategy, completely unconsciously, to express himself. This had the effect of getting the total attention of his audience, as they were left eagerly waiting in suspense. One memorable occasion when Edward's smiling facial expression, his deep breath and hand gestures totally belied the content of his message, was when he came to Elizabeth's door while she was having a cup of coffee and made an announcement.

'There is a *what* at the dispensary?' he boomed.

Eizabeth had pricked up her ears but was totally unprepared for the second part of the announcement. Edward continued, 'A dead body.'

It was very hard for Elizabeth, given the manner of the communication, to maintain the appropriate response. However, as she choked over her cup of coffee, any tendency to an inappropriate response to the news, given in such an incongruous way, was masked by the spluttering and coughing which followed.

On another occasion Edward entered the dispensary while I was doing a clinic. This time he had his two small daughters with him. On looking up from what I was doing, Edward, who had his daughters lined up along the wall beside him, announced – 'I have brought my children to see you. This one,' he said, indicating the oldest, 'is sick, but this one,' he said pointing to the little one, 'is alright. I have merely brought her as the accompaniment!'

Edward's tendency to musical expression was breaking through in every way. People such as Edward were essential in setting up vaccination clinics, mobilising the community on health issues and doing health education. He also enriched the lives and vocabulary of the missionaries who worked with him.

When the maternity ward and some staff housing was finished we felt somewhat relieved of pressure in one or two areas. The mothers had somewhere safe and private to deliver, and the nurses could use the toilet, without waiting until it was dark to use the rather exposed pit latrine. However there were still many other areas to deal with, and facilities to provide, before we could relax or feel free of pressure.

Chapter 9

Early Traumas

After opening the maternity ward, we went to work on completing the medical ward. We had wanted to build a TB ward, but the immediate needs of acutely ill children and urgent adult medical cases were so overwhelming that we realised we would have to meet these needs first. Within a few months we had a medical or general ward finished which, in the meantime, would accommodate whatever urgent cases – men, women or children came along. What we could offer, in terms of treatment, was still fairly basic and we were now seeing more and more seriously ill patients. For some, such as those with AIDS, which was common in the area, there was little we could do. For others, such as those with tetanus, the prognosis was poor, though not entirely hopeless. We could keep the patient sedated and carry out basic nursing care.

Having just come from a 'high-tech' unit where extreme cases were saved, Gudrun found it hard to accept that such people could die under our care, without more sophisticated treatment being available.

'There must be more that can be done,' she would say, and driven by a desire to get more treatment for seriously ill patients she would put them in the Land Rover and drive them to Kampala.

This happened particularly for the first few months after Gudrun arrived, until she got used to the idea that by Third World standards all that could be done was being done.

On one memorable occasion, shortly after the general ward was opened, two seriously ill patients were admitted. One had a provisional diagnosis of tetanus, the other almost certainly had AIDS, though no AIDS test could yet be carried out. Both were in a critical condition. One weekend while I was away, Gudrun got to the point where she couldn't continue to watch these patients deteriorate without doing something more. So she put them in the Land Rover and set out for Kampala to one of the major hospitals. Both were on drips, so someone had to travel with them holding the drips. Also, the tetanus patient could not stand any sudden disturbances, so the journey had to be made very slowly and gently, and took a long time. Gudrun hoped that the Kampala hospital would have anti-tetanus serum, which we did not have. Then just as she drove into the car park of the hospital the first patient with AIDS died. That was a major disappointment. But as they got the other patient onto the trolley he also breathed his last.

Gudrun was devastated. Now, all she had to show for her efforts were two dead bodies. It takes a girl of immense courage and determination to handle such a situation. She had certainly done all that she could, more than could be expected. She had been working flat out all day. She had driven hours to get the patients to a more sophisticated hospital, and at the very last moment they had died. Now she faced the long drive back with the corpses and the task of telling the relatives that the patients had died.

Well, Gudrun had a very positive outlook on the whole situation. She had done all she could and there was nothing more she could do now. Suddenly she felt hungry, and she realised she hadn't eaten all day. Before she faced the drive back to Luweero she would fortify herself with something to eat. So she drove to Bimbo's restaurant in Kampala, parked her Land Rover, containing the corpses at the door, and went in for a meal. Physically strengthened, at least she was then able to go on with her journey. I have often wondered what would have happened if anyone had tried to steal the Land Rover, while Gudrun was in the restaurant. As Kampala had a notoriously high rate of car theft, it was a real possibility. The thieves would have been amazed to discover they had also got two corpses in the back!

Transporting dead bodies was a part of life in Uganda. People were very superstitious about the transport of corpses, and so hiring any transport for this purpose was a very expensive outlay. We were therefore asked on occasions to help. One such occasion arose when the son of a local church worker died in a hospital in Kampala. The plea was made to me, would *we* bring the body back, as it would cost much more than the father could afford to hire a pick-up. I had known the boy. He was one of the many children who had heart disease through rheumatic fever. It was a tragic loss, as the boy's mother had also recently died, so I agreed. However I also had to collect some medical supplies from the airport on the same day. I would therefore combine the trips. The goods at the airport were rather more bulky than I had anticipated and Robbie who was with me raised an eyebrow when she saw how full the car was.

'Where exactly are you going to put the body?' she asked.

'We will find a space somewhere,' I mumbled optimistically.

Over this period of moving between Ireland, England and Uganda I had become expert at packing a large amount of goods into as small a space as possible. However my experience didn't yet cover packing corpses.

When we arrived at the hospital, we found the father waiting with the body wrapped in barkcloth, the traditional burying material. I squeezed it in on top of the barrels from the airport and we set out. We hadn't travelled far before Robbie said, 'Ian, what's that smell?'

It wasn't hard to guess. The body was definitely 'off' in the heat. For the rest of the journey we kept all the windows down and Robbie found a small sample bottle of perfume – very useful for such purposes – which she inhaled when the other odour became too overpowering.

Gudrun was a 'hands on' nurse. If there was a boil to be lanced or burns to be dressed or an ulcer to be desloughed, Gudrun was in working at it. At first I could not understand what the 'puss' was – pronounced as in pussy cat. She would tell me, 'That wound was very pussy'.

After a while the penny dropped.

'Oh you mean pus.'

If there was pus or puss around Gudrun *would let it out*. As we had told our health workers – If there is pus about, let it out –.

Many of these patients who had bad abscesses had AIDS. In the future AIDS would become a preoccupation taking up much of our time, but at this time we were just introducing AIDS testing. Although one always wore gloves, there was a small but definite risk of contracting AIDS while doing such work. This must have been on Gudrun's mind as, when we had our very first batch of AIDS tests, she submitted her own blood sample for testing, unknown to me. At this stage we didn't even have a laboratory, but two friends who were doctors were visiting from Ireland and had brought along an experimental batch of AIDS tests. To test the reliability of the kits, patients were selected until we had 80 samples. The test took about three hours to mix and incubate, so at about 11.00 pm one night we were poring over the test plates with little wells, trying to read the colour changes. No 1 was positive, numbers 4, 5 and 6 negative, number 8 positive and so on. At number 61 Aubrey, the Irish doctor stopped and said, 'I don't like the look of that.'

Then he looked up his reference key, number 61 was Gudrun Troutman. Number 61 was positive.

This was a complete shock for me, as I hadn't even known that Gudrun had submitted a test and she shouldn't have been tested in this batch at all. We sat staring at the test, checking the reference number, checking the controls. Yet according to our controls, number 61 was a definite positive. We were speechless. Gudrun wasn't around, and didn't know we were reading the results at that time. As midnight approached, we all sat around in gloom and despondency. Many thoughts raced through my mind, each one gloomier than the one before. Gudrun had only been working in Africa for six months. If she had contracted AIDS through routine medical work within six months, then the risk to all of us was very high. I had invited her to come, therefore I was indirectly responsible. I could not then, in conscience, ask anyone else to work with me if they could get AIDS so easily. The work would have to close down. We would have to abandon these people. Such panic thoughts raced through my mind, but gradually we began to think constructively. This was only one test, it would need to be confirmed. We would have to get another blood sample from Gudrun and have a reference test carried out in Kampala by the standard Eliza technique.

The following day Gudrun was still blissfully unaware that anything was wrong. 'How do we get another blood sample without telling her?' we questioned.

Finally I approached the subject head on.

'Gudrun, we need another blood sample.'

'Why, do you think I have AIDS?' she quipped.

'Well, some of the tests need to be repeated, yours is not the only one,' I replied without letting her know the anxiety we were feeling.

Although Gudrun had joked about having AIDS she was not seriously worried and accepted my explanation. The sample was taken to a Kampala hospital, where a reference test could be carried out. We would have to wait 48 hours for the result. It was the longest 48 hours I had known. Time dragged past. There were no jokes. Our sense of humour seemed to have evaporated. This was too serious a matter. Finally someone arrived back late at night from Kampala. The result was negative. Our test had been a false positive.

The sense of relief was immense. Suddenly a great weight lifted off everyone, and we felt we could live and breathe again; life would go on. When we told Gudrun that her result was negative she took it all in her stride. She had not seriously expected any other result. She had been spared the 48 hours of agonising.

Getting AIDS through medical contact with AIDS patients is not a common phenomenon but there was a definite risk – if one was accidentally pricked by a needle which had been used on an AIDS patient, if one got cut during the course of surgery on an AIDS patient. In America it had been shown that the risk to medical workers was very small, much less than 1%. However, in Africa, where as many as 50% of patients in a hospital could be HIV positive, the risk was correspondingly higher. Although a doctor or a nurse would wear gloves, rubber gloves would not stop a needle or scalpel going through. The incident with Gudrun, however, made us all realise how closely we lived with the risk of getting AIDS. If Gudrun had contracted AIDS after working in Africa for only a short space of time, the implication would have been that the risk to all of us was very high in routine medical practice.

Although, happily, Gudrun's test was negative, the episode raised the question in all our minds: 'am I prepared to die for what I am doing?' None of us were heroes, none of us wanted to die, we didn't want to be martyrs. But we believed in what we were doing. In many ways we felt privileged to have a sense of calling and purpose as we realised that many people had safety and security in their lifestyles, but not much of a sense of purpose. Although we did not want to get AIDS, neither did we live in fear of it.

One could say that we were having a rather bumpy 'take off' in opening the general ward, and getting involved with AIDS patients and AIDS testing, but we were learning as we went along. We were finding that there were some patients who were beyond help but we could do something for the majority of patients under our care, especially as we continued to develop better laboratory testing and facilities.

Chapter 10

Blue Band Tins

The suspense over the AIDS test wasn't the only drama which involved Gudrun. Much later she developed a cough and chest pain. It didn't seem serious at first and not much was done.

'You have had a BCG?' we enquired.

'Yes I had one as a child, look at the scar,' she replied.

The BCG is the routine anti-tuberculous vaccination given in many countries. It is not fully protective against TB but it helps a great deal. Reassured by the fact that Gudrun had her anti-tuberculous injection and that her symptoms weren't too serious, we carried on, but she had a chest X-ray done as a routine precaution. Nothing showed up. The chest X-ray looked absolutely normal. 'Well, Gudrun it can't be TB. It must be just troublesome bronchitis,' we reassured her.

TB is such a prevalent disease in Uganda that it is one of the first diseases one thinks about if someone has a cough. In the UK it would probably be much further down the list, in fact in my General Practice outside Belfast, I had never seen a case of TB. That all changed when I reached Luweero. TB was common and increasing in frequency due to the spread of AIDS. People with AIDS often reactivated dormant TB, because their immune system was suppressed. As there were so many of these people, they then acted as a large reservoir of TB germs, coughing them up and spreading them around healthy people in the community. So when Gudrun began to cough we thought of TB. However her clear chest X-ray and previous vaccination reassured us.

As the months passed Gudrun developed an odd rattle in her chest.

'Ian, I still feel there is something wrong,' she confided.

She was about to go on holiday, so she decided to have more tests while she was away. Ten days after she left, we got a fax message through the Post Office in Kampala. Gudrun had had a pleural biopsy done, i.e. a sample taken from the lining of the lungs and it confirmed a diagnosis of tuberculosis. We were puzzled. How could an otherwise healthy person get TB when they had taken all the precautions, including BCG? Then we got another fax. By this time Gudrun was back in Germany and she had discovered that the scar she had wasn't from a BCG. She had thought a BCG had been carried out when she was a child, but German children were not vaccinated routinely against TB and her mother told her she hadn't been immunised. So Gudrun had missed getting AIDS but she had got TB. Fortunately with modern drugs the TB was eradicated and Gudrun was back to normal within six months.

The routine test for someone with TB was to stain a sputum sample with acid-fast dye and look for the little TB rods under the microscope, which showed up like double ended matchsticks. In Gudrun's case she had a dry cough which produced no sputum, so we could not do this. But the majority of TB cases would cough up sputum which could be tested. The full course of anti-tuberculous treatment in Uganda lasted 12 months. It was not a course of treatment one usually embarked upon unless the diagnosis was confirmed. If someone has a chest infection, the doctor could try a course of antibiotics for a week and see if it cleared up. This practice didn't really work in the case of TB. If one was on the wrong track they would, at best, waste a lot of drugs and at worst, miss the real diagnosis. Hence I had always made it a priority to get a positive TB test from a patient before starting treatment. At first, before we had our own laboratory, this meant we had to drive the patient to a hospital, where their sputum could be tested and they could be admitted if it was positive. The patient would therefore be coughing and spluttering in the vehicle for several hours, causing an aerosol of millions of TB germs in a confined space. This was definitely not a desirable situation for any medical worker to put themselves in, on a regular basis, as Gudrun had discovered.

It was Karen who solved our dilemma by starting to do TB tests herself, staining the slides in the kitchen sink before the laboratory was built. We were almost in a state of euphoria when Karen made her first positive diagnosis of TB. It may have been a small step forward for medicine in general but it was a large step for medicine in Kiwoko. We were not happy because the patient had TB, but we were happy that our test had worked with such basic equipment. The kitchen sink, a couple of jam jars, a monocular microscope and a hair dryer were not standard laboratory equipment, so we were all the more pleased that we had been successful. The practice of being aerosolled intensively with TB germs, as we drove the patients to another laboratory, thankfully became a thing of the past.

Karen had the onerous task of creating a functioning laboratory out of almost nothing. When the first small dispensary was completed, she was promoted from the kitchen sink to a tiny room at the back of the dispensary. We were all told not to throw out our Blue Band tins or any useful container, as they could be useful to Karen for getting her sophisticated laboratory going. Fortunately she had brought two essential pieces of equipment with her from California, her microscope and violin. The microscope was essential in the laboratory, the violin was essential to her sanity in helping her unwind after the frustrations of a normal day. I think the violin preserved Karen's good natured disposition on more than one occasion. It was very sad when one day someone sat on it in a bus and it got broken, but by the time that happened

Karen had learned to handle life in Uganda and no longer needed the 'crutch' of the violin.

When the maternity ward was finished we also finished an extra room, so Karen got promoted again to a slightly bigger laboratory, where she could have even bigger and better supplies of Blue Band tins. Blue Band tins were an essential part of life in Africa. The Blue Band came in $\frac{1}{4}$, $\frac{1}{2}$ or 1 kilo tins which could be put to good use when the Blue Band had been consumed. Our family were avid consumers of Blue Band – it being the only margarine available in Uganda, we didn't have much choice, but at no time were our used tins actually thrown away. If Karen didn't need them there were plenty of other takers. The small size made an excellent paraffin lamp. A little chimney was fitted and a wick, the body of the tin being filled with paraffin. This made one of the cheapest forms of light for the villages – affectionately known as the smoke bomb because of the amount of smoke and fumes it produced. The smoke was also good in warding off mosquitos but it was a bit difficult for humans in confined spaces, so the smoke bomb was better used outside. Blue Band tins could also be hammered into good funnels. When we needed a funnel to put fuel in the generator, I discovered I was buying my own Blue Band tins back – now reborn as a funnel – and we Westerners thought we were the first to discover recycling!

The clinic also finally purchased its own microscope. Karen's elaborate demands were never very exotic but she urged us to keep all our small empty tablet containers, any spare cotton buds we could find, or any orange sticks. These containers and sticks all had specific uses in collecting and storing small samples of various body fluids and excretions which Karen seemed inordinately interested in.

By this stage she was collecting enough specimens and had enough dyes and stains so that she was offering an impressive range of tests. Blood examinations, urine and stool examinations, sputum examinations. If the patient could produce it, Karen could examine it and report all the details. This was an enormous advantage for our medical work. Diagnosis moved from the realms of an informed guess to an actual confirmed diagnosis. Karen not only had an eye for an interesting stool specimen but she could spot a promising health worker. So it was, that several of our health workers were soon sucked in to the wonders and delights of the microscopic world of patients' specimens.

Of course it took more than a few Blue Band tins and a microscope to set up a useful laboratory. However, being able to do basic tests in the beginning with the limited equipment we had was a great encouragement and incentive for us to keep going. After some time we succeeded in getting a grant from Oxfam to have a fully functioning laboratory, appropriate to our needs.

Chapter 11

Turi

The happiness and welfare of our children was always a big factor in influencing the decisions we made, which would have inevitable consequences for the family. When we had first thought about going to Uganda our initial concerns that the Luweero triangle was not a suitable place to bring up a growing family, were counterbalanced by the knowledge that God cared for our children, at least as much as we did. Therefore if we were walking in faith and a good conscience before Him we need not fear for the ultimate well-being of our children. After all it was Jesus himself who said,

> *'Suffer the little children to come to me and forbid them not for of such is the Kingdom of God.'*

Perhaps many of our fears for the future of our children stemmed more from the values we had unconsciously absorbed from the society around us than any spiritual principles.

Educational standards in Northern Ireland were high. It was a tightly structured system where, if someone opted out, they might not get back in to the level of higher education they wished at a later date. There was a high degree of anxiety among many parents that their children should 'make it' to the appropriate institution of higher learning. To pull one's children out of the system was considered by many to be a great risk, if not downright irresponsible. For some, the fact that we were taking our kids out of school and transporting them to the African bush was unthinkable. Although Robbie wasn't ecstatic about teaching her own children, she realised that in the circumstances there was little alternative. She had started the process in Liverpool, so within a few days of reaching Luweero the books and pencils were brought out and school began again. The children were disappointed to find there were certain immutable, unchangeable points in life, despite vastly changing circumstances, and school was one of them. Sean, Michael and Lauren then aged eleven, nine and seven and a half had, in fact, shown no sign of culture shock or difficulty in adjusting to the new circumstances at all. They took to life in Africa like ducks to water. After all, playing football and games with their new friends, whom they could barely understand, didn't really need any verbal expression. Opportunities for such adventures as skinning snakes had been very limited in life back in Northern Ireland, so they were enjoying life to the full, with the possible exception of the intrusion of school.

Robbie was coping very well considering the difficulties and interruptions which were a normal part of each day. Work on the house was still on-going, so even when she got rid of me, and the line of patients which followed me, there was the noise of the cement mixer outside the window, or the carpenter making a mess in the living room while fitting shutters, or the general hubbub coming from the village women who were preparing food just outside. There were of course the more unusual interruptions to the normal day, like a visit from the Bishop of Namirembe with his entourage. Bishop Kauma was a most gracious and charismatic figure, who was inevitably followed around by at least one Land Rover full of people. So when an invitation was extended to the Bishop to have lunch, it was always wise to have a very large pot of food ready. I don't think Michael had ever seen a Bishop in full Bishop's gear before, but he was not in the least intimidated.

'Do you want to see my chickens?' he asked, probably realising that it would be high priority on the Bishop's crowded agenda for that day, to inspect Michael's three scrawny, ugly chickens.

'Why of course, where are they?' responded the Bishop.

Michael set off across the grass with the Bishop running behind, coat tails flying. The entourage was left standing somewhat bemused, wondering if they should follow or not, as Michael and the Bishop got down on their hands and knees to carry out a thorough examination of the scrawny village chickens in Michael's improvised coop. However such interruptions to the normal school day were a welcome diversion and added greatly to the children's wealth of experience and confidence. After all it is not every day a nine year old gets to show his chickens to a real African Bishop.

Sean was at a more problematical age regarding home school. He was at Secondary School level, at which new maths methods were introduced and science experiments became more complicated. He was just at the stage where he was liable to know more than the teacher, if the teacher didn't do her homework properly. Unlike America, home schooling was not yet popular as a method of teaching in the UK. Consequently the number of courses offered was more limited and usually relied on the teacher or mother actually teaching from a text. American systems were more 'do it yourself' kits. The child could work through the text himself with guidance from the parent, but the parent or teacher would not necessarily need to possess all the methods and skills herself. Sean's science book now contained experiments on such things as conduction of electricity and convection of heat. How were we going to demonstrate these without a laboratory? On some occasions Dad got called in, on the assumption, probably false, that he knew more about science than Mum, whose subject was English. So the gas cooker substituted for a Bunsen burner, and clothes pegs, copper wire and bits of wood were used to demonstrate the conduction of heat in various materials. The improvisation could go a certain amount of the way in demonstrating some aspects of science, but we were rapidly running out of equipment and facilities. Another factor which was becoming evident to us was that as Sean got older he was lacking meaningful peer contact. He was retreating to his bedroom with a book more and more, and while we were glad that he was demonstrating good reading skills we realised that he couldn't spend the next few years of his life lying on his bed reading. He would definitely become 'odd' if he didn't have more friends he could relate to. But where did one find such people in such a remote area? The realisation was dawning on us that we needed to consider boarding school, at least in Sean's case, if we wanted him to grow up as a balanced individual. Michael and Lauren, now aged ten and eight and a half, were not having the same problem, as there were more children around whom they could relate to. As we had been members of a church where family values were emphasised, we had always considered that a child's place was with his parents. The family needed to be together so that love and discipline could be expressed every day. How could this be done if the children were at boarding school? So we had never before seriously considered boarding school as an option. Now we were running into other problems which needed to be addressed urgently and we had to consider all the options.

We had been told about a boarding school in the Kenyan highlands – St Andrew's, Turi, where other missionary children from Uganda attended. Since the time of Idi Amin there had not been a British system boarding school in Uganda. St Andrew's school was highly spoken of by missionaries whose children had attended, so when we bumped into an Irish couple working with Tear Fund, who were sending their children to Turi, we decided to go along with them for a visiting weekend and have a look for ourselves. Quite a number of parents had made the trip to see their children that weekend, families were lolling about on the grass of the playing fields having picnics and chatting amiably. The background was set by the woodlands and rolling hills. It was almost an English scene, so different from the scenery in Uganda, with the tailored playing fields, the neat cricket pitch, the jumping paddock with horses and riders going through their paces, the manicured lawns and ordered classrooms. Since we had no previous experience of boarding schools and didn't know quite what to expect, this was all a pleasant surprise to us. We had thought that we would find austere dormitories with stern-faced matrons, institutionalised classrooms exuding an air of academia, where one spoke in whispers fearing to disturb the aura of learning. What we found were friendly, welcoming staff, pupils who looked happy and a family atmosphere. These were teachers who really cared about the pupils and pupils who liked school. Although the school taught the British curriculum the children were from all nationalities and backgrounds. This was a place where Sean would definitely have the opportunity to have good peer relationships at a very cosmopolitan level. When we had mooted the possibility of boarding school to Sean at first, he was non-committal. His instinctive reaction was that he didn't want to be separated from his parents. However he was happy enough to have a look, and we promised him that if he didn't like it, we would not force him to attend. So a lot depended on Sean's reaction to the school.

At the end of the day we posed the question, 'Well, Sean, what do you think of it?'

'It is not a bad place,' he responded. 'I would like to try it.'

Sean started boarding school shortly after that visit and the house seemed strangely empty without him. At least we still had Michael and Lauren, but for the first few weeks after we left Sean we were anxiously wondering how our small son was coping with being separated from his family. The day approached when we could visit the school again, and as we drove in, we could see Sean running across the grass to greet us. After the hugs and kisses we asked him how things were going and as he started to explain how he felt, the emotion was too great for him and his face crumpled.

'This school is not all it's cracked up to be,' he managed to say between the tears.

It was a hard situation for mother and son. Robbie wanted to take Sean in her arms and take him home with her but she realised this was not the answer. The feelings Sean was going through were normal for a boy who had just started boarding school and were something he would have to work through himself. That day Sean talked more than we had ever heard him talk before. He articulated the feelings of homesickness and isolation; he spoke about the good and bad things he was experiencing. We had not realised that Sean could verbalise his feelings and experiences so well and the exercise was therapeutic for us all. The school had many woodland trails within its boundaries so we could walk and talk. Sean was settling in as well as anyone could expect, but he was homesick and he realised it. He said it was a pervading feeling which coloured everything he did, but being able to identify it for what it was also made him able to deal with it. When we left that day we felt encouraged. The experience of boarding school was helping Sean to mature. We knew he could cope with it. We also felt that the teachers were sensitive to what the children were going through and would offer all the help and care that was possible. It was a school where the Christian values and caring attitude of the staff, combined to make a family atmosphere into which one was happy to entrust one's children.

As things progressed Sean settled well and we were convinced that boarding school would be a positive influence for our children. So somewhat under a year later, we decided also to send Michael and Lauren.

From that point on our way of life in Africa changed drastically. It had been a tough experience leaving behind our oldest son but it was nothing compared to the emptiness we felt when we got into the car and drove off from the school leaving all the children behind. Not much was said that evening, as we realised the implications of what we had done. Large parts of our lives would now be spent separated from our children. We felt a tremendous feeling of loss, we felt lonely and disoriented. However we also felt convinced that the step we had taken was in the best interests of our kids. Home school had been adequate as far as it went, but as the children got older it did not meet all their needs. Sean had benefited from being at boarding school, now it was the right time for Michael and Lauren to move on. Michael was approaching eleven and was at secondary school stage. Lauren was nine.

Although Turi was by no means close to us, we could still drive to the school as Kenya bordered Uganda. The journey took nine hours, but we decided to visit the children as often as possible despite this. There were many reasons for us not to make the journey too frequently, not least that it was a long and dangerous journey. The road we used had an accident rate twenty-seven times higher than the UK average. It was almost impossible for us to make the trip without seeing constantly the evidence of accidents and carnage on the roads – oil tankers over-turned, vehicles crushed and mangled. On one occasion we passed just after a motorcyclist had been involved in a head-on collision. Pieces of the motorcycle and the corpse were strewn all over the road. On another occasion, a bus had gone straight into a matatu killing everyone in the matatu. When we passed, they were laying nineteen bodies along the verge of the road. Once, as a bus approached us, I noticed smoke coming from the rear wheel and immediately pulled off the road, just as his tyre blew out. The pieces showered the car and the bus swerved violently from side to side. If we had still been on the road it would have ploughed into us. Fortunately the driver managed to keep control and came to a halt several hundred yards further on. To make the journey by early evening, we would set out at 5.00 am while it was still dark. In Uganda there was a restriction on heavy vehicles travelling while it was dark. This was to deter thieves from moving goods during the night. However some trucks, especially army vehicles, broke the regulations and travelled during darkness. These vehicles were the most dangerous as they almost always had inadequate lights, or none at all. The army trucks were imported from an Eastern European country and bore the capital letters IFA emblazoned on the front – presumably the name of the manufacturer. However, the Ugandans had styled the initials as standing for 'Imported For Accidents', not without good reason, as these trucks seemed to be poorly designed, lacking brake lights, rear lights and sometimes even brakes. The engineering of the trucks, or lack of it, in combination with inexperienced drivers made a lethal mixture, as we were to find out for ourselves.

It was about 6.00 am and the sun had not yet risen. We were nearing Kampala, on the road from Luweero. On this occasion the children were asleep in the back of the car, as was their custom when we made an early start. They had the blessed ability of being able to sleep in any conditions. We rounded a left-hand bend and suddenly, looming out of the darkness, was an enormous army IFA lorry on our side of the road and totally without illumination! Instinctively I swerved to the right, but the driver of the lorry had the same instinct and moved towards me in the same direction. As the ominous shape bore down on top of us Robbie cried, 'Jesus, Jesus,' and I swerved violently again in the opposite direction. It seemed too late and I could see the huge front wheel about to pass over us, when instead it miraculously missed us and glanced off the side of the car. We bounced away from each other and stopped about fifty yards up the road. We were still alive. I could hardly believe the truck had not mangled us, Robbie could hardly believe that we were still alive. Her words 'Jesus, Jesus,' were a cry for help, but also uttered in the sense that we were coming to meet him and she was committing us all into his hands.

As Robbie and I sat there realising that we had all

95

narrowly escaped death, Sean sleepily roused himself and murmured, 'What happened, did we hit a pothole?'

'No, something hit us, but you can go back to sleep again, it's OK now, we are all right.'

We were still in a daze that we were alive.

We knew that our constant travelling back and forth to Kenya put us at risk on the roads, but we felt we had no option. We had, of course, to bring our children to school, or to collect them at the beginning and end of term, but if we had the opportunity to visit them during term we would often take it. It was at such times that the conflict between our commitment to our work and our children was highlighted. We could almost guarantee that if we went away for a weekend to see the kids, everything would fall apart at the clinic. It wasn't that the people we left behind weren't well qualified or couldn't cope, but it was almost a predictable saga of events. Things would be going along smoothly with no problems and no crises for weeks before we left, then as soon as we got out of the door everything would go wrong. This happened especially in the early days, when we had few facilities. On one occasion we had barely left, when a child with a sickle cell crisis arrived. Children with this form of anaemia have a missing factor in their red cells. At times the cells become misshapen and stick together forming a sludge blocking the small vessels. If the anaemia is severe enough they may die; they require careful monitoring and sometimes small blood transfusions at a critical level. At this time we had no laboratory facilities, but it was obvious that the child was critically ill and needed to get treatment in a hospital where there was a laboratory and the facilities to monitor his condition carefully. Gudrun was about to set out with the child for Kampala, when she realised that there was no petrol in the car. No problem, we usually had a large drum with petrol kept in reserve. However, when she investigated, she found it was also empty. There was more than one vehicle in Kiwoko, so she set out to scout the area for a vehicle which had fuel. None was found, or at least none with ufficient fuel for the journey to and from Kampala. At that time there were constant fuel shortages in the country and there was no guarantee that the petrol stations on the main road would have any fuel either. However Gudrun recognised that the child's condition was critical and she needed to move fast. So what little petrol was available was siphoned from one vehicle to another to maximise resources and she set out. She reached Kampala, but despite her intervention the child later died.

When I arrived back from Turi I had the task of taking the corpse and mother back to the family home. This was the first time I had experienced the wailing of bereavement. The mother had been quiet and full of fortitude with me, but as soon as we reached her village compound, everyone set up wailing. It was the dead of night and it was eerie. However I learned through time that this was the normal village way of expressing grief over a bereavement. It wasn't anyone's fault that the child died, everything which could have been done in the circumstances was done. However I would have felt better if I had been around to save Gudrun the trouble of hunting for petrol and making the journey to Kampala, but I had a simple choice. I could either be welded to my work, trying to take responsibility for every event, or I could recognise that no one was indispensable and I also had a duty to spend time with my children. It was never an easy decision, but I am glad now I did take the opportunities to spend time with my kids, particularly in the light of future events.

I noticed that some missionaries had a highly developed sense of duty to their work which could be to the detriment of their families. On the other hand I realised that many Christians, who would have been interested in missionary work, simply discounted it as a possibility, as they saw a missionary's life as incompatible with their responsibilities to their family. We found that while there were obviously conflicts and compromises to be made, often involving much soul searching and hard thought, it was possible to fulfil one's responsibility to one's family and carry out meaningful service abroad, at the same time. We tended to set our own parameters and it was only when we were prepared to move beyond our own perceived limitations and boundaries that we were surprised how our family or other responsibilities did get taken care of.

When we had signed on with CMS we had assumed that we would only be able to spend two years in Africa primarily due to the educational limitations for the family. Also we were not sure if we ourselves could survive for longer than two years in this totally new environment with all the challenges it entailed. The first night we spent in Luweero, as we lay down to sleep, I had an immense sense of fulfilment.

'This is it,' I felt, 'this is where I should be.' Meanwhile Robbie tugged at my arm. It had been a very trying day and the circumstances seemed completely hostile to Robbie.

'Ian,' she whispered, 'two years, how are we going to make it through two years?'

These were probably entirely natural reactions for a husband and wife. I had the sense of vocation and challenge, Robbie had the sense of the difficulties that lay ahead. However after two years Robbie was the one who was saying about Uganda, 'This is my home. This is the place I love. These are the people I am committed to.'

Nevertheless, we would still have felt we should return to Ireland after two years, but for a significant event which took place at Turi. The school was a member of the association of independent preparatory schools and, as such, their level of education extended only to the Senior Form Two, or age thirteen. Beyond that stage many pupils would go to boarding schools in the UK. However at the time when we had to make decisions about returning home, or sending the children to boarding school in the UK, the Board of Governors of Turi decided to extend their educational level to GCSE. Our children could now attend Turi for at least another three years. We felt tremendously privileged to be able to send our children to

Turi. Some of the teachers got frustrated that they were teaching apparently affluent kids in a relatively privileged setting in Africa. We reassured them of how vital their work was to people like us. Many missionaries and aid workers would have found it very difficult to continue without the service they provided to our families.

Things didn't always go smoothly at Turi, due sometimes to circumstances entirely beyond anyone's control. Uganda had been relatively quiet and stable for a number of years when trouble broke out in Kenya. Unfortunately in Africa, political instability is often accompanied by tribal animosity and violence, Kenya had been moving towards a multi-party democracy and some of the factions were stirring up their followers towards inter-tribal conflict. Kenya had been stable for more than twenty years and most people wished that stability to continue. They need only look over their borders to see the horrific effects of inter-tribal warfare. Sudan, Ethiopia and Somalia were embroiled in conflicts which had brought starvation to millions. Uganda still bore the scars of years of civil war. However there were always some people who were prepared to stir things up in the interests of selfish gain, regardless of the consequences. The area around the school had been inhabited by a number of tribal groups, peacefully co-existing for years, when suddenly rioting broke out. When the situation was examined more closely, it was found that the riots were not spontaneous riots, but were organised. Gangs of men from one tribe would attack isolated villages and wreak havoc. Suddenly the school was enveloped in this sea of violence, death and carnage. The homes of one tribal group within the school were set on fire and they had to take refuge, that night, on the flat stone roof of the main school building. The pupils could hear and see people running around the ground, shouting and brandishing clubs, as the homes of the stable hands burned to the ground. There was certainly an air of anxiety and the teachers kept a wary watch through the night, ready to evacuate the pupils in the event of an attack on the main school. Kids went to sleep that night with baseball bats, hockey sticks or cricket stumps ready to hand. By morning the trouble had passed. The employees at risk were evacuated and school continued. However by this time many of the parents in Nairobi had heard of the trouble around the school on the local news and removed their children. News did not travel so fast to Uganda and especially Luweero, so we remained blissfully unaware of any problems until we arrived five days later in Kampala on our way to collect the children at the end of term. Perhaps it was better that we had not heard anything as we would only have had more time to worry. When we arrived at the school we found very few pupils remaining, mostly those whose parents worked in Uganda. Sean did admit that there had been a few anxious moments, but mostly it had seemed like an exciting bonfire display.

The trouble was not yet over. As we returned at the end of the holiday, with the children, we heard news in Kampala that rioting had started again in Molo, the area around the school. We were not quite sure what to do but decided to press on to Kisumu, the first major town inside the Kenyan border. When we reached there, the next day, we were informed that the school had been closed. The reports in the local papers were terrible. People were being decapitated, mothers and babies set alight in their own huts, hundreds had been killed and thousands of refugees were on the move. At this point we didn't really know what to do. It was a long drive back to Uganda but we were relatively close to the school. We decided to carry on and see for ourselves. After all, coming from Northern Ireland we knew that newspaper reports could be grossly exaggerated and the trouble might be confined to a limited area. So we set out together with the other Irish missionary family, the Brownlees. I suppose Donald and I were in essence a couple of stubborn Irish men who wanted to assess things for themselves. Before leaving we prayed for protection for the journey. We were somewhat apprehensive, and we expected to be turned back by Police if there was serious trouble.

As we neared the area we saw people carrying their belongings in the opposite direction. Some belongings and the contents of houses had apparently been abandoned at the sides of the roads. But there were no Police checks, in fact there was no evidence of security forces or rioters anywhere, so we moved on. As we passed through Molo town, many people were milling about, but there was no evidence of violent intent. We found that the attitude of the people toward us was not hostile, indeed they were friendly, probably because we were white and seen to be uninvolved in this situation.

When we reached the school we realised that all was quiet and it was not under threat. After a week the school re-opened and although violence continued sporadically, the school was never a target. It was in the eye of the storm and although violence flared all around it, peace reigned within the school boundaries. In that whole area of Kenya it was the safest place to be. Some of the teachers got involved with the refugee crisis, collecting money from their colleagues, taking food, blankets and other essentials to the refugees.

In some senses Turi might be a little bit of England, but circumstances like this reminded everyone that it was definitely not in England. Turi had been started sixty years previously by a dedicated Christian couple who had a vision for a Christian school. It had survived the Mau Mau uprising, it had survived a fire which completely erased the school, except the chapel and games pavilion, but had been rebuilt again by Italian prisoners of war. Sixty years later it was still surviving in the midst of a sea of conflict. Through all this time, it maintained a strong Christian ethos and provided an inestimable service to families such as ourselves.

Chapter 12

Snakes and Ladders

I don't think that anyone arriving in a Third World country can escape the bureaucratic machine. On the whole, Third World countries were taught thoroughly about bureaucracy by the colonial Powers. The colonialists obviously did a good job in this area as even though they themselves have disappeared from the scene, the bureaucracy is still alive and well and going strong. It is also fair to say that the former colony could now teach the Imperial Powers a thing or two about the operation of the bureaucratic system.

As relative newcomers to Uganda we were fed into the system. Ugandan bureaucracy is like a mammoth living organism which has a will of its own, a kind of giant amoeba which moves in many different directions at the same time, swallowing up people's faculties and energies, their time and their sanity, and spewing them forth many months later as demented, frustrated, helpless creatures. Many an apparently self-controlled man has been reduced to a blithering, babbling, paranoid, shadow of his former self, by just a few weeks exposure to the process.

In the course of life in Uganda we were automatically thrust into the arms of bureaucracy to obtain special passes, work permits, vehicular registration documents, Ministry of Health registration etc. To a newcomer wandering through this maze, it helps if they are aware of some fundamental principles. First of all they should not make the mistake of thinking that there are no rules in the game. There are very definite and well established rules. It is just that the applicant or player in the game doesn't usually get to find out what they are. The other important thing to remember is that the civil servant is the umpire of the game, so he is the only one who can interpret the rules. The player who becomes over-confident, because he feels he has grasped the rules, will end up in a worse position as he has no control over the interpretation and implementation of them. As we all know in any country a Civil Service's main function is to create employment. This well established and legitimate function, however, often needs to be augmented in the Third World situations. The civil servants are rarely paid a living wage, so they become businessmen seeing and exploiting any opportunities which may come their way. Many an exhausted and frustrated traveller through the maze of bureaucracy is only too willing to advance some smiling, helpful civil servant a few shillings to help him extricate himself. The fact that it may well have been the self-same civil servant who led him into the maze and got him lost in the first place no longer seems relevant.

Living in a rural area, some two hours drive outside Kampala, gave us an added disadvantage. We became familiar with two commonly used phrases which often presented obstacles. The first one was 'the man with the key has gone'.

This was always a particularly difficult obstacle to get around as for any department there appeared to be only a single keyholder. For example, if one got as far as getting all the paperwork completed to the point of paying the duty or taxes, one often found that the cashier's office had closed early, or the cashier hadn't come back from lunch.

'Sorry, the man with the key has gone.'

This piece of information was inevitably followed by the second commonly used phrase, 'Come back tomorrow.'

As this involved another trip to Kampala, another four hours of travelling, it was never very welcome advice. Gudrun had taught us how to deal with this difficulty.

When told 'come back tomorrow', she simply sat on the person's desk and said she wasn't leaving until she had what she came for!

As the civil servant was usually less than happy about the prospect of this German lady decorating his desk for the rest of the day, some extra effort was often made to complete the process and get rid of her.

The reasons for the advice 'come back tomorrow' were myriad. It might be Friday and no one wanted to start a new process on a Friday. It might even be Thursday afternoon and with the weekend in prospect no one was enthusiastic to start something new. It might be 9.30 am and the appropriate person hadn't arrived, or 3.00 pm and they hadn't come back from lunch. As each person normally had their well-defined area of jurisdiction, which couldn't be impinged upon by someone else, the automatic advice given by their colleagues was 'sorry, come back tomorrow'.

Take the process of registering our vehicle as an ambulance, for example. A relatively simple process one might think, but don't be deceived. The process of registration of a vehicle in Uganda involves many steps which can take days or even weeks. In my case I had left the documents with a friend some time earlier, who had assured me that the process was almost complete, but I would have to see an official to complete the final step. I had naively set aside an afternoon for the task. The first civil servant referred me to his boss, who advised that the next step in the process was to visit the Police Inspection depot, where I would get a stamp on the log book. Nothing could be simpler. I had a friend with me visiting from England at the time. Our encounter with Ugandan bureaucracy was to be an education for him of what life was really like in Uganda. We set off for the Police Inspection depot about three miles away. Another official examined the documents.

'But you haven't got the general receipt from the first office,' he explained.

No one had told us about a general receipt. Back we went to square one. Receipt in hand we hot-footed back to the police depot.

'That's better,' said the policeman. 'But now you haven't got a letter from the vehicle registrations.'

'What letter from vehicle registrations? We didn't know anything about that.'

It was like 'snakes and ladders'. We would climb laboriously up, working through the process, step by step, but we kept hitting snakes and getting sent back to the beginning.

After finally reaching the office of vehicle registrations we returned to the Police depot yet again with our letter.

'Now can we get the stamp please?' we asked.

One felt that it was with some reluctance the official acknowledged we had all the correct papers. After all his job was to umpire the game and disqualify anyone who wasn't playing correctly. So back we went to the first office and presented our papers for the final stamp, or so we thought.

'Where's your stamp from the policeman at the door?' we were asked.

'What policeman, what stamp?'

Now we were becoming desperate. There seemed to be no policemen anywhere and the time was approaching 5.00 pm. Finally he was found and stamped our papers, which were fairly well covered with stamps by now. We raced up to the counter and presented the papers.

'Sorry, we are closing,' we were told. 'Come back tomorrow.'

Derek, my English friend, couldn't believe that so much effort could be involved in what we had been told was a simple process, and we were still unsuccessful. In fact in this case it took several more weeks before we had the final document in our hands. However that is how the system works. You can only be told one step at a time. All the steps in the chain could never be revealed all at once, even if it does involve shuffling needlessly back and forth between offices. Actually no one is ever really sure of all the steps involved in a particular process. No one is prepared to advise on anything except the next immediate step, and if they happen to get that wrong it is like snakes and ladders, you have just hit a snake and you slither back to the beginning again.

It seems unjust when some people apparently flow through the process amazingly quickly, after always finding the right ladders and never, apparently, landing on a snake.

The giving of incentives or tips to officials in Third World countries is a well recognised practice. Many people arriving in a developing country are horrified by the widespread nature of the practice. Sometimes it seems that nothing moves or nothing gets done unless a little money changes hands under the counter. In fact bribery and corruption is like an inner rot that is steadily destroying the fabric of many Third World countries. Productive action is strangled by the system so that eventually the country doesn't produce anything and there is no more money being generated to pay the bribes. It is unfortunate that because of modern technology and communication, developing countries are constantly faced with the interface or contrast between the rich and the poor, the haves and the have nots, the old and the new. In Uganda today many people live as they might have lived 100 years ago in Ireland, subsistence farming, the women out with the hoes, the thatched mud huts, the difference being that the Ugandan today also samples modern civilisation and modern technology – fax machines, Mercedes Benz cars, radios, televisions, videos and the latest four wheel drive vehicles are the order of the day.

The Irish peasant of 100 years ago accepted life as it was and slowly worked and struggled to improve his lot. Perhaps a bigger farm, more chickens, another cow, all reachable, obtainable goals. Many Ugandans seek to develop in the same way, to improve their houses, extend their agriculture etc. But some are not particularly interested in this way of development. It seems too slow, too much work involved with little result. They want the modern rewards now, the car, the video and the TV. And they know people who have got there, not slowly and gradually but through being in a position of influence in the city. The policeman who has a job in the vehicle inspection centre made it. He may only receive a salary of ú30,000 shillings per month, but he can easily make ú300,000 per month, unofficially, donated, of course, by grateful clients who are simply thankful for the way he helped them through the maze. It is unfortunate for the development of the country that those areas of activity which could result in real increased productivity get rejected, while people are concentrating on quicker ways to make money. On the other hand, it is best not to become too self-righteous as an outsider. Some people would say that the system of bribery has existed in the culture for hundreds of years and is actually part of the culture and should be accepted as such. It's probably not so long ago in her development since Britain was involved in bribery as a routine daily event. One wonders in Uganda, a country which is just recovering from 20 years of civil war and showing some encouraging signs of development in recent years, if corruption will actually 'kill the goose which lays the golden eggs' or if it will be content to steal some of the eggs. People in Africa accept that some of the eggs will get stolen but when the goose gets killed it is a downward spiral of poverty and deprivation for everyone.

Chapter 13

The Widow's Barrel

Progress at the clinic had reached the stage where we now had a Maternity Ward, a larger Laboratory and a busy Out Patient Department. General Ward was not yet complete but the nurses had a house with a flush toilet. I hadn't given much thought to staff housing, but I was now realising it was going to be a problem. One couldn't run a clinic without staff and there were no decent houses nearby where they could live. The more facilities we provided the more staff houses we would have to build.

Gudrun and the ex-patriot nurses had somewhere to live and the Ugandan midwives had rooms behind the dispensary, but we were still living in the Ugandan farmhouse three miles away from Kiwoko. At first patients had always come to our house, but now as facilities had been built at Kiwoko, more and more patients went directly there. This was as it should be, except when an emergency happened at Kiwoko and I was at home. I got used to hearing the sound of a Land Rover roaring down the road. By the time it arrived, I would be outside waiting for it and we would speed off again to Kiwoko. There was no way of contacting me apart from coming to get me. Personally I didn't mind, but the stress was beginning to show on the nurses as they were having to cope with situations which were beyond their capacity and training. It was obvious that something would have to be done. We would have to build a house for ourselves at the health centre and move to Kiwoko.

Having lived in fairly cramped quarters for more than a year we determined that this time we would have a house with more space, and indeed a garden.

The problem about building a house at the health centre was that we had no money, or at least very little. Yet it was becoming more urgent daily that I be based at Kiwoko. We had a dilemma on our hands which we were to face again and again in the future. We had a need – we believed it was right to take steps to meet it – but we were not at all sure that we would get all the funds to finish the project. The question was simple – did we wait until all the money was in the bank, before starting anything, or did we go ahead with what we believed was right and pray for the money to come?

The Bible had conflicting advice. There was the story of the man who set out to build a tower but didn't have the resources to finish it. It would have been better for him to sit down first and do his calculations. Then there was the example of how Jesus sent his disciples out to meet needs and he didn't even give them money for hotel bills – they were to go out with what they stood up in, and minister in the various towns expecting their needs to be met as they went along.

Both examples could be applied to us. We had come out to minister to the people and were finding various needs as we went along. We could either try to meet these needs as best we could, or hold everything until we were sure of the finances.

If we started a project, because we believed it was right and trusted God and prayed, did that represent faith or foolishness? I still could not answer that question. However, I was aware that in the work we were involved in there was a dynamic, a momentum, which kept us going forward! We were doing things which looked impossible, yet God was giving us grace and providing in most unusual ways. We had a sense that this was not just a humanly inspired project we were involved in, but that there was a supernatural dimension to what we were doing. Too many things would happen which were beyond our control and pushed the work forward.

Therefore we decided we should go ahead with building our house. We selected a site near the clinic where we would build, but as yet we didn't have a plan – a fairly essential element in building any house. Our problem was solved when we visited friends in Kampala. Gary was the pastor of a large Pentecostal church in the city. They had stayed in Kampala right through the eighties when the city was not the most serene place to be. On one occasion they had locked themselves in their home as a gun battle raged outside. On another occasion thieves broke in, tied them up and stole all their belongings. Their house was a simple design – a straightforward rectangular one storey house – but well proportioned. This was a design I favoured as I didn't want to introduce any complicated schemes for the builders.

Fortunately Gary and Marilyn had no objections to me copying their house, so the rest of the Sunday afternoon was spent measuring up. By that evening I had a simple plan and the next day the builders were able to start the foundations.

Before leaving Ireland a small committee had been formed to support the work in Uganda. It had been registered as a charity under the name, Love Uganda, and although it was essentially a small, local group, they succeeded in raising a significant amount of money.

When I communicated with Ian Taylor, the secretary of the group, that we had embarked on building a house but had little money, he wasn't impressed, as he felt somewhat responsible to raise the balance of the funds. In truth it can be a dilemma when church leaders or individuals believe that God has given them faith for a certain project or purchase but in effect the faith of the leader puts other people under pressure. Ian was a brilliant administrator who could produce excellent visual and written presentations of the work going on, but hated asking people for money and was always surprised when they gave it.

I could feel his anxieties all the way to Uganda.

'What is Ian Clarke getting us into now?'

His first big surprise came when someone anonymously gave £5,000 and by the time we had finished building all the money had come in. Many times building the clinic has been like the story of Elijah in the Old Testament when he was being fed by the widow. When he arrived she had just a little flour and a little oil left. She was going to bake her last cake, then she would starve.

Elijah, perhaps some would say, rather presumptuously and selfishly instructed her to bake him a cake first.

The widow complied and after that there was always just enough left to bake the next cake. The interesting thing about the story is that despite the fact they were saved from famine they always seemed to be on the point of starvation. The barrel was almost empty, but not quite. They kept using what was there and the next time there was just enough again. Naturally speaking we all like to have something in reserve. It makes us feel more comfortable. I am no exception. I am not comfortable just having a little in the bank, not knowing if there would be enough to finish the job. However the Kingdom of God often doesn't work that way. Jesus sent the disciples out with what they had got, the shoes on their feet and the staff in their hand and told them to go and minister, heal the sick, cast out demons and preach the gospel.

We were in Luweero in much the same way. We didn't have a big organisation behind us with a big budget but we had something potentially more powerful. We had the Kingdom of God behind us. If we had wanted the security of the big budget and the big organisation behind us we would still be waiting. Plans take time for approval, bureaucracies become involved, surveys have to be done, consultants brought in. There is absolutely nothing wrong with this way of doing things. It is often the right and proper way. However sometimes in God's Kingdom He just needs people to go into a situation and get involved. When the right person is there the right finance will follow, although like Elijah and the widow, it is not always the most comfortable situation if there doesn't appear to be much in the way of reserves.

At the final count, hundreds of thousands of pounds were generated for the work in Kiwoko, but the provision was usually realised afterwards. At the time we always had just enough money to get started on what we believed was the next right step.

Our house was built within a few months and by the time it was completed the general ward had also been finished. Kiwoko was now a Health Centre, that is a small cottage style hospital. It had 35 beds with basic facilities to treat general medical and maternity patients, but no facilities for surgery, X-rays or more specialist treatments. The Health Centre had developed as a result of the community health programme, as immediate needs in the community became obvious through the programme. Now instead of delivering patients in our house or in the small dispensary, we had a proper maternity ward. We could also admit the acutely ill who needed treatment to our medical ward and we could carry out lab tests, screen blood for AIDS and give blood transfusions.

As the work at Kiwoko continued to expand a significant proportion of my time was spent applying for grants, filling in project applications or reports, or writing letters to donors and churches to keep them informed. It was a very important part of my role, even though sometimes the reports might seem tiresome or the administration seemed to be taking me away from my patients. However I realised that although I could train Ugandan health workers to relieve me of some of the clerical work, it was much more difficult for the Ugandan staff to source funds or write the necessary reports. My role was as a link between the aid agency or church in the West and the work going on in Kiwoko.

Sometimes the whole business seemed slow and frustrating. I would write an application and nine months or one year later find that the application had been lost by the agency and no progress had been made with it. This happened on a number of different occasions with a number of agencies. I also found that I often received a discouraging first response, but that I should not be put off by this. I should keep trying. I felt this was because the agency had never heard of me before, so on the first time round they were inclined to be suspicious and negative. However, when I applied the second time they said, 'Ah yes, we have heard of this project, they are doing community health care or AIDS care in Luweero.'

The fact that they had heard about us through our first failed application didn't make all that much difference. I once heard that it was easier to get a hire purchase agreement if the person had borrowed money before. If it was a completely new person with a clean slate the companies were suspicious, but if they knew he had run up debts in the past they could do business with him – they had heard of him. It seemed to be a similar philosophy with aid agencies. Kiwoko benefited from at least three different grants which were initially turned down.

I also found that the smaller agencies were easier to deal with. They had less bureaucracy and could deal with an application more quickly. This was true of War on Want Northern Ireland. This agency depended mainly on thrift shops within the Province staffed by volunteers. The whole organisation had only one paid member of staff so their percentage of funds spent on administration was minimal. As they were a small aid agency they didn't give us large amounts of money. However, they did give us a few thousand pounds every year which over four years mounted up to almost £20,000.

The larger agencies usually had larger bureaucracies which could be a nightmare to deal with. Applications went before committees which usually only met once per quarter. Letters with more comments and questions were returned. Replies were sent to outside experts for their comments. The whole process took many months, if not years, and by the end of it there could be a huge file of correspondence. On the other hand sometimes problems arose simply because of an unreliable postal system. Ugandan postal services could be very fast or very slow. Letters could arrive within a few days or on a few occasions a letter could arrive up to a year or more after being sent. Such a situation caused total confusion on one particular grant from Tear Fund.

Tear Fund had agreed to give us substantial funding for an AIDS project and had written to notify us of the application approval. However, on this occasion they wrote to the Bishop of the Diocese even though all the previous correspondence had been directly to me as the Medical Superintendent. Fortunately they had also sent me a copy letter. Another quirk in the system was that they wrote to the wrong Bishop. This was understandable as Luweero had only recently been formed into an autonomous diocese and they were obviously not up to date in their information. I contacted their Nairobi office to advise them of their mistake and the correct procedure for transferral of funds to the clinic. The grant was duly received, the money spent and six monthly and twelve monthly reports sent back to Tear Fund. Almost exactly one year after the grant had been approved I received a copy of a most unusual letter from the Bishop. It was a letter to Tear Fund thanking them for a grant for Kiwoko. The letter also sought to answer a number of technical questions and pointed out that the typist must have made an error in the date as it was dated almost exactly one year before it was received. Because he was sure that a simple mistake had been made in the year the letter was dated, he even commented on the fast speed of the delivery! Looking at the dates in May it appeared to have taken only a few days to arrive. The Bishop also wrote to our Bishop and informed him that we had received a grant from Tear Fund. Our own Bishop then wrote to me rejoicing that we

114

had received a grant and asking me to call at the Diocesan office.

I was thoroughly confused. I had received letters from not one, but two Bishops informing me that the clinic had received a grant which I wasn't expecting. If this was true it was indeed good news. However I was to be disappointed. When I got out our Tear Fund file I found that the letter the Bishop was referring to, the one with the wrong dates, *didn't* have the wrong dates. It was the one that Tear Fund had sent out over a year earlier. It appeared to have arrived with the Bishop exactly one year and a few days late. So hopes of another grant were dashed. Now I would have to explain to our Bishop that not only had the money been received but it had been spent. The good news about a grant was unfortunately belated.

While the grants from the aid agencies were essential they were usually designated for a specific project. No agency wished to give funds for everyday running costs, which became larger and larger as the clinic grew. Although we charged fees to the patients, these had to be affordable, and on many occasions patients could still not pay the small amount we asked. The fees received covered the cost of medicines and some staff costs, but certainly not the cost of running and maintaining equipment and buildings. For these costs we were very dependent on the donations from churches and individuals. I was blessed to see the wide cross section of denominations which supported the work, an Anglican church in London, a tiny community church on the Welsh border who gave donations out of all proportion to their small numbers, a large Pentecostal church in Belfast, the Anglican Cathedral in Belfast, our own Fellowship church in Bangor, a businessman from the north of England, churches in Canada, Dublin and Germany, doctors in Belfast and England. There was no particular pattern in the support. It could come from an individual who had visited Kiwoko or a church who had sent some young people out for a summer or a church who knew about us and adopted us as their project.

However they all had to have one thing in common – regular communication from me as to what was happening. Writing letters and circular letters was a part of our lifestyle. When a day's work was finished there were always letters to be written. If someone was interested in what was happening at Kiwoko, or gave money for the work, they deserved to be written to. Fortunately I could write letters very quickly. Unfortunately I could not write letters legibly, so it was probably a mixed blessing for people to receive a letter from me. They probably thought it was a nice gesture of him to write to us. It would be even better if we could read it. Robbie wrote much slower than me, but much more legibly.

It may have seemed very mundane to spend so much time trying to raise money, or to fill in reports or keep people in touch once we had received the money. However we realised that although we had the vision to do something to help the people in Kiwoko and although we had the faith to press on meeting needs, nothing would happen without finance, so our lifestyle was a peculiar mixture of prayer, faith, action, communication and begging. Personally we didn't mind who gave us the money or how it came so long as it kept coming in. We were definitely never in a position of wondering what to spend our next donation on. Usually like the widow's barrel, the supply kept up with the demand – but only just!

Chapter 14

Meeting More Needs

When we began to build a clinic, we had in mind meeting the needs of maternity and TB patients. TB patients could now be diagnosed at our laboratory, but we had nowhere to treat them as in-patients, once diagnosed. For those who lived locally, our community health workers would go daily to their homes and give them their streptomycin injections. But if they were outside our area, this was impractical.

Originally I had thought that Kiwoko would stay at the level of a Health Centre, that is a facility with some in-patient beds, a laboratory and out-patient department, but no theatre or specialised unit such as TB ward, surgical ward or nutrition unit. I felt that a Health Centre should meet the medical needs that we saw around us. However now that we had developed to that level we were still seeing many urgent needs which were difficult to cope with. It was obvious that development would not stop at this level.

As the clinic grew, demands grew with it. Demand always seemed to be one step ahead of supply and as one was dealing with people's lives the need couldn't be ignored. It was true that we couldn't meet every need that was presented to us but we had to do our best where we could.

The local people appreciated what was happening at the clinic and were eager to be involved. Some were employed as village health workers, some as laboratory assistants, some as nurse aids. Ever increasing numbers of patients kept coming with more serious medical complaints. The demands on the service increased as the level of service offered to patients expanded. As people saw that we could do more for them, more patients came. People saw that drugs were available, babies were delivered safely, lab tests carried out and patients received good treatment, so more and more people came.

However this gave us problems. If a mother couldn't be delivered by normal delivery or forceps delivery we had to take them to Kampala for caesarian section. If a man came with a strangulated hernia we had to rush him to a hospital. This was expensive and time consuming and the extra delay could be dangerous. It was becoming obvious to all that we needed an Operating Theatre.

The Memorial Fund for Barbara had generated a significant amount of money but at this point money was again in short supply and there certainly wasn't enough to build and equip an Operating Theatre.

The main building had been completed. It now housed an Out-Patient Department, Laboratory, General Ward, Maternity Ward and Delivery Room, but there was apparently no space left for a Theatre. I prowled up and down the building assessing what we were doing with each room. The Maternity Ward was the best equipped and most spacious and it had two delivery rooms. I finally decided that we could use one of these rooms. It would be small and the midwives would not like losing a delivery room but it could work. We had to make some alterations but a few weeks later we had a room ready for Theatre.

We had overcome the problem of space for a theatre, now what were we to do about equipment? I was a little daunted by the prospect of equipping and running a theatre, after all being trained as a GP I knew little about surgery, but I knew enough to appreciate it was a very expensive business to equip a theatre. What about anaesthetics, theatre lights, instruments etc? How would we sterilise our instruments?

Also the running of a theatre within a hospital was very much a sub-speciality. Most of our nurses knew little about theatre techniques. We would have to find someone with theatre experience. I knew that a high specification theatre would take tens of thousands of pounds to set up and equip. Thankfully we were not in that category, but even a simple theatre required certain basics – there must be a light which moved in every direction and gave good illumination for the surgeon. There must be an operating table which could be raised or lowered and tilted forwards and backwards. Because of the hydraulics necessary in an operating table and the mechanisms for the different positions of tilt, a new one could cost over £10,000. A new operating light would also cost £2,000 or more, depending on the degree of sophistication. The cheapest autoclave to sterilise the instruments was in the catalogue at £3,500. The smallest simplest anaesthetic machine was £1,500. Then there would be many different types of surgical instruments required, all of them expensive.

Once the theatre was equipped, how would we staff it? Who would act as theatre nurse? Who would give the anaesthetic? And most important of all, who would operate? I certainly hoped that I would not be expected to take up the role of surgeon. I didn't see myself in that role but I had a dreadful suspicion that I would get sucked in.

Sometimes when I was faced with apparently insoluble problems, which I could do nothing about, I had to just sit back and wait and see what happened. There was nothing I could do, so there was no point in me fretting needlessly. However over the next few months equipment began to arrive for the theatre. An operating table was supplied through Mengo hospital. An operating light came from Northern Ireland. A mission support organisation was sending out containers of medical equipment, school books, clothes and scripture teaching materials from Northern Ireland to Uganda. As the National Health Service cut back and hospitals were closed, they received hospital supplies which were sent out to Third World hospitals. Among equipment which had been sent was a dental operating light. It was rather small for general surgery but it could be raised or lowered and moved in any direction. If an assistant kept it focused on the exact area where the surgeon was operating, it worked well. Being a medically designed light it was also shadowless, a great advantage when peering into the depths of someone's abdomen.

Joint Medical Stores, an organisation in Uganda, who supplied mission hospitals with drugs, had received a consignment of autoclaves which were being sold to hospitals at subsidised prices. Unfortunately we were not on their allocation list. I knew they had one left, but they refused to part with it. If I wanted an autoclave I would have to pay £3,500. Then it came to my attention that JMS were looking for a small generator. What a coincidence! We just happened to have a small petrol generator which we were prepared to sell or even swap for another piece of equipment such as an autoclave. So a deal was struck and we got our autoclave.

Now all that remained were theatre instruments, an anaesthetic machine and the staff to run the theatre. As I was due to go on leave we had arranged for a doctor to replace me. As it happened, the doctor who came, Dr Amos, had experience in surgery and was very enthusiastic to get the theatre working at Kiwoko. Even more surprising was the fact that Lawrence, who had been working quietly as a village health worker, came forward to tell us that he was a trained Theatre Assistant. In the 1970s he had been working in the main theatre in Mulago Hospital, the main Government Hospital in Kampala. In the early 80s he came back to his home village near Kiwoko. When the war broke out in the Luweero triangle he was trapped in the area. He survived for four years hiding in the bush when soldiers or rebels were around, coming back to his home when it was safe. Lawrence told us that Museveni's army were the soldiers of the night, the Government troops were the soldiers of the day and the ordinary villagers were caught in the middle. If they helped one side they were treated as rebels, if they helped the other they were treated as collaborators.

Usually they had no choice. The rebels would come at night and demand food. The Government troops would come in the day and demand that they take them to the rebels. The safest thing to do was to hide from both sides.

Lawrence was a very experienced Theatre Assistant who was invaluable in getting the theatre going and in keeping a high standard of sterility in theatre practices. He was also responsible for the training of the student nurses in theatre techniques.

The anaesthetics problem was overcome by Gudrun herself. She had done a course in anaesthetics in Germany and with a little more training in a hospital in Kampala she became our anaesthetic assistant.

When I went on leave in Ireland I visited a small hospital and asked if they had any theatre instruments they didn't need, explaining what they were for. Theatre Sisters didn't usually give away their instruments, but I thought it was worth a try. The Sister looked pensive.

'Yes,' she said, they did have a caesarian section set which was now obsolete, since sections were now done in the other maternity theatre. If I returned the next day I could collect them. The following day, when I returned, the bottom cupboard (where the old instruments were stored) was raided and I had some of my precious instruments.

'How did you get around Sister?' one of the nurses asked.

Could it have been my natural charm and good looks?

Probably not, Sister recognised a good cause and just wanted to help.

More instruments were found through the missionary support organisation and finally, when some money was available, the drawover anaesthetic machine was purchased.

When I returned to Uganda after my leave, Kiwoko had

a functioning Operating Theatre. There would now be no more necessity for those hazardous trips to Kampala in the middle of the night.

Karen was especially concerned about the lack of facilities for treating TB patients. After all she was seeing positive TB sputum results every day. Was there anything she could do about it?

'Why don't we build some mud huts?' I suggested. These TB patients didn't need intensive medical attention, they just needed to be getting regular treatment. So if they lived on the clinic compound they could get treated.

We had been told that mortar could be made from a mixture of sand and cow-dung. If mud bricks were used with this, a low cost building could be erected. Karen was torn. Mud huts could be built for next to nothing, but she had been given $1,000 so she had some money with which she could build a better building. The question was, could we build a TB Ward using low cost materials which would cost less than $1,000? I was dubious. Even if a large low budget building was put up, the roof alone would cost $1,000 as it would be preferable to use iron sheets. In theory, thatching was more appropriate, that is, it was cheaper, it was cooler and it used local materials. In practice the local thatching was of very poor quality. It leaked after a short period and had to be renewed and it was the ideal home for rats. The local people themselves preferred tin roofs, if they could afford them.

If someone would donate the iron sheets then it would be a different matter, the $1,000 would then cover the cost of the walls and floor, but who would help us, we wondered?

'What about our friends in Kampala, the Ruparalias?' I suggested.

This was an Indian family with whom we did business. They had always been very interested in our work and had given us milk powder for malnourished children and some money for the clinic in the past. They owned a Hardware Shop which sold iron sheets. Perhaps they would give us the sheets for the roof. Well there was no harm in asking. They could only refuse.

So Karen was dispatched to Kampala with our request. She had completed some other business with the Ruparalias when she took a deep breath.

'We would like to build a TB Ward, but we don't have enough money. We can build the walls but we need iron sheets for the roof. We wondered if you would like to help us?'

She got it out in a rush. She was having palpitations because she wasn't used to this type of situation and had no idea what the response would be. She might have got a downright refusal or just a withering look. After all, these people were in business to make money and she was asking them to give away part of their stock without payment.

Paresh, the son in the family, with whom she was dealing, didn't even look up.

'No problem,' he grunted. 'How many do you need?'

Karen's heart was beating even faster now. She hardly dared to say a figure.

'One hundred' she suggested timidly, ready at the slightest sign of disapproval to cut the number by half. After all anything was better than nothing.

'No problem,' murmured Paresh again. 'Send your truck.'

Karen rose quietly and floated out of the shop. She could hardly believe it had happened. This man had just given $1,000 worth of iron sheets and he hadn't looked up from what he was doing. The Ruparalia family were in fact to give us much more money and materials as the work went on. They were a devout Hindu family whose practice it was to give regularly to charity. Mr Ruparalia had lived in Uganda all his life, even during the time of Idi Amin. He had not been expelled. He loved the country and wanted to see it prosper. He explained to me on another occasion when he made a donation of £2,000 worth of cement.

'I want to help the poor, the orphans and the sick. I can't do it myself but I can help people like you who are doing it.'

It didn't matter to him that we were a Christian Hospital and he was a Hindu. Many of us, when we make a donation, have some vested interest in the Organisation we give to, for example they are usually people with the same beliefs. It didn't even matter to this family what our beliefs were. The Ruparalias always gave us strong encouragement in what we were doing. Here was a Ugandan Indian family giving money so that a Christian Hospital would help the poor and the sick in their adopted country. If Uganda had more people of the same spirit the future would be bright.

So the TB Ward took shape, with enough space for twenty patients. The first patient was admitted even before the roof was completed and within a few weeks it was overflowing, sometimes with as many as thirty patients. Before it was plastered we got some money for cement, so it was finished in the conventional way with a layer of cement plaster. No one looking at it would ever have realised that this building was really held together by cow-dung!

As we now had medical and surgical facilities, TB Ward, Laboratory and Maternity Ward, we had moved beyond the realms of being a Health Centre. I consulted the regulations governing requirements for various categories of medical units in Uganda and discovered that we came into the Hospital category. It would be necessary for us to take steps to be re-registered as a Hospital with the Ministry of Health. I sighed inwardly, envisaging many trips to the Ministry of Health Headquarters at Entebbe, many forms to fill in and endless bureaucracy. Dealing with bureaucracy was not my strong point or indeed my favourite pastime.

I set off for the Registrar's office and found that the Registrar was away on a course and his duties had been delegated to the Assistant Director of Medical Services. I was given the appropriate forms to fill in which were remarkably uncomplicated. When I returned the following week the Assistant Director of Medical Services said he would like to visit the Hospital and inspect it for himself.

A few days later he arrived. He was extremely pleasant, helpful and commented that it was excellent to see a hospital develop in such a rural area. These were the places that really needed medical services. By the time the doctor left, he had given us the certificate which showed that Kiwoko was now 'officially' a Hospital. Nothing could have been simpler.

The work had developed from Community Health Project to Dispensary to Maternity Centre, Health Centre and then Hospital in less than three years. At no point since the day we arrived in Luweero had patients stopped coming, although on many occasions we had wished they would. The patients themselves had created the pressure for the rapid development of facilities. As I remembered the times we had rushed to Kampala with very ill patients, sometimes only to see them die when they reached the hospital, I was grateful that there were now facilities on hand so we could deal with the emergencies ourselves.

There were many deficiencies in what we had and we would continue to develop and expand for some time to come, but we could now intervene in many of the common and preventable causes of death which had hitherto gone unchallenged.

Chapter 15

Media Exposure

'Julian who?' I asked.

'Julian Pettifer' repeated Richard.

I was just completing a clinic, when a mini bus had arrived filled with camera equipment, tape recorders and a BBC film crew! Sometime before I had been told a BBC crew would be visiting us as part of the filming of a series of programmes entitled 'Missionaries'. However I was somewhat sceptical about this information and I thought it most unlikely that they would actually turn up. Why would they come to Uganda, much less all the way to Kiwoko to see me? If they really were interested in filming missionaries there were far more interesting missionaries than the Clarkes to see. Whatever their motive for coming I was definitely surprised at being introduced to a BBC team in Kiwoko.

It was 6.00 pm and filming was impossible for that day so I invited the crew to come home with me.

'I'm sure I can find somewhere to put you up,' I assured them, thinking of the building we euphemistically called 'The Guesthouse'. The latter had once been an old church which, when we arrived, was minus the roof. With the addition of the tin roof, some bunk beds and an outside shower and pit latrine, it had become the only accommodation we could offer to guests even if they were from the BBC. Of course it had the usual colony of rats. These particular rats seemed to be ardent climbers as they were continually spotted scampering among the rafters.

The BBC team were a rather considerate lot and they had brought an assortment of food along with them including, most notably, a bottle of Heinz tomato ketchup. I am not sure if they had been 'tipped off' that missionaries in Africa suffered withdrawal symptoms from such things as Heinz ketchup which were not readily available in Uganda, or if some of their own team had secret cravings and had to travel with a bottle. At any rate never before or since, have we had a whole BBC film crew come to deliver us a bottle of ketchup.

When we arrived back at our house I duly introduced the members of the team. My wife was understandably somewhat taken aback by suddenly having six extra people for dinner but even more taken aback to meet this person called Julian Pettifer. Apparently I hadn't been watching the same TV documentaries as Robbie. She recognised him as a well known TV presenter. The crew were thoroughly nice people. They had been travelling round the world filming all sorts of 'odd bod' missionaries, which explained why they had come to Kiwoko. And they intended to spend at least another year making their series of programmes.

Julian who was co-producer and presenter explained that in the course of his filming various travel documentaries he had met many interesting people, who turned out to be missionaries. When he explained about these missionaries to his friends back in London they would invariably comment, 'I thought that species of person had become extinct. Do missionaries still exist?'

I suppose people had in their minds a stereotype of the old missionary explorer in the bush – 'Doctor Livingstone, I presume.' So he was making this whole series on that interesting species of mankind which was not yet extinct – the missionary!

Filming was to start the next day at the crack of dawn. It was to be roughly 'a day in the life of the Clarkes'.

The final product, after all the editing, turned out to be three minutes of 'a day in the life of the Clarkes'.

Maybe we didn't turn out to be 'odd' enough to warrant much space in the final programme.

At 7.00 am the following day we were up on the roof filming Julian Pettifer interviewing the Clarkes.

Question: 'Ian, why did you leave a comfortable practice in Northern Ireland to come out to Uganda to be a missionary.'

Answer: Giggles and stutters from Ian!

Sean using the clapperboard: '589 take 2.'

Then later the breakfast scene – The Clarkes at breakfast.

Very natural – cold coffee and stale toast – small talk at the breakfast table. Just ignore the melon sized mike dangling over you and the man with the camera hovering about two feet away.

Family devotions after breakfast.

'Michael, would you stop praying into your hands, people are supposed to hear what you are saying.'

'Lauren, could you repeat your prayer again, the camera has run out of film.'

'Sorry, Lord for all these interruptions.' The cameraman apologises and promises to make up for them tonight in his own prayers.

Then school with Robbie and the kids.

'Now children, try not to ask too many dumb questions and look interested and intelligent.'

Now a shot of Ian leaving for work. 'Get into the car and drive round the corner, then you can come back.'

Later in the morning we all set out for a clinic. As it happened it was a clinic in the remotest area I covered – two hours drive away. The road goes north, then northwest through a beautiful forest, then through a swamp and finally grassland. Half-way through the forest I had to stop so they could take a shot of the jeep coming through the trees. The cameraman planted a tripod in the middle of a road then instructed me, 'Drive right back to the next

corner, then come down the road as fast as possible. Don'
slow down as you pass me.'

Then as an afterthought, 'You do have enough room to
get past me, don't you?'

As I came down the road again trying to measure the
distance between the camera and the side of the road, I
thought 'I wonder how much a new BBC camera costs
these days?'

Later I have to ferry the crew and their equipment over
the swamp. The road is so bad that their van cannot pass.
They debate if six of them plus their equipment can get
into the jeep. I think that our capacity is at least nine.
What are they worried about? They are obviously not used
to travelling in Uganda.

The clinic turns out to be very busy. Absolutely in the
middle of nowhere, not even a mud hut in sight.
Livingstone and I see the patients, we examine them on a
sack placed on the ground.

Julian asks, 'Is this your examination couch?'

As I look at a child with a greatly enlarged spleen and
liver, he asks again, 'Ian, can you tell us what the diagnosis
is?'

'Gulp', I didn't think I would get an oral examination on
TV as well.

By the end of the day we are travelling home in the dark
and I am suffering from nervous exhaustion. Whoever
thought that one could come to the African bush to get
away from it all and have a quiet life!

The team had spent ten hours getting their film. When
the final series of programmes was shown, 18 months
later, the slot on the Clarkes lasted exactly three minutes.
However we were not unhappy with our limited spot. It
had seemed fairly impartial, even favourable, in contrast
to many other missionaries in the series who ended up
looking ridiculous as a result of BBC editing. It was sad to
see that good well meaning people, who had given their
lives to help others, were being portrayed as 'latter day
Colonialists' simply interested in imposing their own

cultural ideas and values on people who didn't really need them or want them.

We experienced an entirely different aspect of the media when we were visited by a journalist from a local newspaper in Northern Ireland. The newspaper had been very helpful in publicising fundraising events for the work in Uganda so they decided to send out one of their journalists to investigate what was going on and do a series of articles.

Colin seemed the most unlikely investigative reporter. He was very quiet and seemingly introspective. Perhaps he was overwhelmed by all these vociferous Christians he suddenly found himself among. Perhaps it was the hostile environment with soldiers carrying sub-machine guns going through his belongings on the way from the airport. Colin really did get thrown in at the deep end. There were several road blocks on the road from the airport where the army were a little over-enthusiastic about carrying out their duties of stopping and searching. Taciturn soldiers pulled out our bags and searched everything, with frequent suggestions that we could have improved their mood and general attitude with a small gift. Finally one soldier found $20 in Colin's wallet. Seizing the notes he waved them triumphantly in his face.

'What is this?' he snarled. 'Undeclared foreign currency?'

'But it is declared,' protested Colin, confidently producing his currency declaration form from his inside pocket.

'This is no use,' snapped the soldier and handed it back.

Colin found himself staring at a completely blank form. The carbon hadn't come through when he filled in the copy.

The soldier now felt himself to be in a strong position. At this point the ritual was to press on with the show of intimidation so that we would finally be glad to go without protest leaving him with the $20. However this particular soldier had not reckoned on having to deal with my wife!

In fairness to Robbie I have to say she is normally a

131

moderate, self-controlled person, who doesn't go round intimidating people, much less soldiers with sub-machine guns – that is until she gets her hackles up.

The soldier, who until now, had felt very much in charge of the situation suddenly found himself facing this irate white lady demanding his 'name, rank and serial number', and further demanding that she speak to his Commanding Officer. It also happened that we knew a Captain in the army. So she was also threatening dire consequences for this soldier through our 'inside' contacts in the army. Actually, I don't think that our nodding acquaintance with one captain in a huge army would have made much impact, but the soldier wasn't to know that.

'Who is this woman?' demanded the soldier, visibly shaken.

'Sir,' he said, pointing at me, 'keep your wife under control.'

However at this point he didn't appear to have any heart in pursuing the matter of the dollars further. Handing them back to Colin he waved us on our way. Hence, that is how, when Colin came to write his article in the local newspaper, I was described as 'cool, calm and collected' and Robbie was described as 'fiery'. Robbie still protests that this description is totally unfair, however personally I feel that Colin had a lot of insight.

Colin shared the guesthouse, at the time, with Gudrun and other staff, Gudrun's own house not having been completed. There was also a small group of Irish young people visiting. The 'cross fertilisation' in cultural values and language between this sceptical reporter, the German nurse, the Ugandan staff and the Irish young people was rich. On one occasion one of the Irish group described Gudrun as a 'quare gag!'

Now for anyone outside Northern Ireland they would be totally mystified by this term, as indeed was Gudrun. It means, roughly translated, that someone is a 'good sport' or a 'good laugh'. However it was all lost on Gudrun.

'What is this "square peg"?' Gudrun kept insisting. 'I don't understand.'

Rosie, one of the Irish team was from the Randalstown area in Northern Ireland, where accents are 'thick' and they have their own particular colloquialisms, usually understood by few outside the immediate Co Antrim area.

'Wud ya luk at the cut o thon' exclaimed Rosie.

One really can have some sympathy with Gudrun and the Ugandans in trying to understand what was being said. Translated it means, 'Look at the cut, as in clothes, of that one.'

Colin wanted to see all the clinics and the work we were doing so we would set out each day with the Suzuki full of people. One Friday we had to travel about two hours to do a clinic on the other side of Luweero. It was a beautiful, cloudless day when we set out and the car was crammed full of people. Part of the roof was detachable, but we didn't have space to put the part back inside the car. So we decided to go without it. After all there was not a cloud in the sky.

'You are making a mistake,' Robbie warned as we left. 'It will rain.'

The journey to the clinic passed without incident but as we were finishing, clouds began to gather. Seeing our predicament a Ugandan handyman helpfully cut a piece of plywood to fit over the hole, so we set out. Unfortunately the plywood wasn't quite a snug fit. It was a little bowed in the middle and tended to collect water. This didn't bother anyone until we went round a right-hand corner, then the water poured down the back of the front seat passenger's neck. Everyone was thoroughly amused except the front seat passenger. However when we went around a left-hand corner, water poured down the driver's neck, who happened to be me. I should have listened to my wife.

It always surprised me how many visits we received in Kiwoko from people from all over the world and in particular from various media people. Some of these visits concerned the AIDS epidemic which was obviously of great interest abroad. On one occasion we were visited by a Ugandan reporter who was living in London and freelancing for the BBC. The circumstances which brought about this visit were somewhat unusual. Robbie and I were in Kampala on our 'Wednesday' trip getting supplies. While I was in a shop ordering iron sheets for roofing Robbie was approached by a man and woman in business suits. They were black, but spoke English, not with the usual East African accent, but with an Oxford English accent. The man explained that he was a reporter and he had been told to make contact with an Irish doctor working somewhere in Luweero, but he didn't exactly know where the place was or what the person's name was. He had seen that our vehicle was a hospital vehicle and wondered if Robbie would know of such a person.

'I do know him rather well,' Robbie was able to reply. 'Actually I'm married to him.'

It transpired that the journalist had been born in Uganda but had gone to boarding school in England and was working in London for an English newspaper. He had been commissioned to do a programme for radio about the effect of AIDS on families in Uganda since he himself had a family there, and would have first hand knowledge of the epidemic. A colleague had heard of our work in Luweero and had advised him to visit us. So through this fortuitous meeting in Kampala an appointment was set up. As he wanted to talk to Ugandans who had friends and relatives who died of AIDS I asked some of the staff if they would like to be interviewed by him. Three of the staff volunteered and as I listened to the interviews I was impressed by their insight and courage.

Janet had lost a brother and two sisters to AIDS.

'What do you think of the attitude of Ugandan men to AIDS?' the reporter asked.

'Men have two attitudes depending on whether it is light or dark,' Janet replied. 'During the day they agree with all the propaganda about AIDS but during the night they forget it as they have other things on their mind.'

The reporter turned to Rose next. Rose had full-blown AIDS and I was surprised she was still alive. She had suffered two episodes of herpes zester, one severe episode affecting the face which had been painful and disfiguring. She had also had marked weight loss, a cough and a pleural effusion. Yet her spirit was undaunted and she kept going. She continued working and if she became tired or flagged her colleagues covered for her. She knew she had AIDS and she didn't try to hide it from anyone.

'Rose, have you had any relatives who have died of AIDS?' the journalist asked.

Rose didn't beat about the bush. 'I have AIDS', she replied.

She then went on to say that even though she had AIDS she didn't fear death because she trusted in God. She had a strong faith and she put her trust in God for every day. It was God who was taking care of her so why should she fear death? The journalist then turned to the last nurse who was HIV positive and whose baby had died of AIDS. She told him the same thing – she didn't know what the future held, but her life was in God's hands.

I was mesmerised. These girls had said little to me. They had not previously struck me as very confident Christians, but they were sitting in front of me unafraid, telling this reporter that the secret of their courage in the face of AIDS and the pain and suffering which each of them had known, was their faith in Jesus Christ. I was moved by their simple testimony. Let no one scorn their faith in Jesus Christ unless they too have suffered what these girls have suffered. It is easy to be a cynic on the sidelines but for these girls their faith was a stream of hope which ran through their sufferings.

Media people who came and went from Kiwoko all went back with their own particular perspective. Some, like the BBC team, appeared to have their mind made up on their angle or line for their TV series before they arrived and were simply looking for ammunition to propagate their particular point of view. However others seemed genuinely affected by what they saw and experienced.

Colin Bateman went back to Bangor and became involved in fundraising for Kiwoko. He commented in his newspaper article about his own agnostic state but said, 'It strikes me that it is only religious people who are prepared to go out to these troubled countries to try and do some good.'

Colin's visit gave him a new perspective on our own troubles in Ulster.

'I arrived back in the UK on a Sunday night and the first thing I saw was newspaper headlines about the murder of seven soldiers in a bus bomb. Nothing had changed here.

'If we can't help ourselves, is it too much to ask that we think about helping others a lot worse off than us?'

Chapter 16

Punctures

Rev John Olhausen approached me looking pale and anxious.

'Ian, I have done an awful thing,' he said.

John was the vicar of Holy Trinity Church in Hazelmere, a church that was becoming increasingly supportive of the growing medical work in Kiwoko. He was visiting Uganda for the first time. I was intrigued to hear what he had done. I had never been in the position of hearing the confessions of a vicar before!

'What is the problem?' I inquired in my best bedside manner, as John was obviously under some considerable stress.

'The wheel of your car has come off,' he confessed.

'But that is not your fault,' I reassured him.

'Oh, but it is,' he replied. 'You see I was the one who put it on in the first place.'

'I see,' I said, not sure where to take the counselling session from there.

John had only had good intentions and been trying to help. We had had two punctures the previous day and he had volunteered to change the wheel, since I was busy with some patients. That morning we were to leave for the airport. As the car had not sounded quite right, he had taken it for a 'test drive'. While travelling down the dirt road the wheel had flown off and rolled into the long elephant grass. The car bumped to a halt but John had no idea where the wheel had disappeared to. Fortunately while he was standing disconsolately beside the car a local boy emerged from the elephant grass with the wheel, so no real harm was done, apart from a slight dent to John's ego. The small dent in John's ego was to be nothing compared to the annihilation my own ego would suffer over the next day as we made the journey to Entebbe.

I don't understand why, but I've always had problems to do with punctures. When I was in Liverpool I finally had to give up riding my bicycle because of punctures. Actually the problem was not the punctures themselves, but my inability to repair them. I would follow all the instructions, remove the tube, find the hole, apply the glue, stick on the patch, replace the tube and tyre and inflate. The patch would promptly blow off and the tyre would deflate. After repeating this procedure several times I would be throwing bicycle spanners and muttering incoherently to myself. The children would be giggling behind their hands but staying at a discreet distance as they had learned that it wasn't safe to be near Dad when he was fixing a puncture. By the time we left Liverpool and set out for Uganda I was so disgusted I gave the bicycle away, but I was still to be haunted by the spectre of punctures.

As recorded in an earlier chapter, the first one happened on our very first journey from Kampala to Luweero and had been a matter of ardent prayer on Robbie's part. Since that time we had been averaging two punctures a week. This was probably due to a combination of poor tyres and even worse roads, but as we also had two spare tyres for the car, we usually managed to keep going and the local puncture repair garage did a roaring trade. I wondered what it was about my destiny which doomed me, or rather the vehicles or bicycles which I was responsible for, to get constant punctures. I didn't know it, but my worst test was yet to come.

We set out to take John back to the airport. We now had two spare wheels and a foot pump, having learned from previous experience. Unfortunately both our spares were now flat and we had not yet had an opportunity to repair them. Halfway to Kampala the inevitable happened! We got another flat tyre. However with a quiet word of prayer and some vigorous pumping we managed to get enough air pressure into one of our flat tyres to enable us to get to a garage. This garage didn't have the normal modern facilities for puncture repair but with some old Land Rover springs, a piece of an old tube, a stone to roughen the tyre tube and some very dubious looking glue, the tyre was repaired. So we were on our way rejoicing. We still had four inflated tyres and two flat ones, but as long as the score was four:two, we could keep moving.

By this stage I felt that I had probably gone through my severest testing on punctures and I had passed with distinction. I had remained cool, unflapped and had stayed in faith. After all hadn't everything ultimately worked out on every occasion we had a puncture?

The tyre held firm until we had deposited John at the airport. But on the way back from Entebbe, bumpity, bumpity bump! The score was three:all again. There was the offering of yet more prayer. This time not so quiet – a slight edge of desperation creeping in. However scarcely had I opened the boot to reveal the foot pump when a young man appeared beside me with a 'Vespa' scooter tyre. My own tyres were now beyond redemption by simple inflation, but his only required pumping. Ten minutes later he appeared with his scooter, complete with inflated tyre. He indicated that I should bring my tyre and get on the back. I made a precarious sight perched on the back of the Vespa, clutching the wheel, but a mile up the road was a petrol station, where the Land Rover spring, the stone, the old bit of tube and more dubious looking glue appeared. An hour later we were on our way rejoicing and reasonably confident that we could get back to Kampala to get all the tyres properly fixed. It was not to be.

Another mile passed and we thought we detected the dreaded 'hiss'. Of course by this time we were sensitized to that sound and we hoped we were imagining things.

Unfortunately the 'hiss' was followed by the rattling that indicated we were driving on the rim. This is the point where the head of the family, that is me, reminds the other members of the household that we are Christian missionaries and in situations like this we need to keep cool and trust God to look after us. At least that is the theory. Things were getting desperate now. It was getting late, my money was getting low and to crown it all the jack had broken. However one should never despair. As somehow only happens in Uganda two helpful, or perhaps hopeful, local lads were hurrying down the road toward us. I hadn't quite realised at first but the sight of a muzungu (or white person), standing pathetically beside his flat tyre has the same effect as a newspaper announcement that there will be a distribution of free gifts. 'Hopefuls' appear out of the woodwork looking for their share. If you help a muzungu to get his puncture fixed you can count on at least 500 to 1,000 shillings.

By this stage I was slightly dazed and in no position to argue. I had three flat tyres and now my jack had ceased to function. Ten minutes later I found myself in the next village in a puncture repair shop with one of the helpful Ugandans. Another fact was, that on a Sunday afternoon, on this particular stretch of road, this puncture repair shop had a monopoly on business and prices were increasing in direct proportion to the muzungu's state of desperation. As I was pretty desperate by then the price was high. Out came the inevitable old tube and dubious glue again. One and a half hours later I was back at the car with my tyre repaired and very little money. A crowd had gathered by the car so at least the problem with the broken jack was solved. We physically lifted the car and changed the wheel. Soon we were on our way. There were audible sighs of relief and muted thanks but I could tell that the members of the family were listening out for the dreaded hiss. Unfortunately they didn't have to wait long. The dubious glue really didn't hold out long this time. A few miles along the road and we had another flat tyre. At this point the missionary's faith will either have risen to new heights of trusting God and overcoming in any situation, or it will be as flat as the tyre. I will make no comment as to which end of the spectrum my faith was at. I suppose a man of greater faith than mine might have got out, laid hands on the car and prayed. I had to admit, at this point, I wasn't feeling calm or rational. I jumped out of the car and gave it a kick. I could now understand why Moses struck the rock!

All things considered, since darkness would soon fall, I decided to abandon ship and hitch a ride to Kampala. Two passing cars stopped and the whole family was ferried safely back to Kampala.

Although this may have been my severest, most concentrated trial regarding punctures, my trials continued in one form or another throughout my time in Uganda. Perhaps because I never really licked the problem in the first place, God felt I needed to be reminded of my weakness in this area from time to time. After all Paul had his 'thorn in the flesh'. However one had to see the funny side of many of these situations.

On one occasion I got a puncture on the way from Kiwoko to Luweero and when we checked the spare it was also flat. So I set off to Luweero with my wheel. On the journey there I got a lift in a lorry and having successfully inflated the tyre in Luweero, I had to make my way back.

The road from Luweero to Kiwoko was a dirt road which didn't have any police checks. Hence all the old vehicles which were totally unroadworthy plied the Luweero Kiwoko road as taxis. Since a large number of people travelled out from Luweero to the hospital every day, this had become a busy road which was very profitable for the local taxi drivers. The taxi stand looked like a scrapyard – a line of ancient vehicles usually without windscreens or interior upholstery. Most of them dated from the 1950s or 60s and seemed to be held together by faith and bits of wire. The amazing thing was that they could run at all; in any other country or situation they would have been scrapped years earlier.

So I arrived at the 'scrapyard' taxi terminus with my tyre and negotiated a special hire to take me back to the stranded Landcruiser. The first taxi in the line was an ancient Ford Popular probably dating from the late fifties. It was without a windscreen, as was usual, and the seats inside had frames and webbing, but at some point in the distant past the upholstery had been removed. When we had successfully completed the negotiations as to the fare, all the other taxi men gathered around the Ford Popular to give it a push. My driver ran around to the front of the car, opened the bonnet and led a rubber hose from somewhere in the recesses of the engine through the missing windscreen to a five litre jerrycan at my feet. He then started to suck on the tube and I realised he was syphoning petrol to start the car. The fuel tank was the five litre jerrycan at my feet! When the fuel was sucked and the rubber tubing attached to the appropriate place, he ran back around to the driver's side, jumped in and as the other drivers pushed he jump started the car into life. Black smoke belched from the exhaust and we were on our way. I had never experienced this system of fuel fed through the windscreen before. However, it seemed to be fairly effective and we rattled and banged on our way until we reached the Landcruiser, where my taxi driver insisted on changing the tyre. What the taxi lacked in basic parts, the driver certainly made up for in good will. I must say I have found taxis at home very boring and predictable since this experience.

These taxis were the standard way for visitors to get to the hospital if they didn't have private transport. A ride in one of these taxis was a rude introduction to life in the bush and more than a few visitors wondered what kind of a place they were coming to if this was a sample of things to come. I had had spacious accommodation in the Ford Popular since there were only three of us, but normally the driver would keep putting in more people until there was literally no single space left and arms and legs were sticking out of the absent windows. Four people could fit into the front of the Ford Popular and four or five in the back – with their belongings. It was particularly distressing for new muzungu on their first trip to Kiwoko when, having secured a ride in a 'taxi' they found more and more people getting in literally on top of them. The driver had a way of driving with his right arm and shoulder out of the window and someone sitting on his knee. I could never understand how he managed it but he didn't seem to find anything unusual in this peculiarly cramped driving position. Unfortunately I personally was not the only person in Kiwoko who was afflicted by problems with punctures. Sometimes the whole project ground to a halt because of punctures. Perhaps it was because I was like Jonah in the boat – my problems followed me to the detriment of others. When we acquired a tractor, I became used to the sight of the large rear wheel lying on the ground as a group of men tried to remove the inner tube. I didn't need to ask what the problem was – a puncture of course. I had to admire the stamina of the tractor driver as he pumped up the tyre again with a simple foot pump – it takes a lot of energy to inflate a rear tractor tyre.

Cathy, a Dublin medical student, who helped at Kiwoko for two summers, became conversant with the difficulties a puncture could bring. One afternoon as the regular driver was away at another rural clinic, Cathy was asked to drive the vehicle for the AIDS home care team. This involved going around the outlying villages visiting the homes of people with AIDS. Everything went smoothly, or at least as smoothly as anything could go over the dirt roads, until they got a puncture. Now this was one of those occasions when Cathy was badly advised. Bosco assured Cathy that there was no jack in the vehicle. In fact we were fairly careful by this stage to ensure that all the vehicles had the proper equipment and the jack was there, stowed away in a side panel at the rear of the car. However Cathy didn't know this, so the decision was made that someone should go back for another jack. One of the Ugandan staff was about to leave, but then it occurred to Cathy, probably quite correctly, that he would not be able to carry the jack back and she should go with him and come back in the pick-up. So off they set. A few yards down the road they met a man with a bicycle, so after some judicious haggling the man surrendered his bicycle for a small fee and Cathy and Moses, the Ugandan health worker were under way again. Cathy was perched on the back corner of the bicycle and Moses pedalled home. Fortunately Cathy is of slight build and didn't cause too many problems for Moses.

When they arrived back at the hospital their problems were only just beginning – they had Hannington to deal with. He was in charge of the equipment including the big jack, and he wasn't about to part with it. The reason was very obvious. The tractor had a puncture, the wheel had been removed and the tractor was sitting on the hydraulic jack. No amount of pleading or cajoling on Cathy's part could persuade Hannington to part with his jack. The tractor was on it and the tractor would stay on it as far as he was concerned. Unfortunately I was not around to help solve this dilemma, as the tractor could easily have been propped up on concrete blocks and the jack removed, but Hannington wasn't about to listen to a mere woman and the idea of the blocks hadn't occurred to him. So Cathy had to make do with borrowing the pick-up and the tiny jack belonging to it. They set off again to find the Land-cruiser with the small jack, the bicycle and the spare tyre for the pick-up loaded into the back. They reached their destination and thankfully were able to get the tyre changed before dark with the help of the small jack. So all was well that ended well – except for one thing – when they were about to set out they looked down to discover that the pick-up now had a puncture. They could hardly believe their eyes. It was just as well they had brought along the spare tyre for the pick-up.

Cathy learned two things out of this incident: Number one – get tough with the men. Even though she was only 5ft 1in she wouldn't be misled or obstructed again. Number two – the difficulties involved in medical work in

Uganda were not usually complicated medical problems but simple everyday things like getting a puncture.

I could verify it was true that punctures were an everyday sort of problem. Sometimes I got one every day – and it did try my patience. Nevertheless when I thought about the tremendous problems or obstacles the early missionaries overcame in travelling, my small problems with punctures paled into insignificance and I felt very shamefaced. I could go on ad infinitum with stories about punctures but I won't bore you with more details. Suffice to say that, on the other hand, when I thought about the early missionaries I also wondered if I was a man born out of my time. After all these people did have tremendous obstacles to overcome but getting a puncture wasn't one of them. Perhaps I would have done better in that era.

Chapter 17

The Man With The Key Has Gone

I cannot recall the number of times I'd reach an office or a store, sometimes after many hours of driving, and often with an urgent need for some medical supplies or stores, to be told – 'The man with the key has gone.'

It seemed that the problem reflected not just a problem in bureaucracy but an attitude to life in general. My Ugandan colleagues would seldom raise any complaints like: 'Well, why is he gone? He's supposed to be here, this is during working hours.'

But they would accept the statement as an explanation in itself.

'The store is closed.'

'Why is the store closed?'

'Because the man with the key is gone.'

End of story.

Perhaps in Uganda people accepted there were so many legitimate reasons why the man with the key should be gone that it was not their place to raise the question in the first place. He could be at a funeral, he could be at a meeting, there might have been some urgent business to attend to. It was only when irate foreigners like me arrived, demanding explanations, that anyone got upset. After all, why was this muzungu going on about it? The man with the key had gone, no one could do anything about it, so why make a fuss? It only caused embarrassment. Everyone knew that there was always only one key

146

for an office or store and when the man with the key went, he didn't entrust it to anyone else. It really didn't matter who wanted in, it didn't matter if it was an irate white person or indeed a Ugandan big shot. Once the man with the key had gone the case was closed.

As the work expanded in Kiwoko the demands for supplies increased. Everything from drugs to dressings to plumbing, electric and building supplies. So it was usually necessary to make a Kampala trip at least once a week. The Kampala day started about 6.00 am and finished around 10.00 pm. It involved hours of driving and going from office to office, from place to place, seeing people about various hospital needs and getting all manner of supplies. Eventually we would arrive home late at night, tired out and laden down with goods – needles, syringes, catgut, drugs, paint, nails, plastic sheeting, whatever we could get our hands on. It was definitely not a restful day.

On one occasion I had to bring back a fan belt for the large generator which had frayed and broken and almost caused the generator to seize. Since we were entirely dependent on the generator for light such as theatre light, and power, especially for the laboratory equipment, this was an urgent need. So in the morning when I reached Kampala I went immediately to the appropriate supply depot. It was 8.45 am. The mechanic in the yard informed me that he thought they probably had the fan belt in stock, but just when I was getting my hopes up he dashed them with his next statement.

'But sorry, the man with the key to the stores is not here.'

8.45 am was obviously too early, although the rest of the staff were around.

'When will he be in?' I queried.

Perhaps 9.30 am they estimated. I had learned from past experience that it wasn't a productive way to spend a day waiting for someone who might come in, so, wondering how their business could run when the spares department wasn't open, I went on my way.

The day itself proved very tiresome, with many of the usual small frustrations and by 4.30 pm I still had not managed to get the fan belt from another supplier, so as a last resort I decided to try the main dealer again. I raced back, at break-neck speed, and arrived to find to my immense relief that the depot was still open. But my hopes were to be dashed again, as although the man with the key had returned later that morning, he had now gone again.

By this stage I was fuming. 'How do these people expect to do business? What sort of way is this to run a depot?' I muttered.

The employees just stood around looking at me philosophically and pityingly. 'What is he getting himself worked up about?' they were obviously thinking. After all there was nothing anyone could do about it, and I would lead a more calm and peaceful and probably longer life if I accepted some of these everyday little hiccups with a little less frustration and a little more equanimity.

Living in Uganda does take a particular type of temperament and although I am an Irish man, I didn't learn 'Murphy's Law' until I came to Uganda. Murphy's Law sums up a certain view of life, that 'Anything that can go wrong, will go wrong.'

Now if one accepts this law as part of life, one should be psychologically prepared for the daily frustrations. However somehow knowing the law still didn't help me to cope with the things which did go wrong. I still got frustrated. On the other hand I realised that if one became too philosophical about things going wrong, nothing would ever get achieved. I had heard many visitors to Africa say – 'well this is Africa!' as an explanation for all the things which went wrong. I had also heard people use the term 'Africanised', meaning the person had now become thoroughly adjusted to the ways of Africa. However if a person became too Africanised then they had nothing more to offer. The person would accept things as they were and bring no change and no new ideas. I had found living in Africa had to be a process of 'give and take'. No one had ll the answers. I had to learn from the local people and be hanged by them. I could also contribute to them and help hem to change, if the need arose.

I'm afraid that I have never been able to accept 'the man with the key has gone' as an explanation in itself and on a ew occasions I did try to change things.

One such occasion was when I was trying to get a supply f catgut for theatre. It was Wednesday afternoon and I vas in a hurry as usual. I had done 12 things on my Kampala day list but 8 more were still remaining. I arrived t a mission supply organisation where I knew they had a onation of suture materials. The young girl in the dispen-ary was quite charming and I always enjoyed doing busi-ess with these charming Ugandan ladies.

'Yes, we have the sutures but sorry the man with the key o the store is gone,' she apologised. 'I can't get them out or you.'

I looked at my watch. It was only 3.00 pm. Why should he storeman not be here at 3.00 pm on a working day, specially since no one had another key? However there as nothing I could do apart from complaining to this oung girl. So on this occasion I just went on my way. The ollowing week I returned. It happened again to be a Wednesday afternoon.

'Could I have the suture material please?' I asked, nowing that our supplies for theatre were now perilously ow.

'Oh, sorry the man with the key is not here again,' the ice young lady told me, obviously embarrassed to be iving me the same message again.

This was too much for me. I definitely became very anAfrican' and demanded to see the manager of the nstitution.

'He's in a meeting,' his secretary told me.

'Well, ask him if he will see me,' I told his secretary with hat steely look in my eyes that said I wasn't about to go way. Within a very few minutes the Manager appeared.

'I seem to have a problem,' I explained. 'I keep coming

here to get supplies but the man who has the key to you store is never here. How can I get supplies if your store i always locked?'

The Manager looked concerned, then enlightenmen dawned.

'Oh, you always come on Wednesdays,' he replied. 'Ou storeman goes to a prayer meeting every Wednesda afternoon.'

Now, even though I approve of prayer, I was no impressed with this explanation. My immediate thought were 'why is he allowed to go to a prayer meeting durin, working hours?' and 'why does he take the key with him?'

It seemed that this process had been going on for year and so no-one in the management had ever seen an' anomaly in it or any reason to question it. However ques tions were going through my mind like 'what about worl discipline? What about responsibility to one's employer? It might be a brilliant prayer meeting and not to be missed but how could this man leave his employment in the mid dle of every Wednesday afternoon, and go with the key i his pocket and none of his bosses object? As we were now critically short of catgut, I for one was certainly unwillin to let the matter rest there. I found out where the praye meeting was and went to fetch the man. When I arrived h didn't question why I had come. He simply got into the ca and came and opened the store! Perhaps after all he had guilty conscience about being away, or more likely, he jus wanted to get rid of me! In this case I had made a fuss an not just been prepared to accept the situation at fac value. Maybe the people concerned just thought I was bit of a nuisance. However, maybe I did make a smal contribution to the efficiency of their organisation becaus I never again had the problem with this man going to prayer meeting with the key.

Sometimes things happened which were basically no one's fault but made me ask myself the question, 'D people have a fixation about keeping keys?'

One such incident involved Michael making a trip to th

dentist. Michael had toothache, so the driver, James, took him to Kampala where he was to meet a friend who would take him to the dentist. It was Sean's birthday, so we had planned a special meal in the evening. James was asked to make sure Michael was back by late afternoon. By 5.00 pm the meal was prepared and everything was ready. By 6.00 pm Michael still hadn't returned. 7.00 pm passed, 8.00 pm, no Michael. At this point we were very worried. James was reliable, he knew Michael was to be brought back much earlier. What could have happened? We had visions of a terrible accident and Michael lying injured, or worse, in a pool of blood at the side of the road. As we had already invited guests for the meal, the meal went ahead but was eaten in gloomy silence. It was a disappointing birthday celebration for Sean. Then I had an emergency and had to deal with it.

By this stage it was 10.00 pm.

'We will set out for Kampala as soon as I have finished this,' I told Robbie.

By this stage our imaginations had taken over and Robbie and I were in a state of complete nervous tension. After all anything could have happened to our son. We should have gone with him to Kampala. This was the first time we hadn't accompanied him. We blamed ourselves, we would never forgive ourselves. We indulged in the kind of self-flagellation that most parents go through when they are in a state of extreme anxiety.

At 10.30 pm a door banged and Michael breezed into the house.

'Hi Mum, I'm back,' he announced nonchalantly.

The poor boy didn't know how to react when his mum threw her arms round him and burst into tears, except to burst into tears along with her.

'Now Dad, don't blame James, it wasn't his fault,' Michael was quick to point out, just as James arrived into the house.

'What happened?' I questioned.

'You see, while Michael was at the dentist's,' James

explained, 'I left the car in the garage for repair a[s] arranged. However when I went back to collect the car th[e] mechanic had gone with the ignition key in his pocket. No one knew where he had gone. He finally returned late i[n] the evening. I just had to wait until he came back an[d] obviously there was no way I could get a message to you.[']

So that was it, the cause of all our worry and frettin[g] over our son was of course that the man with the key ha[d] gone. We should have known.

Sometimes despite all our efforts the problem of th[e] man with the key having gone extended to the hospital[.] One morning I was surprised to find all the laboratory staf[f] seated outside the lab at 10.00 am. While the patient[s] might be expected to be seated outside the lab at this tim[e] of the morning, the staff were definitely supposed to b[e] inside working.

When I inquired as to what was the problem I was tol[d] that one key had broken in the back door, one key was o[n] the wall inside and Christopher, one of the senior techni[-] cians who happened to be off that day, had the other ke[y] in his pocket. The old problem again! Was this proble[m] going to defeat us in our own hospital? We could loo[k] inside and see the key hanging on the wall – but there wer[e] bars on the windows. We rounded up all the other key[s] from the hospital and tried every key in the front door – t[o] no avail. Finally I decided we would learn from the Bibl[e] again. There is a story in the New Testament of a man wh[o] couldn't get in the front door to see Jesus – so he cam[e] through the roof. The laboratory was next door to outpa[-] tients for which we did have the key. If I climbed onto [a] table I could cut a hole in the ceiling. From thence I coul[d] move through the roof space and let myself through [a] trapdoor into the lab. So a saw was sent for, a hole wa[s] rudely cut in the ceiling and I disappeared into the voi[d] above. I found the trapdoor into the lab easily enough an[d] just as I was contemplating the long drop to the floor th[e] door was opened and everyone walked in – someone ha[d] produced another key!

152

That was great. I could have saved myself a lot of trouble – now could someone rescue me before I broke an ankle in the jump? It didn't feel very dignified, sitting up in the rafters like a bat waiting for someone to bring a ladder. A medical superintendent wasn't really supposed to do this kind of thing, but the staff weren't in the least perturbed, they were used to me by this stage. At least on this occasion they didn't laugh at me which was more than could be said for my experience with the bees.

African bees have the reputation of being dangerous and bad tempered, but not being especially interested in bees or bee keeping I had not had occasion to find out anything about bees for myself. This all changed one morning while we were having staff prayers.

This was a meeting we held every morning at 8.15 in the classroom. Many of the staff came and we had a lovely time of singing followed by a short Bible meditation and some prayer. I often found time there encouraging and uplifting. It was a great way to start the day. The praise and worship would minister to my spirit and the Bible meditation usually gave me something to take away and chew over for the rest of the day. We were finishing prayers when we were disturbed by shouts and people running hither and thither in front of the hospital. A boy with an ulcer on his leg came hobbling over to the classroom, crying. He was being attacked by bees and he couldn't shake them off. We got him inside and killed the remaining bees. Now we could see none outside the hospital, all seemed quiet. Apparently a swarm had been disturbed outside the surgical ward and had started attacking everyone. Fortunately there was mosquito screen on the windows so those who rushed inside and banged the door were safe. Nevertheless we couldn't stay inside all day while the bees terrorised the hospital. Someone would have to show some initiative and deal with these bees – leadership was called for. I looked around to see if there was anyone to fit the bill. Then the realisation dawned. I was the person in charge, I was the one who would be expected to take the initiative and show leadership. I couldn't sit cowering in the classroom all day even though I hated bee stings and was dreadfully allergic to them.

So I sneaked out to the carpentry shop to ask Kigongo's advice. Kigongo was a man who would know what to do in such situations. He advised that we burn down the dead tree from which the bees were attacking. At first I thought that this was in order to set the bees alight, but I later learned that it was the smoke which had a calming influence on the bees. Under the influence of the smoke they would settle down and become law abiding bees. Kigongo volunteered to do the deed . That was a relief. I didn't think my powers of leadership would extend to being attacked by a whole swarm of bees as I tried to burn them out of their home. However, I could help Kigongo. I had the ideal beekeeper's protective clothing for him. We had received some secondhand clothing for distribution and among it was an arctic ski suit, fur lined, complete with hood tied at the sleeves and ankles. Why an arctic suit had been sent to Uganda I will never know, but it was about to be put to a use which had never been dreamed of by the designers. We still needed some protection for Kigongo's face – this was provided by mosquito netting so off he went with his paraffin and matches. After the second attempt the mission was successful and Kigongo returned unharmed. However he was followed by a trail of frustrated angry bees who when they spied or perhaps smelled me, immediately deserted Kigongo and attacked me. In fact any stray bee which happened to be chasing someone else at the time immediately forsook its primary target and stung me instead. To add insult to injury the rest of the staff tended to break into fits of giggling when they saw me rushing around frantically beating the air. Within a few minutes my face was beginning to swell and by the next day it was bloated and jelly-like with only two slits remaining where my eyes had been.

I felt that in each one of these situations there were times when I could learn from the incident and there were other times when I could change things. The problem was knowing which was which. It was always easier to make the júdgement in retrospect. For example, I could have sat back and kept calm at the fan belt garage. I wasn't going to change anything anyway and I would live longer if I was more philosophical about such difficulties. On the other hand I was able to change something at the mission supply depot and the hospital got its catgut. As for the laboratory my strenuous efforts at gaining an entrance through the ceiling proved unnecessary and as for giving leadership in the bee attack I could have saved myself a lot of discomfort if I had hidden inside, but then Kigongo would not have gotten the protective arctic clothing. All in all I saw my role as a catalyst. I provoked a reaction. Sometimes that reaction was good and sometimes it was bad, but it always got something going.

Chapter 18

Technical Difficulties

In retrospect one usually doesn't remember the important things which may have been accomplished. These are few enough in our day-to-day experiences, nor do we look back and remember the quiet, peaceful equilibrium which surely must have been the pattern of most of our days. However one does seem to remember the frustrations of life – such as punctures or getting our paraffin fridge lit.

We had been away on our first holiday in Mombasa. It was a wonderful experience – lying in the golden sands with palm trees swaying in the background. We had a little cottage by the seashore, complete with a cook who prepared us our meals – the full cooked breakfast, served on the verandah after we struggled out of bed, and dinner prepared from the local seafoods. This was the life! We could put up with this style of missionary existence.

Coming home was all the more daunting. As we came through Kampala we stopped off at the butcher's and Robbie stocked up with two kilos of mincemeat as none would be available locally.

'Are you sure that you will be able to get the fridge working Ian?'

'Don't worry Robbie, I'm an expert with that fridge now.'

The fridge in question had given me more than a few difficulties in lighting and regulating it in the past, so it was understandable that Robbie was a little apprehensive.

Before coming to Uganda I wasn't aware of the existence of fridges that could run on paraffin. So in my ignorance when CMS provided a paraffin fridge without instructions, I didn't realise it was a very delicate piece of equipment which required just the right adjustment, balance and trimming of the wick to keep it running. However after many months of practice I now felt in command of the situation.

While we were on holiday we had allowed the fridge to go out, so I was now faced with the challenge of relighting it. Our supply of meat for the next two weeks was at stake if I failed. I am now of the opinion that every missionary candidate should take a course in regulating paraffin fridges. This aspect of our own preparation was sadly lacking and I think that such a course would not only impart the technical skills necessary for the job, but would serve to strengthen the moral fibre and resolve of everyone undergoing it. It would also probably bring to light those people not suited for missionary life. In my case I would have failed!

Robbie was understandably worried about me getting the fridge lit. She had watched my performance many times before and had reached the conclusion that when I was lighting the fridge, it was better if she stayed well out of the way. However this time I knew it would be different. I was calm and in control of things, the family were depending on me and I would rise to the occasion.

First of all I pulled out the tray underneath the fridge and checked the level of paraffin. Then I detached the globe from the wick assembly to clean it. Horror of horrors I dropped it and it smashed into numerous pieces. Robbie's worst fears were confirmed, I had been defeated even before I got going and our meat would go green. A fridge seems such a basic household appliance that usually we give no thought to it. It's different in the bush. To have one there is a tremendous blessing and a luxury. To keep it in good working order it is necessary to spend large parts of your evenings lying under it, trimming the wick, adjusting the flame etc. Now I had broken the glass and there were no spares.

Still with a remarkable feeling of detachment and poise I said, 'Don't panic, there's always "superglue", we can glue it back together.'

In this case there wasn't actually superglue but there was Araldite. One mixes a little from the two tubes together and it forms a glue which will set rock hard, or so the instructions say. After about two hours of mixing and sticking I had the globe back together again. However not quite in its original shape. It was now roughly oval instead of round but it was the best I could do. The problem is that the globe should be a snug fit over the mantel so that the flue gives the correct draught. I now had a roughly oval globe, with a few pieces missing, wobbling about over the wick. A snug fit it definitely was not. Undaunted or at least at this stage, only somewhat daunted, I soldiered on. I managed to get the flame lit, usually an exercise requiring at least a half box of 'lucky strike' Chinese matches – aptly named I have always thought, meaning 'you'll be lucky if they strike'. However having overcome all difficulties, I sat back to watch, but was horrified to see – not a clear blue flame as it was supposed to be, but black smoke billowing from the fridge. The flame had heated up the Araldite and black toxic fumes were pouring from the back of the fridge. I have to be entirely honest and say that I had now completely lost my cool. Robbie had long since returned to bed where she was pretending to be fast asleep, probably a very wise move. Finally I had to admit defeat or be suffocated by the toxic fumes, so I too went to bed in complete frustration. I had been defeated by the technicalities of our paraffin fridge once again. I would like to say that I emerged from the experience a more mature missionary and I was ever after in a state of control when I had to relight the fridge, having learned from my mistakes. However someone has said we never learn from our mistakes and I feel there is a grain of truth in that statement. I still continued to spend many evenings lying on the floor beside the fridge, using up many boxes of 'lucky strike' matches and adjusting the flame, trying to get it just right. I once heard a preacher say that the children of Israel had to go round and round the wilderness because they failed to learn the lessons God was teaching them the first time, so God kept sending them round one more time. This perhaps was also true in my case, as I still found each time of lighting the fridge a major trial.

When we moved to our new house at Kiwoko I personally supervised the moving of the fridge to make sure it was handled carefully. As I started to light it again that evening, I discovered that despite the care in moving, a tiny but vital part, called the flame spreader, had been damaged. The function of this part was, as its name suggests, to spread the flame evenly. Now since this part didn't work, tongues of yellow flames shot out at all angles. I laboured with the thing until 2.00 am but each time, just when I thought I had it adjusted, another tongue of yellow flames would spring out of the side where it wasn't supposed to be. Again I went to bed defeated.

This little part didn't appear to be available anywhere in Africa, so I finally showed the damaged part to one of our most able staff, John Ando, to ask him what he thought. He returned in a few minutes with the part repaired and proceeded to light the fridge in a remarkably short time. 'Well,' I thought, 'some people have the gift and some don't!' After that I just got John to light the fridge. I asked myself if I had learnt something from all these frustrating experiences – was I a calmer individual? Was I a more mature person? Was I a stronger Christian?

'Yes,' I could honestly say that I had learnt something from these experiences. I had learned that – if you are not up to the job, get someone else to do it for you!

Fridges were not the only piece of equipment that I had trouble with. I sometimes thought that in Africa any piece of mechanical apparatus was doomed to failure. Sooner or later, something would surely go wrong with it, which couldn't be fixed. We tend to take things for granted in developed countries, like a constant power supply, or a main dealership where the spare parts are available, things which cannot be taken for granted in a Third World country. We also make the mistake of thinking that because something is good enough for Britain or Ireland it will work in Africa. This can happen particularly with vehicles. Someone donates a second-hand Land Rover which has been running well for years. It is sent to Africa and falls apart as soon as it leaves the port. People do not realise how bad the roads are in some parts of Africa, or how different the conditions are. Even a new vehicle will often last for only three or four years. Like everyone else we made the same mistake. We bought an old Land Rover in Ireland and had it sent over to Mombasa. In our case the Land Rover was doomed to failure as soon as it hit African soil – literally – someone dropped it off the boat during unloading. This didn't do our Land Rover any good at all. The chassis which was already weakened from all the bad weather and rust in Northern Ireland, gave way under the impact. Our Land Rover probably had the shortest record of any vehicle which was sent out to Africa, of developing mechanical problems. Unfortunately the broken chassis was only the beginning of its problems. The transmission was also cracked and the Land Rover could not be driven. However the shipping firm which had been engaged to transport it to Uganda didn't inform anyone of the mishap or claim from the shipper's insurance at this point. They simply towed the disabled vehicle to Kampala, a journey of over 600 miles. The Land Rover was then deposited on my doorstep with no-one prepared to take responsibility for what had happened.

We should probably have realised at this time that the Land Rover was doomed and abandoned it, but since so much money had already been spent on purchasing it and sending it out by this stage, it was a case of the proverbial throwing of good money after bad, we were reluctant to give up. Hence, more money was spent on repairing it, the transmission was fixed and the chassis was welded.

I have always found certain people to be ardent supporters of Land Rovers. The Land Rover company seems to create a brand loyalty among a particular group of people, usually people who have driven old Land Rovers for years. I am inclined to think, somewhat cynically perhaps, that these people have an intense loyalty because they are among the select band who have overcome the difficulties of survival with a Land Rover and have lived to tell the tale. They are also usually tough, rugged individuals who have developed immense practical mechanical skills. This leaves people like me who have never really succeeded in mastering the simple technical skills of everyday living like operating a video, repairing a puncture or lighting a fridge, somewhat out in the cold. I suppose that I should be an encouragement to all the less rugged unskilled individuals like myself, that it is possible for us to survive in Africa.

I have to admit that I am the sort of person who likes to get into a car and drive it away with never a thought to what goes on under the bonnet. I certainly don't like getting all dirty, lying under it checking things and tightening up bits and pieces which might otherwise fall off. However this procedure seemed to be necessary before or after every Land Rover journey, otherwise parts dropped off along the road. This was Heather and Robbie's unfortunate experience one afternoon when they went out in the Land Rover to a neighbouring village, to conduct a church Bible Study. On the journey back they were caught in a freak thunderstorm which turned the dirt road into a raging torrent. With Heather at the wheel they bumped and rocked through the flooded potholes, hardly able to see ten feet in front of them in the driving rain. Suddenly they were brought to a halt by a fallen tree and as Robbie got out to act as guide around the obstacle Heather negotiated the track. Robbie noticed that the Land Rover appeared to be listing slightly to one side but after checking that they had no punctures, she concluded that the list

161

was due to the uneven road and was nothing to worry about. When they arrived back at the house I was waiting for them as I was immobilised indoors by the storm. As the Land Rover pulled up I looked in horror at the sight and exclaimed, 'What happened to the Land Rover?'

Robbie and Heather looked at me in surprise and with more than a touch of annoyance. After all, they had been through a life-threatening tempest and all I showed interest in was the old Land Rover and not their welfare.

'There's nothing wrong with it,' they replied irritably.

'Then why does it look like that?' I rejoined.

As we all stared out at the Land Rover we could see that it was leaning over at a forty-five degree angle as if it was very, very tired.

'Well, I have to admit that I thought it was listing a bit,' said Robbie, 'but when I saw it didn't have a puncture I thought it must be the road.'

This had seemed like a very reasonable explanation to a non-mechanical person such as my wife. The true explanation was that the U-bolt had dropped off the axle and the chassis had come adrift. Not only that, but the chassis was broken in numerous places. It was surprising that they had arrived back safely. I did take some comfort from these lady drivers because they were even worse than me. They could drive a Land Rover which had a broken chassis with the axle hanging half off and not even notice, though in mitigation, I had to admit that the weather conditions which they were battling against were pretty atrocious. From that point on we decided to give up on the Land Rover. We had it towed to Kampala where we sold it for a surprisingly high price, considering that by this stage the chassis had completely folded in on itself and the Land Rover looked like 'Herbie' on a very bad day.

Equipment of any kind could cause problems. The hospital was dependent on a generator for its power supply. The generator ran the distiller to make the intravenous fluids, the theatre lights, the laboratory equipment, the autoclave and was even wired to run a maize mill. Unfortunately we had a problem with the maize mill which no-one seemed able to overcome. When it was switched on, it would not run at the speed required to grind the corn. This problem baffled everyone, including a visiting engineer from the UK. Starters and motors and wiring and connections were all checked, but although we thought we had the problem solved many times the maize mill would not work. Eventually we decided to look at the generator, so we asked an engineer from Kampala to come and investigate. Within a few minutes he had discovered the cause of our difficulties. We had the generator wired wrongly, bypassing the voltage regulator. Hence it only developed a fault when it was under heavy load, such as when the maize mill was switched on. We had been looking in the wrong place for the fault. If anyone had thought of starting with the generator and working back, we would have solved the problem months before.

The engineering problems encountered in Africa were not so difficult in themselves but it was often difficult to find a specialist engineer who had the appropriate knowledge in a particular field. I discovered that engineers were like doctors, they all had their own peculiar speciality. Someone who knew about generators might not know much about Land Rovers, or someone who knew about water systems probably didn't know much about electrics or electronics. The hospital had equipment in all these fields and even if we did find someone who was good at everything, it was still difficult to find the spare parts. The Ugandan mechanics were very good at improvisation, but not so good at maintaining things. They could often fix engines in very ingenious ways, but one realised that if the thing had been maintained properly in the first place it would not have broken down. They also seemed to have a knack of having some nuts, bolts and screws left over after repairing a vehicle. Even though they reassured me that these were not vital to the process I was never quite happy that everything had been put back together properly in its rightful place. I did remember my own boyhood days of dismantling and reassembling my bicycle and it was never quite the same without that handful of bolts which I had left over.

Our difficulties sometimes lay in more basic mistakes. We had acquired a very old portable X-ray unit, which we wanted to use, but at that stage we did not have a radiologist at the hospital. So Gerry, the hospital manager, and I decided to have a go at taking X-rays ourselves. It didn't look all that difficult and we had the instructions. We filled up three jerrycans with the developing chemicals and set up a dark-room – a store off the intravenous fluids making room, which we had commandeered. Gerry disappeared into the dark-room to load the X-ray film into the cassette while I read the instructions about exposure times, distances and voltages for taking chest X-rays. When Gerry returned with the cassette, loaded and ready, I donned the lead apron and carried out a chest X-ray on a TB patient. We certainly looked as if we knew what we were doing, even though we were novices. While Gerry again disappeared into the gloomy depths of the dark-room to unload the cassette and immerse the film in the developing and fixing solutions, I called out the time for each process. Finally he emerged from the dark-room triumphant, X-ray in hand, or so he thought. As he held it up to the light we realised that we had just spent the last half hour taking and developing an X-ray with a piece of cardboard from the packing material! In Gerry's efforts to load the cassette in the dark so as not to expose the film, he had carefully removed the cardboard from the pack instead of an X-ray and loaded it. We never were very successful at getting that X-ray unit working, even when we did use proper X-ray film and not cardboard, and we were delighted when we were given a large X-ray unit from Joint Medical Stores. We were even more delighted when Isaac, a trained radiologist, arrived to work it. By this time we were convinced that there was more to the mysteries of taking X-rays than met the eyes, and we were happy to leave the job to a trained professional.

As far as equipment was concerned we were often in the

position of not having a trained professional on whom we could call, and as a result we sometimes spoiled equipment through not knowing something simple – such as the time when a battery blew up in the laboratory. The explosion knocked Henry off his feet and the other laboratory staff ran out as fast as their legs would carry them, under the mistaken belief that they were being attacked by gunfire. When Henry picked himself up off the ground he found he had no physical injury, although he was very shaken. The cause of the explosion had been very simple. The battery had been charged up very fast with a resulting build-up of gas inside. If the caps had been loosened off it would not have happened. We made Henry the person in charge of seeing that this was done in future and, not surprisingly, he never forgot and was very faithful in carrying out his duties.

Chapter 19

Baby Henry

We had been without a second doctor for about three months, so I had been working seven days a week without a break. I was gradually becoming more irritable and strained. It wasn't that I couldn't cope with the work. It was because I was having difficulty relaxing or sleeping when I wasn't working. Sometimes things went well and everything seemed worthwhile, such as the time when a mother started to haemorrhage profusely and we were able to take her to the theatre immediately and save her and the baby. However at other times the effort seemed futile when it appeared that in spite of what we did the patients would die anyway. The brother of one of our workers was brought in unconscious one Saturday afternoon. I did a lumbar puncture which showed he had meningitis. He was immediately started on large doses of penicillin. But it was too late. He died within twelve hours. If only he had been brought earlier, he might have responded to the treatment, but he had been kept at a small Health Centre for three days before he was brought to us. It was only when his condition deteriorated that he was moved to the hospital.

One evening while I was in the ward a mother came in with her nine-month-old baby. He didn't look terribly sick and he was obviously a well cared for, well nourished little baby, but his Mum said he had constipation and he had been passing blood. My ears pricked up. A baby shouldn't be passing blood. I did a rectal examination and found he had a condition called Intususeption, where the bowel invaginates into itself. The bowel is like a long flexible rubber tube, and in this condition one part of the tube gets pushed inside the other. The natural wavelike motion of the bowel, which usually pushes the food along in digestion, pushes the inside part further and further along. When I examined this baby I could detect that the small bowel had been pushed all the way along into the rectum. When this happens the blood supply to the inside part gets cut off and it goes gangrenous, the resulting infection usually killing the patient. This beautiful little baby, who looked healthy and happy, was in fact in a critical condition. I explained to the parents what I had found and told them that he needed an immediate operation to disentangle his bowel which they agreed to readily. At operation, when the abdomen was opened, the condition was found to be severe. Part of the bowel was necrotic and this had to be removed. However, the baby's condition during the operation was stable. That is until the lights went out. A fault had developed in the generator line and it couldn't be traced. So the operation was finished by torch light. However our problems were not yet over. Henry needed fluids and the IV line was not working. Thinking that perhaps the light would be better in my own house where we had a permanent solar system, we wrapped him up in blankets and rushed him down to the house. By this time Henry had recovered from the anaesthetic and was kicking his feet and responding well. 'Please let him live, Lord,' we prayed as we tried with everything we knew to get a drip running. But we failed. By this stage everyone was involved and was praying 'Lord, let Henry live.' Everyone identified with his struggle for life and was willing him to live. If he lived he would be one we had rescued, just one who had cheated death but it was not to be. At 2.00 am I was called. Henry had died. Disappointment washed over me. I couldn't sleep. Death seemed to be all around me. I could see the faces of so many patients who had died, young girls who had died of AIDS, the boy who had died of meningitis, a beautiful young mother who had died of hepatitis, babies emaciated, wasting away from TB and AIDS, children who had died of measles. In a space of a few hours that baby had become personal to me. He could have been my own child. I wanted him to have a chance to live. The operation had been 'technically' successful. Our staff had given of themselves, poured themselves out for him. We had watched him fighting for his life and he seemed strong. We prayed for him. We were on his side cheering him on, willing him through the crisis, but he didn't make it. As waves of discouragement and death washed over me and I tossed and turned in the night, I spoke out my feelings to Robbie.

'Where is God in all this?'

I felt like one of the prophets of Baal in the time of Elijah who jumped up and down, worked themselves into a frenzy, cut themselves to try and bring down fire on the sacrifice while Elijah stood by and jeered.

'Call louder, perhaps your gods can't hear, perhaps they have gone to the bathroom.'

Except this time it seemed every unbeliever was jeering at me.

'Where is he, has he gone to sleep?'

It was so easy to produce glib answers when one was not too close to the situation. In our Christian fellowship groups we could produce the answer about a loving God and how tenderly He loved us and wanted us to experience His arms around us. But when one was working in a situation where one faced the effects of poverty and disease daily it was not so easy to feel all warm and glowing inside. That night I didn't have any answers. Perhaps it was the effect of working without a break for months, perhaps it was because I saw people die of AIDS every week, if not every day. Perhaps it was because I had let a little baby get under my skin. A doctor wasn't supposed to do that. He was supposed to maintain a professional impartiality. But as I was in the midst of a plague of death all around me I looked for one little situation where I could cheat death. Baby Henry was that situation for me. Also in his case it wasn't just me but all the staff working with me who were saying 'please Lord, let this one live.' But he died and we were filled with disappointment.

At prayers in the morning a pall hung over the staff. No one could utter a prayer. We rigidly went through the motions. The episode pushed me back to reading about the life of Jesus again, especially to the story of Lazarus. Usually at such times I found it hard to get answers. The pat answers didn't help. But Jesus as a person stood out as a real human being who had gone through these situations himself. He had constantly put himself with the people who were suffering. He was always in among the sick. He worked seven days a week without any breaks. He had constant demands on him but he didn't turn anyone away. He simply loved people and kept giving of himself. He identified with people in their need. In the case of Lazarus when he died, he listened to Martha and Mary his sisters in their grief, and he wept with them. Then he prayed and asked His father to raise Lazarus from the dead. He could have stood aside from their grieving knowing that he had the power to raise him from the dead. But he did not. He wept along with them and that seemed to be his example to us as his followers. We ended up weeping for the life of a baby who never got a chance to live. Although Jesus *was* the answer to people's needs he didn't *give* glib answers and he never stood apart. He wept with those who wept and he suffered with those who suffered, he laughed with those who laughed. Perhaps his approach didn't seem to make any sense in the face of all the human suffering and misery there was in the world but what other approach could we take. In the dead of night when I woke up and said, 'God where are you in all this?' He said

'*I* am not in it, but *you* are.'

We were always looking for God to intervene supernaturally and change things. It was disturbing to realise that I could be a part of his intervention.

Chapter 20

Theft

No one likes failure, and missionaries are no exception. We are only too aware of our failures and weaknesses and sometimes we are only too aware of our desire to give up. One such period was sparked by a theft.

There had always been a certain amount of petty thieving around the hospital. The builders working on the hospital liked to help themselves to cement if someone didn't keep close supervision. However, we had a police guard, and one night they caught a worker stealing iron sheets. He was arrested and put in jail. I was sorry for him as I had liked him, but at least, I felt, the forces of law and order were at work. Unfortunately a few weeks later we discovered that our chain saw had been stolen from the workshop. This saw had been especially imported from England and the theft represented a great loss to us. So I called the workers together and explained the situation. The saw had obviously been taken by one of them so someone must know something. How could the hospital function if our own workers were stealing the equipment? It was the responsibility of anyone who knew anything to let me know. As a carrot I offered a substantial reward for information leading to recovery of the stolen saw.

A few days later a worker came forward. A friend of his had been asked to transport the saw to Kampala where it would be sold. The friend – who proved to be another worker – was brought in and questioned. All the information pointed to one man – Kyanga, our roofing expert. Kyanga denied everything and seemed untroubled by the whole affair. The 'friend' changed his story and denied having been involved. Then the saw was suddenly produced. It had been traced to the house of the relative of Kyanga in Kampala. Kyanga could now only admit he had taken the saw and pleaded for leniency. I was somewhat suspicious when the police also pleaded for leniency.

'This man has an aged father and is responsible for orphan children. If he goes to jail it will go hard for him,' they insisted.

I was confused. Why were the police suddenly so concerned with the social welfare of thieves. This was not a normal stance for the police. Thieves were beaten when caught to teach them a lesson. It seemed perhaps that Kyanga had influence within the system. I mulled over the problem and finally decided that the due process of the law should take its course. The rest of the workers would have to learn that crime didn't pay and the fate of Kyanga would be an example to them. So I instructed the police to continue with the prosecution and Kyanga's case went through to the local court. One week later I was dumbfounded to find him free again and walking around Kiwoko. I dashed quickly to the police post with the information that Kyanga must have escaped. I had seen him walking around the area. The police didn't get too excited.

'He has been released,' I was informed.

He had been fined a small amount and paid the fine. I was nonplussed. The due process of law had indeed been followed, but instead of it being an example that crime didn't pay, it gave the message to the other workers that the punishment would be lenient. The penalty didn't seem to fit the crime. This man had stolen equipment worth 1,000,000 shillings and received a 40,000 fine. I knew that the fine for a traffic violation was 5,000. Another anomaly was that the worker who had stolen a few iron sheets was still in jail after several months. I began to realise that Kyanga must have some inside contacts.

'Why?' I asked myself, 'am I inferfering?'

I was an outsider here and perhaps I was trying to impose a way of life and standards which they were not interested in. It was a relatively small incident in the scale of things, but I was disappointed. If they had their own values and their own way of doing things what was I doing here trying to impose my ideals – perhaps my ideals of equity and justice were inappropriate? However several months later my belief in the fairness and impartiality of the system of law and order were to be revived. More importantly the incident demonstrated that the vast majority of the local people did not wish to see the hospital cheated or stolen from and some would not stand idly by if they saw evidence that this was happening.

It started with an anonymous note delivered to the nurse on duty in the medical ward. The note read – 'your workers have stolen three bags of cement and they have other schemes.'

The note was immediately brought for my attention and I set about investigation. I was becoming quite adept at this amateur detective work.

'How much cement did we issue from the store yesterday?' I asked the storeman.

'Ten bags,' he replied.

'Then let me see the work which was carried out using it.'

I had a reasonable idea by this time of how much cement we should use on any job, the complicating factor was that if the mix was diluted the work would appear to have been done but the mortar would be weak. In this case it was fairly easy to tell – the amount of work carried out would not have justified ten bags, even if the mixture was weak. The foreman should have kept a better check. However we all had our lapses. So the evidence seemed to confirm the anonymous accusation. In my experience as a detective I had discovered that one didn't usually have

173

actual proof – at least not to start with – but what was essential was a high index of suspicion and dogged perseverance until an admission was drawn from the suspect

In this case my suspect was David, the builder who wore the funny hats. Uganda had a well developed system of local representation known as the Resistance Committees. Committees were elected at all levels of society from village level upwards. It was an excellent system which gave true representation to the people, although not along party political lines. In a case such as this, where a member of the community was suspected of theft, the first step was to involve the local resistance committee. The defence representative on the committee could then make a complaint to the police who could proceed with investigation. We went through the necessary steps and the police took David in for questioning. After a night in custody he admitted his guilt and the full story was revealed. As usual he had been short of money, and to relieve his financial straits he made a deal with a local headmaster to sell him three bags of cement for the school building programme. The headmaster had apparently not questioned where this cement would come from. David, having secured his market, waited for a moment of laxness on the part of the storeman, ordered extra cement and secreted it in the elephant grass. At an opportune moment he loaded the cement on his bicycle and delivered it to the school. It all seemed very simple. What he didn't reckon on was that another teacher at the school would see the whole transaction and alert me anonymously. So he confessed. Two of the bags of cement were retrieved and he went to jail, this time a more deterrent sentence being fixed by the court. The interesting twist to the story was that when David confessed he not only implicated the headmaster as the receiver of stolen property, but the other teacher. In fact he might have been believed but for the fact that the anonymous note was produced in court and matched the teacher's handwriting. David had obviously been informed as to who the 'grass' was and decided to try to implicate him in the crime also. After all, to his way of thinking, it was worse to be a 'grass' than to steal.

It was sometimes a real dilemma for members of the local community. Was their loyalty to the hospital or was it to their fellow tribesman or kinsman – even if they knew that he was committing a crime, or harming the hospital in some way? After all, the hospital was seen to have foreign money behind it. It could stand the loss of a few shillings. It was an attitude that we strongly resisted, as we knew that the end point of that way of thinking would be continual corruption in the hospital. The attitude would seep through to people who were essentially good, but who would then justify their thefts on the basis that their need was greater than the hospital's. Government health workers were badly paid and few people felt a moral responsibility to the institution they were working in. They felt that their needs were greater than those of the hospital and consequently stealing and corruption flourished. We worked hard to stamp out this attitude, as we knew that both the local community and the members of staff needed to have a sense of ownership, and not feel that this was an impersonal institution. If people saw it as their own hospital then they would not tolerate others harming it. There would always be the minority who didn't care, but the responsible members of the staff and community would look after things.

Hence we had to have a strict policy about stealing. For the hospital staff, we had a rule that if a member of staff was caught stealing they would be automatically dismissed, no matter how small the amount. This is the normal policy of any institution in any part of the world, but in our case I sometimes found it hard to enforce, because I would find a conflict in my heart between compassion for the individual and what I knew to be for the good of the institution.

One such case involved Dora, a nursing assistant who helped in the TB ward. Dora was at first enrolled in our nursing aids' training course, but after some time we found that she was not able to keep up with the other students as she was not very academic. As she could not complete the course, we suggested that she look for another job. A few weeks later Margaret, the nurse in charge of the medical ward, came to tell me that Dora had not been able to get any other employment. She had no immediate family to support her and as this was a genuine case of hardship would we employ Dora in some capacity? The TB ward had many patients who were getting injections every day but otherwise did not require many nursing skills, so I decided that I could employ Dora in this situation. Her duties would be routine, not requiring any degree of academic ability.

Dora worked happily in the TB ward for more than a year and I felt that a good compromise had been reached. Then an irregularity arose with the receipts from the ward. Patients had been issued with receipts differing from the amount of money which the cash office had received. Investigation showed that Dora was pocketing the difference. The amounts involved were not large but Dora had clearly broken the rules. If she wasn't dealt with according to the rules then we might as well not have them. However I still found it very hard to dismiss her, I knew that she had nothing to look forward to in the future, she wasn't very bright, and she had virtually no chance of getting another job. When she went back to her village she would just be 'seated' as the Ugandans said, ie she would do nothing, apart from digging her garden. As she was a single girl she was at the bottom of the social scale and she would feel pressure to get a 'husband' – or at least a boyfriend who would give her some financial support. Her risk of getting AIDS was extremely high in such circumstances. Knowing all this I was reluctant to sack her but I didn't see any alternative, it was a case of the good of the one being sacrificed for the good of the many.

Then to make matters worse, Dora's grandfather, who was her closest surviving relative, paid me a visit. He was a little frail old man who walked bent over supported by a stick. He had made the journey all the way down from his home village to plead Dora's case. I could feel nothing but compassion for this old man who was deeply concerned for his grand-daughter. However if I took Dora back it would be extremely detrimental to the rest of the hospital in the signals it would send out. I was even more distressed when the old man got down on his knees to plead with me. This situation was killing me but there was nothing I could do. Old men from the village do not prostrate themselves except in extreme circumstances. I had never seen such a thing before and I was deeply moved by his care for his grandchild yet there was no compromise that I could offer, I had to appear like the hard callous employer. I knew that the Ugandan staff hated such situations and were very happy to leave them to me. I also knew that because such dilemmas were often not addressed a hospital would end up short of drugs and equipment and patients would die because of it. However no one would be prepared to associate the death of the patients with the failure to address the original root. There were a lot of parallels with God's dealings with mankind. How did he show his justice and mercy at the same time? By Jesus taking the penalty and demonstrating God's justice so that God could show us mercy which was not weakness. Unfortunately I was never able to find a way to show Dora mercy.

We were not the only people who had to deal with thieves. Jay and Vicki Dangers, American missionaries, who ran an orphanage/school in the area, experienced two hold-ups at gun point. Armed robbers burst into their home threatening them menacingly with machine guns. Everyone in the house was rounded up and made to lie on the floor while the thieves ransacked the house. Then the booty was loaded into Jay's own van and they made their escape. It was a most unpleasant and frightening experience for the whole family especially for the children, the youngest of whom was only three years old. Six weeks later the gang returned again, and this time they were even more menacing, threatening to shoot Jay if he didn't disclose where the money was hidden. They did not seem to accept the fact that they had cleaned them out in the previous robbery and there was no more money left. Finally the thieves made their escape in Jay's van which had been recovered after the last robbery.

When the coast was clear Phil, a teacher who was staying with them, cycled to Kiwoko on one of the children's bicycles to raise the alarm. While we sent our driver off to the town of Luweero to alert the police at the main Police Station, I decided that I would take Phil and some of the local police in our car and try to follow the gang. We had a rough idea in which direction they had headed, so we set off, asking in the villages we passed if they had seen a vehicle pass this way. We also examined the earth for recent tyre tracks. At one point, where the road forked, we were not sure which direction the thieves had taken, so I went to the nearest mud hut to ask the occupants if they had heard or seen anything. They were understandably reluctant to answer as it was 1.00 am and they were frightened by the commotion, so it took me some time to rouse them. When I returned to the car I found Phil on the ground doing his press-ups! I did find this rather strange behaviour at this time. It hardly seemed the most appropriate time to do one's exercises, but we all had our strange little quirks, so I passed no remarks.

We reached the next town called Nakaseke in the middle of the night and alerted the local police to the robbery, as we thought the thieves had passed that way, though by this time we were only guessing. Hence at 3.30 in the morning we were laboriously filling in a Police report and I was wondering why I had initiated this wild goose chase, as obviously nothing would come of it. Having filled in the report we had to decide whether to press on or admit that the trail was now completely cold, and go home. We were stubborn, so we pressed on. About five miles further down the road we spied a vehicle.

'That's it,' cried the police and everyone immediately jumped out of the car.

'What am I supposed to do?' I asked.

'They are armed,' explained the police 'and they may still be in the car, so you drive slowly towards them while we walk behind the car.'

That's great, I thought – you hide behind the car while I get shot at.

'Perhaps you should fire a few shots to let them know that we are also armed,' I suggested, 'then they might not try to attack us.'

So the policeman let off a few rounds from his rifle. I slunk down as low as possible in the seat and drove the car slowly towards the parked van as the police crouched behind. However we hadn't reckoned on Phil's nervous energy; the adrenalin which had made him do his press-ups in the middle of the night also sent him striding out in front of the car. None of this crouching behind the car for safety for him. There he was, illuminated for all to see by the car headlights. Fortunately for all of us the thieves had long since gone. They had secreted their booty somewhere and abandoned the car. When we got in we realised why. The fuel gauge was registering empty. Nevertheless we were determined to take the van home with us. We started it with an old key and headed for home. I expected to see it chug to a halt at any moment but it kept going despite the empty tank until we reached Kiwoko.

Jay was understandably upset that the thieves had come back a second time. Not only was their house ransacked twice, but they were left feeling very insecure. Since the thieves had come back once they might try again. Vicki had heard of an instance where someone who had their handbag stolen during a robbery of their house, had later recognised it in Kampala and was able to catch the thief. So with this story fresh in her mind she prayed that when they went to Kampala they would recognise some item that had been stolen. In a city of one million people it seemed like a long shot, even if God was on their case. However that day they were going to Kampala, so she would be able to see if her prayer had worked. Later in the day they were travelling along a road in the outskirts of the city, in an area they seldom had cause to visit, when Vicki suddenly grabbed hold of Jay's arm and yelled,

'There is a man walking down the road wearing your shirt!'

As the van screeched to a halt and they all turned to look at the man, he saw them and took to his heels, confirming that he was indeed one of the thieves, or at least he had a guilty conscience about something. They gave chase and caught him. So with a lot of amateur detective work on Jay's part, the trail begun that day eventually led to the capture of the whole gang and the recovery of much of their property. With the thieves safely behind bars the family were at least able to sleep more easily, knowing that they could not return a third time.

In most of the large cities in Africa thieving was rife, and we quickly learned not to leave our car unattended if it contained anything of value. In fact it was preferable in certain cities not to leave it unattended in any circumstances. Our first big robbery, before we learned our lesson, was in the town of Kisumu in Kenya. We had collected the kids from school for the Christmas break and were doing some shopping on our way home. While we were doing our Christmas shopping the thieves were also doing their Christmas shopping – in our car. I had left the car parked in a busy main street where I thought it would be safe, but that was no deterrent to the street gangs, who worked at lightning speed. One would break into the car, another would enter, passing the goods to another, who would make off down the street, and it was all over in a matter of seconds. When we returned after a few minutes to the car our suitcases and a considerable amount of our worldly goods had disappeared. We never left the car unattended again, even for a few minutes. However it was surprising how things disappeared even while we were watching. I was collecting goods from the market in Kampala one day and was 'watching the car' while the market boys fetched the shopping. They warned me that the street where I had parked had a reputation for thefts, but I wasn't overly concerned as I was there myself watching everything. However after a few minutes I noticed that the money which I had been paying particularly close attention to, had vanished. I could not believe my eyes. It was like a magic trick, now you see it, now you don't. I thought I had been watching it all the time but obviously I had not been watching it closely enough – as it had disappeared. The market boys who had been doing my shopping were very upset. I was their valued customer and they didn't want their reputation or business destroyed, but the money had gone and there seemed to be nothing anyone could do. A week later it was announced on the radio – 'would the doctor who had his money stolen at the market please come back to reclaim it' – the market boys had recovered the money. After all, I was their valued customer and they were not going to let some thieves destroy that profitable relationship. They knew who the thieves were who worked that territory and arrangements were made to have the money returned.

Robbie's first experience of theft was rather personal. We had arrived in Nairobi late one evening and were looking for somewhere to stay. Robbie was crossing the road to the hotel when she suddenly felt her ear being yanked, then a man ran past her – he had stolen her golden hoop earring. She was so surprised by this audacious attack that she just stood staring after the man as he ran away. However he dropped the earring and as he bent to pick it up, he looked back and their eyes met. 'Ha, ha,' laughed Robbie, 'it was only a fake one anyway, you didn't get much.'

We learned to have a philosophical attitude about losing our worldly possessions and although we did take all the sensible precautions, we didn't get too uptight if we had something stolen. We realised that we were living among people who had nothing and we recognised that the temptation to steal was great.

Chapter 21

Fishing

We were now at the stage of having fifty to sixty beds in the hospital, but development was by no means complete. We still lacked adequate X-ray facilities. Theatre was terribly cramped and uncomfortably hot. The separation of medical and surgical patients was inadequate. Maternity was now too small and the Laboratory needed extra equipment. We had come a long way since examining patients on the floor while holding clinics in the Church, but we still had many pressing needs.

Like an Irish Wolfhound I was continuously sniffing around as to where we would get money and supplies. I was in such a frame of mind when I visited Joint Medical Stores in Kampala and noticed Sister Marliss, a Dutch sister show someone a picture of an X-ray machine. When the person had left I picked up the picture and enquired,

'What is this about X-ray equipment?'

Marliss and I always teased each other and gave the other a hard time but generally enjoyed the verbal sparring. She was responsible for allocation of drugs to the Mission Hospitals, so we saw each other regularly when I came for supplies. It appeared that a friend of Marliss, a doctor working in Holland, had given her a complete X-ray unit. It was secondhand but in good working order. Marliss had been anticipating giving it to one of the Catholic hospitals but when I asked her for it she saw no reason why we should not have it as our need was greater than

183

any of the Catholic hospitals. I didn't need any further encouragement. The next day I sent the pick-up to collect it just in case she changed her mind. We still had to build a room to house it but that was a minor detail, we knew we could build a room fairly quickly. When we did get a room ready and the equipment installed we found it worked perfectly. I was not to know then how vital having this X-ray equipment would be later for me personally.

Another piece of equipment which was needed was an Eliza reader for AIDS testing. Without this we could only carry out rapid tests which were not as accurate as the reference methods and not nearly as cheap. The rapid test required little equipment to read but cost £3.00 per test. The Eliza tests required an Eliza reader and some expensive pipettes but could be bought for $1.25 each. In a country which had a budget for health services of around £5.00 per head, neither test could be considered cheap, but the advantage of Eliza testing in accuracy and price was beyond question. Nakasero blood bank, the national blood transfusion service, supplied us with blood for transfusions on a weekly basis, so we got to know them well. After some time we found they had a small Eliza reader which they could make available to us, on loan. They could also supply us with AIDS testings kits at a very competitive price, provided we paid for them in hard currency. This would save all the business of sourcing and importing the testing kits ourselves. We could draw our supplies on a monthly basis from Nakasero blood bank as we needed them.

Initially AIDS testing had been provided free through the National AIDS Control Programme but their supplies had ceased and the World Health Organisation no longer seemed interested in providing money for AIDS tests. WHO and EEC did provide funding for screening for transfusion but not to hospitals to do AIDS testing on patients. I wondered how one could build up an awareness of the problem in their community or counsel adequately without AIDS testing being freely available. We were endeavouring to carry out the service by subsidising most of the costs ourselves, but we knew that most Mission Hospitals and all Government Hospitals did not do testing of patients unless the test kits were supplied free. It seemed an anomalous situation that hospitals should not be able to carry out AIDS tests in the country which had one of the worst epidemics in the world.

The Official Line was that an AIDS test was not necessary to diagnose a case of AIDS and a list of major and minor symptoms and signs had been drawn up. If a patient had enough of the appropriate signs a clinical diagnosis could be made. This was true of full-blown AIDS cases but by this stage they were in the terminal process of the disease. Their life expectancy was limited and they were not usually in a position to continue spreading it. It was the less obvious clinical cases which, with just a few early signs, needed testing. These people, perhaps with only a skin rash, would go from hospital to hospital, each time getting different diagnoses and treatments until they finally developed more symptoms and the correct diagnosis was made.

Having obtained our Eliza reader and test kits we set about training our laboratory technicians to do the tests. Karen was assisted at this time by Lesley, a final year Microbiology student from the UK who had been sponsored by her church to help us during the summer vacation. Lesley was a very conscientious person and having carried out a number of test batches successfully herself she was ready to instruct Henry our lab technician. Then she noticed that some of the equipment was missing – a filter for the Eliza reader. Further investigation revealed that the necessary filter had been soaking in a bucket of disinfectant. However the said bucket of disinfectant had been disposed of by Lesley that morning. It was an opaque liquid and when she poured it down the placenta pit, for safe disposal, she had not realised it contained part of her AIDS testing kit. The placenta pit, as its name suggests, was a very deep pit where we disposed of placentas and also any dangerous hospital wastes. It had a concrete top with just a small hole remaining through which we could pour the wastes. Lesley obtained a torch and peered through the hole. She could see the missing part winking back at her from the recesses far below. She was horrified. She had come out to help and had instead destroyed some vital equipment. She realised that she must retrieve the filter at all costs. It could be disinfected safely and used again, if she could get it back. What she needed was a fishing line and hook.

Lesley enrolled Gerry, the hospital engineer's help, so all that morning Lesley and Gerry spent their time 'fishing' in the placenta pit. It was a frustrating experience as they could see the article but could not quite hook it. Finally they decided to take a break for lunch – the filter wouldn't go away – they had almost got it, they would come back in the afternoon and finish the job when they felt more refreshed.

When they returned they could no longer see the filter. Where had it gone? Then they realised that it was still there but in their absence some 'fool' had poured other waste down the pit on top of it. It was an understandable mistake; however I was glad Lesley was of a placid disposition or she might have strangled someone.

Gerry decided to take some definitive action, enough of this fishing around in the pit. Someone would have to go down there and get it. However, understandably, no one was volunteering so as Gerry had had the good idea himself he had to carry it out himself. The concrete top was removed by the tractor with no real problem. So while the tractor was working Gerry got dressed like a spaceman and then climbed down into the pit. The filter was retrieved and both Gerry and the filter were disinfected. Gentle Lesley never forgot her experience with the filter and the placenta pit, but no harm was done, and she obviously made a vital contribution to the lab in other ways as she was asked to come back the following year, when she had qualified, to help teach on the laboratory technicians' course.

By this time the lab employed fifteen people and carried out twenty-two thousand tests per year. Many of the people employed there were from the surrounding villages and had been trained 'on the job'. We had sent our most senior person to the large Catholic hospital in Kampala for a two year lab technicians' course, but meantime we had commenced our own training course. At the end of two years the lab assistants would sit the National Examination and obtain a recognised qualification. Despite all these advances in the laboratory, Karen was still using her Blue Band tins as part of her array of laboratory jars and containers.

At the other end of the building was another enclave of activity. This was the theatre and autoclaving room. Lawrence had the place going well with about seventy operations being carried out per month. It seemed that a high percentage of people in the community had hernias, as we had a huge influx of patients for hernia repair. All these people in Luweero must have been nursing their hernias but had nowhere to go to have them repaired. When we got theatre operational they reported to us in droves. Presumably at some stage in the future we would have fixed all the hernias in the community and the numbers would decrease. For the present, any doctor working at the hospital got great experience in the procedure of hernia repair.

There were many other operations carried out besides herniorraphies – caesarian sections, laparotomies, hysterectomies, cystectomies, removal of tumours etc etc. However the most difficult operations were referred to our visiting Consultant Surgeon, Doctor Christina, who came once a month. Christina had been a surgeon in Africa for many years and it seemed that she had seen and done nearly anything to do with surgery, and could do plastic surgery, orthopaedics, trauma, urology, general surgery.

She had a special interest in urology which was vitally

187

important, especially in Uganda, as so many old men, and not so old men, had urethral strictures, as a result of gonorrhoea, and couldn't pass water. Understandably this was a serious problem for the patient and it was also extremely painful. It was often overcome by the doctor passing a catheter directly into the distended bladder through the abdomen. This relieved the immediate problem but did nothing to remove the original obstruction. Consequently some of these old gentlemen had been using an abdominal catheter for years and had not been investigated to see if they could pass water again in the usual way. The other dangerous complication was that through the catheter the bladder and kidneys eventually became very infected and the patient could die of renal failure.

Christina had used a special instrument called a urethrotome to reopen the urethra in a number of these old men, so that after years of inability they could now pass water. Hence her fame spread in Luweero and she had a following of old men who inevitably turned up if she was around. I never understood quite how they knew that she was coming but the bush telegraph was a reality. On the second day of her visits to Kiwoko a very motley assortment of admirers would be waiting for Christina outside theatre.

Christina also believed that the patients wanted to see the bits of them which had been removed, so that they knew the problem had been definitely dealt with. As almost all of her patients had the operation carried out under spinal anaesthetic she could talk to them during the operation, and when she removed the tumour she would show it to them. These were not usually minor tumours but huge masses which could weigh up to nine kilos. I always found her rapport with a patient intriguing as she held up melon sized tumours and said, 'See, Mama, we've got rid of it now! It won't cause you any more problems.'

The patients appeared completely calm and detached as Christina chatted with them about what she was doing and demonstrated the finished product. They all took it as a matter of course that this was how surgery was carried out everywhere.

One afternoon after an operating session Christina bounced into the house.

'Do you have any patients with harelip?' she asked no one in particular, 'I like fixing hare lips.'

Robbie was around and knew exactly the case for her. She and Heather taught a scripture class at one of the local primary schools where one of the children had a hare lip. The school consisted of a long mud hut and the children sat on stones on the floor. Nevertheless they were bright kids and when Robbie introduced a system of incentives for memorising verses, she was nearly trampled by the crowd. The incentives consisted of small gifts such as a pencil or a rubber or even small toys. These were highly prized. One of the brightest pupils was Sarah, who was thirteen, but she had a gross hare lip, with the teeth in her gum growing through the gap and pointing in all directions of the compass. Sarah was from a very poor family and had been hidden in the village all her life because she looked like a hideous freak. Robbie had been about to ask Christina if she knew of anyone in Uganda who could do plastic surgery to correct her deformity when Christina posed the question. On finding out about Sarah she was enthusiastic to do the repair. She had done a number of these cases and they had good results, so the following month Sarah was brought to theatre and the operation to correct her hare lip was carried out. The result was amazing and Sarah's life was transformed. She completed her primary school exams and we obtained sponsorship for her to go to secondary school where she excelled academically. Were it not for Christina, Sarah would still have been the village freak. Afterwards Christina said that now she was so pretty she would find a husband.

'No,' replied Sarah. 'I don't want a man, I don't want to get AIDS.'

Wise girl.

The theatre was very small and hot. Worse still, the

autoclaving room was just beside it, making it even hotter. When autoclaving was going on at the same time as theatre, streams of sweat would pour down the surgeon's body. By the end of the operation the green gowns would be soaked. I found it rather uncomfortable as sweat ran down my chest and soaked my theatre trousers, and Christina found it almost unbearable. The other problem was that because of the small size of the theatre there was a constant threat of desterilisation by touching the walls. Indeed it was virtually impossible to work if there were more than four people in the room, the Surgeon, the Anaesthetist, the Scrub Nurse and the Runner. The conditions were inadequate and troublesome but at least we were able to carry out most of the necessary operations. Nonetheless provisions for a larger theatre would have to be made. Since the theatre was too small and the maternity ward was also too small the obvious answer was to build a bigger maternity ward and move the theatre to the old ward. As this required a completely new Maternity Wing, I started looking for funds again.

As part of my efforts to get money and equipment for the hospital I had visited the British High Commission in Kampala the previous year. The girl whom I dealt with was keen to help but the proposal got stuck at a higher level. Nothing more was heard for almost a year until I received a note from the British High Commission to say if I was still interested in applying for a grant I should contact them immediately. I didn't need a second invitation. As I met with my contact again she explained that it was the end of the financial year and they had underspent in their small projects budget. In the usual Civil Service scheme of things, if they did not spend the money this year, they would be allocated less next year, so they wanted to spend the money quickly. I was delighted to help them out! I had the maternity ward project in mind which could go ahead immediately. All that they required were the receipts for materials purchased. By British aid standards the amount which the hospital received was tiny amount of money – £7,000 precisely, but it was given immediately and enabled us to get the ball rolling for the new maternity ward.

The speed at which the hospital was developing often meant that funding from a large bureaucratic organisation was difficult. In fact many of the grants and donations we received were very small by international aid standards, but as they came at the critical time they enabled us to make the next logical step in development. Consequently our development which took place step by step was always relevant to the existing needs and never out of date by the time it took place.

As work began on building the new maternity ward, deliveries on the old cramped ward continued as usual. Some of these deliveries were extremely unusual, like the one which happened one day while I was in theatre. I was carrying out a caesarian section when Christine, the midwife, poked her head around the door.

'Doctor, a mother who hasn't delivered the second twin yet, has arrived!'

This was not such an unusual situation. Women sometimes delivered the first twin at home and came to hospital because of delay in delivering the second. However this was usually within a few hours of the first delivery, or because the second twin had died. In this case the mother was from far to the north of us. She had delivered a live baby and then realised that something was not right. At this point she did not know she was having twins. However she made contact with a local midwife who told her that she was having twins and hadn't delivered the second one yet. The midwife also thought that it had died, so the mother started to make her way to the hospital. It was a long journey. She was first carried on a makeshift stretcher, then got a ride in a pick-up and finally a bus. The journey took two days. By the time she arrived at the hospital it was a full three days since the first twin had been delivered. I was thinking about how we could remove the second twin who was now certainly dead when

191

Christine broke into my thoughts to inform me that the baby was not dead but was still alive. This was extremely unusual after all this time, but an hour later the mother delivered her second baby now three days after the first. She was understandably delighted. African babies are born pink and they then increase their pigment over the next few days. Because there were three days between the twins she now had one pink baby and one brown one.

I had never heard of someone delivering twins three days apart before and neither had any of my medical colleagues. I went to the ward to take pictures of this medical phenomenon and the mother blushed with pleasure at being the centre of all this attention. The incident confirmed my admiration for African mothers. They were survivors, no matter what life had to throw at them they had the ability to keep going, usually without complaint.

However very few stories of delay in labour had such a happy ending. Most ended in disaster for the mother and the baby. Sometimes a delay in getting to the hospital was inevitable and couldn't be avoided especially if the mother came from a distance. For this reason we had commenced building a mud hut village beside the hospital where some of the huts were reserved for mothers waiting for delivery. The others were used by relatives and attendants of patients. They could come some time before they were due and await delivery without incurring any cost. On the other hand some of the delays could have been easily avoided and involved 'quack' midwives or husbands who didn't seem to care. A village midwife could usually carry out a normal delivery with no real difficulties. In our Community Health Programme we trained them to use a new razor blade to cut the cord and have a clean scrap of cloth ready for tying it. However, problems arose when there was malpresentation of the baby and the village midwife (or, traditional birth attendant, as she was also known), tried to forcibly pull the baby out. If an arm came down first she would grab it and pull as hard as she could. This was the worst thing she could do. The baby would become wedged at the shoulders in a position in which it was impossible to deliver. If enough pulling, pushing and delay took place, the uterus would eventually rupture and both mother and baby would die. Even if this didn't happen the baby would die and infection would set in so that the mother became critically ill. I could understand why this situation would arise when a mother lived far from medical help. I had absolutely no understanding, and even less sympathy for the relatives and midwife, when it happened around the corner from the hospital. In one such case a relative eventually came for help. We sent out a vehicle and brought the mother in. By this stage the baby was long dead and we could see from the marks to the tiny protruding arm that it had been thoroughly pulled, levered and yanked in an attempt to remove the baby. I felt sadness and sympathy for the mother who must have endured terrible agonies, but I was incensed at the relatives and the traditional birth attendant who had done this. The position of the baby was such that only a caesarian section could remove it now. Fortunately, in this case, the uterus had not ruptured but infection had set in. This young mother survived with heavy doses of antibiotics but others died despite what we could do.

One morning I was called by our midwife Donata. She seemed none too pleased and I soon discovered why. A young girl had just been admitted who had been in labour for three days. She lived exactly three miles away and Donata was giving the relatives 'a tongue lashing'. I couldn't understand the language but I could understand the spirit of the conversation and I knew that Donata was telling the husband exactly what she thought of him – which wasn't much. The baby was already dead and if the mother also died, he would be directly responsible she concluded, pointing the finger at him. The beleaguered looking husband cringed and looked away under the midwife's fiery gaze. I took the patient to theatre and found she had a ruptured uterus. Worse still was the fact that it had obviously happened many hours, if not days ago and infection had set in. She was stinking. In such a situation, with so many complications, the odds were against survival, but we pressed on and did what we could. We removed the damaged uterus which was providing a focus of infection and gave her massive doses of intravenous antibiotics. Unfortunately despite what we did she died as we were closing up. She must have had overwhelming septicaemia.

I stripped off my gown and gloves and went to tell the relatives. I hated such situations because even though there was decided neglect or even stupidity on someone's part in this case, they were still people who had lost a relative. A mother had lost her eighteen year old daughter. A husband had lost a wife. These people were the poor and downtrodden, not just by western society's standards but by Ugandan standards. I told Donata that the mother had now also died and she spoke to the relatives. Then she turned to me, her eyes full of a mixture of frustration and compassion. 'I am sorry for them,' she said, 'but I am mad at the husband. He doesn't really care, he will just go and get another wife. Here life is cheap and the men regard the women as expendable.'

I knew she was right. The mother would grieve for her eighteen year old daughter but the husband would soon go out and take another young wife to bear his children. I thought of the young girl herself who had died so pointlessly because no one had cared enough, or been informed enough, to bring her the three miles down the road to the hospital where she would have had a safe delivery.

Some of the more fortunate ladies who survived such obstructed labour were still left with a hole in the bladder. As the baby's head had been pressing down on the bladder and urethra for an abnormal length of time, the tissue lost its blood supply and a hole later developed. This was a terrible condition for the patients. They had absolutely no control over passing water and were incontinent all the time. It was easy to pick out those to whom it had happened by the strong smell of urine. It was inevitably a young girl who was very small. That was why it had happened in the first place. The pelvis was too small for the baby's head to pass; she had cephalo pelvic disproportion and the head had got stuck. These holes or fistulas were very hard to fix surgically. Christina hated to see our line of small smelly girls awaiting her attention. They often required repeated surgical procedures, especially if the hole was large. Hence Christina established quite a relationship with some of these young mothers. It was a very frustrating condition both for the patient and the surgeon. The operation would be carried out and the patient would be dry for up to fourteen days, then when everyone was getting excited that things had worked this time, a leak would develop again. At least Christina tried and a number of these young girls were helped, otherwise no one would do anything for them. They were poor, they were smelly, very few surgeons in the country could help them and even if they could find such a person they couldn't afford the operation. So they learned to live with a constant stream of urine trickling down their leg and people moving away when they sat down beside them.

When our new maternity ward was complete it had twenty-six maternity beds, so we had capacity for all who would come. The hospital now had a total of 100 beds, a reasonable sized district hospital. We had also continued to construct mud huts for the mothers who came from afar and to spread the word through our community health programme and ante-natal clinics that the hospital was a good safe place for delivery. It was hard to judge success as it was always the exceptional cases that one remembered – so often the horror stories. However I had a feeling that things were improving, many more mothers were being delivered at the hospital, the vast majority with a happy conclusion. We still got the extreme cases which made us sad or sometimes frustrated but we were running a hospital and that's what we were there for. If people came to us, even when it was late and they had already tried traditional healers, witchdoctors, herbs, or local midwives, or just been neglected in the mud hut, they still came because they believed that we could help them and that is why we were there. We were there to help the poor, the ignorant and the downtrodden.

Chapter 22

Strenuous Relaxation

Life at Kiwoko wasn't all work and no play. There were also lots of opportunities for leisure activities such as visiting the National Parks both in Uganda and Kenya. Many of Uganda's National Parks had suffered greatly from the period of civil war with soldiers or bandits taking pot shots at the animals. The elephant population in particular had been vastly depleted. However there were some scenic areas in Uganda where there was still much wildlife. One such place was Murchison Falls National Park on the banks of the river Nile. The falls themselves were spectacular and the river teamed with hundreds of hippos and crocodiles which were said to be the biggest in the world.

On some occasions we took visitors to Murchison Falls to show them another side of life in Uganda. The falls were several hours drive north of Luweero and on one occasion I decided that we would make the trip there and back within a day, to save us the bother of making an overnight stop. Besides we needed to be back for a church service the following day. Accommodation in that area tended to be expensive with the hotels demanding payment in dollars for the very basic facilities being offered. So we set out before dawn. The journey was rather longer than I had anticipated, and we didn't reach the park until 10.30 am. This meant that we had missed the morning boat trip up the river which was the highlight of the excursion. However we were informed that the boat would leave again at 2.00 pm, so we explored the falls, had our picnic and did some animal spotting. Most of the animals would be seen best from the boat as they came down to drink at the water's edge.

By 2.00 pm we were assembled, waiting for the launch which had not yet returned from the first trip. 3.00 pm passed and the boat had still not returned. I was becoming somewhat agitated as I now knew that the journey back would take four to five hours. I also realised we needed diesel. The boat trip would normally take three hours so if we had boarded at 2.00 pm we would have had plenty of time to make the journey home. Now it was 3.30 pm and the launch had only just returned. Perhaps they would cut short the trip, after all they would not want to be on the river later than 5.00 or at the least 6.00 pm. In fact our party made up all the members of the excursion. Then I noticed that was not quite true, a man and a woman had boarded after us and sat unobtrusively in the corner. I now felt relieved. Since we made up almost all the passengers, we would ask the pilot to be back for 5.30 pm. Normally the boat travelled the few miles up the Nile from the docking site to the Falls offering a good view of the crocodiles and hippos on the way and the cascade of the falls viewed from below. We didn't mind if we turned back before we reached the falls so that we could reach a garage before closing time and make the journey home.

The views of the bird life, the animals in the water and on the banks were spectacular. Brightly coloured kingfishers hovered and dived beside the boat. Fish eagles sat majestically on the trees by the shore – flocks of waders searched for food in the shallows and huge crocodiles basked with open mouths on the rocks at the shore. Hippos, by the hundred, appeared and disappeared in the water. As the boat chugged along, these large fat pig-like animals would disappear into the murky depths leaving only a few ripples. Under the surface the river must have been seething with hippos and crocs – not a place to go swimming. On the banks were elephant, water buck, cape buffalo and giraffes and towering overhead, on the far bank, was the remains of what was once a luxury hotel. This had been the tourist lodge for the park but in 1986 it had been looted by guerillas. It now stood empty and derelict, a patent reminder of Uganda's former days of prosperity. The trip on the Nile had been worth waiting for. We had now seen all the sights and were ready to return. I had a quiet word with the driver about our predicament – we had a long way to travel and I needed to get back to Masindi, the next town, to get diesel before the petrol stations closed. As far as the driver was concerned there was no problem, he could turn back now, but he would need permission also from the other two passengers who were not members of our party. I had anticipated that, so I had my speech prepared and I approached the couple. They looked like reasonable people and when I explained to them that we were in danger of being stranded without fuel for our car I was sure they would understand. After all the boat was way behind schedule and it would soon be dark for everyone travelling back. No one would wish to be travelling in a remote National Park during darkness. The man listened to me impassively.

'We paid our money to see ze falls; we are going to see ze falls!' he stated coldly with a thick German accent.

My heart sank. I was not dealing with a fellow Irishman here or indeed an English man whom I could reason with or persuade. This man had his mind made up and I knew enough of the German temperament to realise that there would be no argument or appeal in this case.

As I sat disconsolately, Robbie thought she would have a try. She would appeal to his sense of compassion, she would throw us on his mercy. He could not want us to be stuck in a National Park all night. We needed to get back to our patients, there were lots of humanitarian compassionate arguments she could use. So she made her impassioned plea. The German sat stony faced and stared straight ahead during the monologue. Finally he made a response.

'We have paid our money and we are going to see ze ze falls.'

Robbie had obviously made a big impression. The boat chugged on. By now it was getting very late and we were desperate. Instead of enjoying the trip everyone was sitting as stony faced as the German. Finally he broke the silence – had his heart at last been touched, had he been moved with compassion? We held our breath.

'We will make ze trip to ze falls,' he announced.

Our hopes were dashed again. But all was not yet lost. Somewhere under that stony exterior beat a real human heart.

'However I think I can help you to get fuel, I know the garage owner in Masindi.'

At least a little ray of hope had been lit.

When we made it back to the docking point it was about 7.00 pm. We raced to our car and set out along the long dirt road. I decided this was the time to put my rally cross experience of driving around Kiwoko into action, so we covered the distance to Masindi at breakneck speed – much to the discomfort of my passengers. However the rally driving was to no avail. When we reached the town all the garages were closed; we had missed the last one by a mere twenty minutes. There was nothing we could do but park at the garage and wait to see if the German was as good as his word. It was now after 9.00 pm and we had a three hour journey left. We settled down to wait. We would either be spending the night at the garage or our friend would return with someone who could get us diesel.

An hour later a four wheel drive vehicle rolled up and the German sprang out with four mechanics who immediately proceeded to roll out a drum of diesel – we were saved! Now the stony faced expression of the German had gone and he was grinning all over his face. We couldn't help but laugh as well and there was lots of hand shaking and back slapping. We had finally become friends. So we were able to make it back to Kiwoko that night, or rather sometime early the next morning we finally arrived back home. When we contemplated the day's adventures it had been a 19 hour day with hours and hours of driving. Much of the time which we had not spent driving we had spent worrying. There had been a few hours of sailing on the Nile and seeing the animals – but was it worth it? This was supposed to have been a restful, recreational day out. I did wonder sometimes why our leisure activities seemed to be more demanding than our routine working days. I knew we needed time to relax and rest, but somehow these relaxing times had a habit of turning into demanding marathons of activity which resulted in nervous exhaustion instead of relaxation.

One such occasion was our half term trip to Masai Mara. We had been told about the delights of Kenya's best known big game park – Masai Mara. This was the game reserve which linked with Tanzania's Serengeti. This was where the wilderbeast migrated in their thousands, where lion, giraffe, elephant, rhino, cheetah or leopard could easily be spotted. The only problem was that the costs quoted for accommodation in the lodges were horrendous. So the Clarkes decided to do it on the cheap and camp. There were a number of camping sites listed in the brochures and finding a safe site to pitch our tent didn't seem to be any real problem.

We picked the kids up from school and headed off for the Masai Mara. This would be an opportunity to see big game in large numbers and we were all very excited. We were not disappointed. On our first day's safari we saw almost all the big game listed in our brochure. As the afternoon went on it was time to find our camp-site, before darkness fell. We followed the roads, or rather tracks indicated on the map, which would lead us to the camp-site, but although the maps indicated dots for camp sites we could find nothing where the camp site should be. We stopped to ask some tribesmen, who were most anxious to help. One got into the car and authoritatively told us to drive north. After some miles we began to have our doubts as to where this fellow was taking us and on further questioning we realised the man couldn't speak English. As we couldn't speak Swahili there was a definite communication problem. We decided that it was safer to retrace our steps and get back to the road indicated on the map. More inquiries yielded similarly fruitless results. The tribesmen were most anxious to help – they sniffed financial reward in the air – but the only problem was that they did not understand what we were asking. The afternoon was drawing on and we appeared to be lost in the middle of nowhere unable to locate a camp site. Finally another Landrover arrived laden with tourists and camping equipment. Perhaps they knew where the camp site was, so we followed them. They led us down a track to some sheds – some semblance of life at last, but still no sign of a camp site. They stopped to speak with someone and then headed out across a field. We asked the same man if he knew where the camp site was.

'Follow that Landrover,' he instructed, 'they are going to it.'

At last it seemed we had arrived. However the Landrover stopped in a field. No sign of other campers, no sign of tents or toilets, no fence or security, nothing except an open field by the Mara river! Could this be the place marked on the map as a camp site? We thought a camp site was like those we had stayed in while on holiday in France – with a shop and table tennis room, toilets and showers. Well, if that was too much to hope for at least it should be surrounded by a fence and have some security. This was on the banks of the Mara river, the same river we had seen scores of crocodiles basking in the sun earlier that day.

We decided there would be safety in numbers and sidled up beside the other campers who were pulling belongings out of their Landrover. At least if we were attacked by crocodile, or stampeded by cape buffalo they might hear our cries and come to the rescue. As we unpacked our things one of the campers came over to us. This was nice, a friendly welcome from our fellow travellers.

'You are not thinking of camping here?' he said indicating our site.

'Well, yes we were,' we admitted.

'Do you mind moving away from us? My friends are teachers. They want to get away from children and I see you have children.'

So much for our friendly welcome from our neighbouring campers. We definitely had the feeling we were getting the cold shoulder. So we moved away at least around the corner where they would not be offended by the sight of our children. The man in charge of the camp appeared to collect his camping fees. There may not have been any facilities but we were certainly not going to spend the night scot free.

'You will need a guard,' he mentioned casually.

I was inclined to agree with him. The site definitely felt very exposed and insecure. 'In fact you will need two guards,' he went on, 'so that one can guard while the other sleeps.'

I had always been under the impression that a guard was supposed to stay awake while guarding, but if he wanted to give us two guards so much the better. He would arrange it, he said. That would cost us an extra 300 shillings. The guards were not part of the camp site fee, that was just for the privilege of setting one's tent up. The spirit of commercialisation had certainly reached Masai Mara, if nothing else.

As we set up our tent and got our cooking fire going our guard arrived. One look and we realised that this was not part of Securicor's franchise. The 'guards' were Masai tribesmen, clad in sandals, scarlet wrap-around cloak, brightly coloured bracelets and loop earrings – no those weren't loop earrings, those were their ears which had been extended in the traditional Masai way by making huge holes in the lobes. To complete the costume with the necessary accessories for every well dressed Masai warrior about town, they had spears.

These warriors might have been introduced to western

commercialisation, as no sooner had they arrived than they were trying to sell us bracelets. However they were still unspoiled in the arts of western social graces. They joined us around the camp fire and indicated in the universal sign language – by rubbing their stomachs and sticking their hands out – that they wanted food. That was no problem, we were happy for them to join us for our camp fire meal. As the night wore on things did become a little more awkward with our guests, as we realised that they didn't have any idea of the concept of interpersonal space. They were naturally curious about everything and tended to stand at least three inches away from us at all times. This practice was somewhat inconvenient for us as well as downright unnerving. We appreciated their attentions in guarding us, but if they could just stand or squat a little further away we would all be more comfortable. We decided we would make a tactical retreat – to our tent – early in the evening, however this was probably a mistake as it allowed us extra hours to lie awake in the darkness listening to the night noises and worrying about every sound. I could hear the Masai guards talking quietly over the camp fire for the early part of the evening, then all fell silent.

This worried me more than the noise. What if they had both gone to sleep? I fretted. There would be no one left to guard us. What if we were charged by a herd of cape buffalo – animals which were known to be very bad tempered. I lay awake straining to hear every sound. Was that a crocodile I could hear slithering through the grass, was that the roar of distant hoofs thundering across the plain? We would be found in the morning trampled to death or half eaten by crocodiles. Or perhaps that sound was an elephant which had gone mad. They were known to do that from time to time – we had heard of an incident where an elephant had gone berserk and attacked a tent with people sleeping in it. They had escaped but the elephant had run off with the tent, waving it victoriously like a flag. It had been retrieved the following day, no longer in pristine condition, about a mile away. Such thoughts were circulating through my mind making sleep impossible, but my problems were nothing compared to Robbie's. She had been reading in the newspapers about the Julie Ward killing in Masai Mara. This was an English girl whose car had broken down in the park. Much later parts of her body were found and one theory was that she had been killed and dismembered by tribesmen.

As Robbie lay silently in the tent, every nerve strained to hear what was going on outside, she thought of what she had read in the papers. She was now convinced we would all be murdered. The guards had gone off to get their fellow warriors! They would come back, sneak up on us and brutally kill us before dawn. There was no doubt in her mind that this would happen. It was merely a question of when. She lay awake waiting for the soft foot falls. Meanwhile, as I was waiting to be crushed to death by stampeding cape buffalos and Robbie was waiting to be murdered, the children slept peacefully. It was an interminably long night but eventually we were surprised by the first glow of the dawn and we found we were still alive.

As we ate breakfast we could see that our fellow campers were having some trouble starting their Landrover. The battery was apparently dead and as it was uneven ground they had no chance of getting enough momentum to get it push started. After watching them for about ten minutes, as we munched on our cereal, I said to Michael to go and ask them if they would like some help. I felt after our night's trauma I would enjoy this. I was about to fulfil the biblical injunction of blessing those who rejected us and thereby heaping coals of fire on their heads. I hoped they burned. Michael came back with the message that they would very much appreciate our help. So I produced a tow rope, hitched up their Landrover and had it started within a few minutes. I must say I enjoyed watching the expressions on their faces. I had rarely seen five such sheepish looking people. Of course I was generous and magnanimous – as a Christian should be. The fact that we had been cold shouldered and snubbed only the previous evening meant nothing to me!

As we packed up to leave our camp site, we were thankful to be moving on. Tonight, we promised ourselves, we will find a proper camp site with lots of people and proper guards there. We set off to see more wild life that day with hopes renewed and spirits high. There were no sign posts but we felt we knew the direction to the concentration of wildlife so we drove on and on and on. Finally we decided we had better stop and ask directions. We had been driving for rather a long time and didn't want to become completely lost in this barren wilderness.

'Masai Mara?' the old man repeated, 'but you are going in the wrong direction, you are heading for Nairobi!'

That did it. We were now thoroughly fed up, we had had enough of this adventure safari. If we were going in the wrong direction, so be it. We would carry on to Nairobi. A secure night in a comfortable bed beckoned. Who wanted to see any more big game anyway?

Half terms spent with the kids may have been nerve racking or exhausting but they were never boring. Sean had signed up to climb Mount Kenya with a school trip during one half term. This was fine by me. I was delighted he was to have the experience. The only problem was that he had signed me up as well, and after my experiences of Masai Mara I fancied something more relaxing in the way of a break – preferably some sort of activity that involved sitting by a pool with a good book and a cool glass of lemonade with just enough activity to exercise my elbow and eye muscles, not actually anything which would involve working up a sweat or even getting wet. However Sean had signed me up and no matter how much I yearned to lie by the pool I felt it was my duty to climb this mountain with my son. This may have been a product of my Presbyterian upbringing sense of values, which dictated that if there was a difficult way I should choose it, so this particular half term break found me struggling up a mountain instead of relaxing by a pool. The first night was spent at base camp, a series of huts at 10,000 feet which boasted no amenities apart from what we had brought along ourselves. The school headmaster had generously allocated supplies so we were able to feast on a hearty meal of meat and spaghetti.

The following morning we set out for the next camp at 14,000 feet. This involved a climb up what was called the vertical bog. We were fortunate it had not rained for at least a month and the bog was dry, so although the thigh muscles objected, the going was not too tough. The camp at 14,000 feet consisted of a long store house, a set of pit latrines and an icy spring. The rooms were packed with bunkbeds which had mattresses of dubious hygienic standard. At this level water boiled at a low temperature and it was hard to get a really hot cup of tea. It was also cold – very cold.

We were informed that we would set out at 3.30 am to make the summit by dawn. It was apparently spectacularly beautiful to see the sun rising over the peaks – but was it worth it? It was too cold to sleep anyway so rising at 3.30 was not so difficult. It was pitch black so we formed up in a line and moved off behind the guide. Our climb involved several hundred feet of a shale slope which we appeared to have to go straight up. It was perhaps a blessing that it was dark as we could neither see what lay ahead or what was behind. The air was becoming decidedly thin and breathing was difficult. Altitude sickness was also setting in with several of the boys, causing disorientation and lack of co-operation – or was that their normal personality? Whatever the cause, several of the boys decided they could not and would not go any further and they would prefer to lie down in the ice and end it all there and then. They were fortunately blessed to have a parent who was an Anglican theologian following them, who believed in perseverance under trial and motivated the mutineers to get going again with a few strategically aimed kicks. As we neared the top I understood at last what it meant to have a breathtaking experience. I could not breathe, I could only walk five or six steps and then stumble to a halt gasping. Meanwhile Sean waited patiently for me. He was taking the whole experience with his usual nonchalant air. We struggled on. As we approached the final peak, the dawn broke and the peaks were outlined against the red sky. I also heard voices. Was this the effect of the altitude sickness and was I beginning to hallucinate, or was that the voice of Christina De Wind, our visiting surgeon to Kiwoko? She had not come with our party, so how could she be here at 6.30 am on the top of Mount Kenya? It wasn't the kind of place where one bumped into friends who happened to be passing through. But as I clambered to the peak there was Christina in the flesh. We shook hands on the summit. Christina had climbed the other face of the mountain and we had arrived at the summit together. It definitely was a small world after all.

The view was stupendous and the experience was probably exhilarating but I was in no condition to appreciate it at that moment. I felt cold and sick and wanted to get down as soon as possible, now that we had accomplished what we set out to do. So Sean and I didn't hang around breathing in the thin mountain air at 16,500 feet and taking in the view. There were still two days of half term left and a swimming pool beckoned us. Our record for getting up the mountain was hardly spectacular, but our speed at getting down was. Our senses told us that if we could get off the mountain quick enough we would not have to spend another night at base camp. The prospect of a hot shower, a tasty meal and a comfortable warm bed ignited our afterburners and we zoomed down the mountain as fast as our little legs would rotate. We were also pursued, or in fact pursuing most of the time, the Anglican theologian who had also got the scent of home in his nostrils.

By that evening we had made it back to the club where Robbie, Michael and Lauren were staying. We felt proud of ourselves. 'It was an exhilarating experience,' we told Robbie. We were delighted that we had done it – now that it was over! Since it was such an exhilarating experience, they asked, would we want to do it again next year? Well, we wouldn't want to rush into that, after all it was the kind of experience which we could enjoy, so long as it was behind us, not in front of us. Retrospectively we could tell everyone how wonderful it was, especially if we were expounding on the delights of mountaineering from our sunbeds by the pool.

Our experiences at Murchison Falls, Masai Mara and Mount Kenya were a part of life in Africa which had an addictive quality. The uncertainty, the danger, the challenge, the stupidity, the exhaustion, the perseverance, whatever the ingredients were, they certainly got the adrenalin flowing. There was nothing spiritual in these experiences, we were just being tourists and discovering Africa, but what a tremendous perk it was with the job. What a tremendous breadth of experience our kids were able to have. It certainly beat sitting at home watching the telly, and we were very grateful for such experiences, even though they were sometimes uncomfortable.

Chapter 23

Dedicated Staff

Sometimes I found myself acting as assistant to the electrician or engineer. This was particularly with regard to our generators. It was not that I knew a lot about either generators or electrics but I could tell when something was going wrong and I often had enough common sense to be able to trace a fault. Kassana the electrician was good with electrics, it was just that he couldn't see very well and sometimes made the wrong connections. An electrician who has difficulty with his vision is definitely at a disadvantage in the trade! Occasionally the live and neutral wires would get mixed up, with consequences immediately felt by all, but more commonly Kassana couldn't get the little screwdriver accurately into the junction box or switch and, unknowingly, left the connections a bit loose. This would not usually show itself until some time later. Then at some critical time a short would develop and the generator would go into overload. I didn't mind my role as Kassana's assistant, nor did I object to helping Simon, who was the generator supervisor, I just didn't like doing it in the middle of an operation. However sometimes in order to get an operation carried out my role in helping with the generator and the electrics was more vital than my role as the surgeon. After all one cannot do an operation in the dark.

One day in the true Kiwoko style and in keeping with Murphy's law, everything went wrong. A very old man had been brought in with a strangulated inguinal hernia. Since the hernia had been strangulated for almost two days, his condition was critical and the prognosis was poor when he arrived. At this time we had three generators – a small petrol Honda which could run one or two items such as the theatre lights, a medium sized diesel generator which could run on a single phase, and a large three phase diesel generator which could run all our heavy equipment. As it was early in the morning and as only the theatre lights were required, I asked Simon to start the Honda while we prepared the patient. Within a few minutes it was evident that there was a problem somewhere. The theatre lights were flickering off and on and the generator was labouring. So in order to save time in tracing the fault I asked if we could use the medium sized generator. After a further ten minutes there was still no light, so I got on my bicycle (a convenient form of transport round the hospital compound) and pedalled off to the generator house. There I found the men all standing around contemplating the generator.

'It has refused,' Simon reported.

Then he pointed to the problem. A notch had broken off the starting handle and the handle kept slipping off the crank.

'Well, we have wasted enough time now,' I remarked, 'let's start the three phase generator.'

I knew by the scramble of activity which followed that starting the large generator wasn't going to be a straightforward matter either.

'Does the battery work?' I queried.

The men looked sheepishly at the ground and admitted the battery hadn't been charged and was flat. Now I was becoming a little frustrated.

'Three generators and not one of them works,' I commented and cycled off in disgust. However all was not yet lost. Simon went to get more workers and they returned with ropes to attach to the pulley in order to start the generator manually. With six men pulling the rope and a large heave they got it going.

Back in theatre I was now preparing for the operation. But there was still no light although I could hear that the generator had started, so I asked one of the nurses if she could go and see what the problem was.

A few minutes later the young nurse reported that there was still a short and the large generator was overloading when they put on the lights.

'Then could you ask Kassana to set up the Honda generator with a direct line to the emergency free standing theatre light?' I suggested.

Shortly thereafter this was done and we finally had light. Now we were ready and I was about to commence the operation when the patient starting vomiting profusely. The light was disconnected again so that we could use our suction pump. The poor old man was deteriorating now but eventually he was sorted out and I was ready to begin again. Scalpel in hand I instructed,

'Switch the light on.'

The nurses connected up the plug, pressed switches and generally looked as if they knew what they were doing but they didn't produce any light. As I was scrubbed up I couldn't touch anything so I was telling anyone who would listen, to try that connection, or check that switch, or make sure the power was on at that generator. Finally I could bear it no longer, so stripping off my mask and gloves, I raced outside to check things myself. Gown and hat flying I was calling,

'Someone get Kassana, someone get me a screwdriver,' all the time muttering under my breath.

The workers at the carpentry shop nearby were mesmerised by seeing the doctor rush out of theatre in his gown and start fiddling with the generator. Within a few minutes I had checked the connections from the generator back to the light and asked the staff to try the switch.

'It doesn't work, doctor', they responded.

So I tried it myself. Miraculously the light came on. I looked at it in amazement. It simply hadn't been switched on properly. Then I looked at the staff accusingly.

212

I was now almost in apoplexy. They however continued looking at me blankly until my Northern Irish temperament boiled over and I muttered, 'Buck Eejits!'

The theatre staff just continued to stare at me blankly. Although to be called a 'buck eejit' in Northern Ireland is definitely very unflattering, it didn't have an equivalent meaning in Uganda. In fact it was meaningless, which was just as well, as it isn't becoming for a medical superintendent, no matter how frustrated by events, to be abusive. After that events went smoothly and the old man survived the operation. However I did feel guilty about calling them Buck Eejits. So I apologised profusely. We were very fortunate to have excellent theatre staff who worked hard and rarely complained.

Lawrence was the main theatre supervisor and the most experienced, but he lived about five miles away from the hospital. As this was a little far if he was needed urgently in the night, the junior staff did most of the emergency night calls. I understood his reluctance to move to the hospital as he had a small farm, or shamba, which couldn't be tended from afar. He had a wife and nine children and in the usual tradition his wife tended the shamba while Lawrence went out to work. He was also a devout Catholic, a Catechist, who had responsibility for a local church. I was very impressed by Lawrence's character and integrity. After the ninth child was born they decided that 'enough was enough'. So one day while I was preparing for the next operation which was to be a bilateral tubal ligation, Lawrence informed me that the patient was his wife. He was very 'dead-pan' about it all. The following day the general discussion in the theatre came around to marriage. I was chatting to Grace our anaesthetist, about the subject, when Lawrence interjected that he was getting married that year.

'But you already have a wife and nine children,' I objected.

'Yes, but we are going to get married this year,' he reiterated.

'You already are married,' I persisted. 'How can you get married again?'

I was a little concerned that he meant he was taking a second wife.

'I am married,' he replied, 'but we have never had a proper church wedding. We intend to have one this year.'

Then the other staff joined in: 'Which means you have lived with the lady for fifteen years, had nine children, she has had a tubal ligation carried out, and then you get married. Do you not think that is the wrong order?' and laughter broke out. Actually Lawrence's sequence of events was not so unusual. Many people lived together until they could afford the 'official' wedding. However even by local standards he had taken rather a long time to get round to it and it was unusual to have a tubal ligation and then a wedding.

At that time our student nurses lived in Kiwoko village a short distance away from the hospital, so if there was a call during the night for an emergency operation, I would send for them, or rather I would go myself and collect them, as it was less trouble than waking up the hospital driver. At first I found it difficult to see where all the people lived in Kiwoko. The village consisted mainly of 'dukas', or little shops which had grown up along the sides of the road, mostly since the hospital developed. The growth of the hospital had also caused the local economy to expand. Some of the dukas constructed earlier with mud and sticks were now being replaced with brick buildings as the owners became more prosperous. The little dwellings behind these were still of mud and sticks, usually with old tin sheets on the roofs and a corrugated iron door. Windows were either very small or missing altogether, as the residents felt that windows were an invitation to burglars. So in the dead of night I would be creeping around a line of these little mud terraced houses calling quietly, 'Sarah and Ida, we have an emergency laparotomy.' Eventually they would appear, rubbing the sleep from their eyes and climb silently into the car.

The theatre staff never complained about these unsocial hours and usually just made jokes about the long hours they had to work. After waking the nurses, we would get the keys for theatre, which usually stayed with Grace the anaesthetist. As the nurses went to prepare theatre and set out the instruments, I went to wake up Kassana so he could start the generator. If everything worked we could be operating within twenty minutes. Usually this was the case, but not always. One such instance was the time when the doctor was scrubbed and ready to commence when Grace realised that she hadn't enough scoline. Scoline was a drug which was needed to cause muscle relaxation so the intubation could be carried out. The scoline was kept in the fridge next to the theatre but no one could find the key. There was a back-up supply in the laboratory fridge but again the key could not be found. As the doctor stood gowned and gloved, no doubt drumming his fingers and tapping his foot, a hunt ensued all over the hospital for the keys. Eventually scoline was produced and the operation went ahead after an interlude of more than thirty minutes. Afterwards when an inquiry was held it was acertained that the first key had been hidden near the fridge by a well-intentioned midwife, who didn't want anyone to steal supplies. However in the second case 'the man with the key had gone!' One of the laboratory technicians had gone home with the key in his pocket. However the more usual cause for a delay was due to mechanical problems. The person in charge of the generator was always reminded to have fuel ready, and not allow the generator to get empty. This was because the diesel generator was hard to start again after it ran out of fuel. It first had to be bled by a mechanic until it spluttered into life. We wanted to be ready to switch on the lights immediately if we had an emergency operation. However despite the constant warnings the generators often ran out of fuel, much to my frustration. Then Kassana would be running round the hospital compound in the middle of the night, waking up the storeman to get into the fuel store. Petrol or diesel had to be siphoned off and taken to the generator. It all took time and was doubly difficult to do in the dark. Life at night would have been more straightforward if the generator had been prepared during the day. But some people were not good at anticipating a problem and taking pre-emptive action. However as time passed I noticed the empty generator problem was becoming less frequent. Despite our little hiccups we were usually able to cope with emergencies within a matter of minutes rather than hours. Our student theatre nurses had been trained at the hospital and were fast and efficient in the basic theatre skills. As I compared the high tech hospitals which I knew from the past with our low tech and low key operation, I was encouraged and inspired by the people working around me. The students lived in very basic accommodation; they didn't have high educational standards, they worked long hours for little pay and the demands on them were high. However I never heard them seriously complain. They learned quickly and were good at their job. They also had acquired skills which many western nurses considered beyond their domain, but were essential for nurses in Africa.

It hadn't always been easy for us to get nurses. When we had opened the Medical Ward we needed qualified nurses to be in charge but at that time nurses didn't want to leave Kampala to come to Luweero. They considered the place primitive. They didn't want to be isolated from their friends and they still had a mental picture of the atrocities that happened in the Luweero triangle during the war. The hospital was developing well but it still didn't hold out much allure. Staff housing was basic, electric light was intermittent, and transport back and forth to Kampala was expensive. We were therefore delighted when Margaret and Pulcheria, two experienced nurses who had been working in Kampala, volunteered to come and work at Kiwoko. The reason they decided to come was not because of the money, or job security, or any special perks. They had heard that a Christian hospital was developing in Luweero where they could put their faith into practice. We were particularly keen to attract nurses who were Christians. Although we took nurses of any religion, we knew that committed Christians would fit in best with the ethos of the place. Margaret and Pulcheria had a real sense that they were called to work at Kiwoko. They came in the spirit that they wanted to serve the underprivileged. They knew that the vast majority of our patients were poor and they wanted to live out their faith by reaching out to them. There was no spirit of pride with Margaret or Pulcheria. They were gentle and sympathetic with the patients.

One of our poorest, most miserable patients was Nakato. This was a lady whom I had first been introduced to by the Rev Livingstone. She lived in his parish and he thought that she had AIDS. He had good reason to believe so, as she looked like a living skeleton. She was emaciated, her hair had fallen out, her large eyes stared out from their sockets and she was totally crippled. She could sit and crawl on her knees with difficulty, but she couldn't stand or walk. Contractures had developed in her knees, hips and elbows. She was one of the most pathetic sights of a human being I had ever seen. At first I too thought she might have AIDS but through time it became obvious that she did not have AIDS. She was suffering from a slowly progressive wasting disease. I saw her from time to time but there was not much I could do for her. Then one day she was brought into the hospital by the community health workers who had been endeavouring to help the handicapped in the community. The village health worker in her area decided Nakato was a logical case to help. He had first obtained a dress from our supply of second hand clothing as she literally didn't have anything to wear, except rags. When I saw her in her new yellow dress, perched on the bed, my heart sank, because I knew there was little I could do medically. Nevertheless we decided to keep her in hospital for a few days, at least to carry out tests and make some attempt at rehabilitation.

After about a week I talked to her village health worker about her going home. He told Nakato that she would have to leave and the big tears appeared. I had never seen her express any emotion before and I was surprised at this show of sadness. She normally had the totally blank-eyed staring look of so many victims of malnutrition or starvation. After another few days during which Nakato stayed at the hospital, the village health worker returned to say that there was a problem in Nakato going home. There was no one prepared to look after her. I knew that she lived alone but the last time I had seen her at her hut there was a child with her. I had been told that this was a relative's child who looked after her and the neighbours provided food. This arrangement, which was tenuous at best, had now broken down. The neighbours probably saw an opportunity to get rid of the responsibility and the child had gone back to her relatives. Whatever the reasons, Nakato had been abandoned at the hospital. She couldn't stay indefinitely, that was completely impractical. Patients at hospital always had relatives to tend to their everyday needs, like cooking, washing and taking them to the toilet. Nakato had no one. The village health workers and nurses had worked out a rota to ensure she was fed. We had also discovered she was incontinent, so she required a lot of care. This was no problem in the short term but in the long term we knew we didn't have the staff or space to cope with her. Although she couldn't stay at the hospital I saw no real reason why she couldn't live beside it, in the village where attendants, expectant mothers and relatives of TB patients stayed. A number of our staff such as Sentongo, the warden of the TB ward also stayed there. Nakato could cook for herself if she was supplied with a few basics and Sentongo could keep an eye on her. When we made the suggestion, it was the first time I saw her smile. It transformed her appearance. So she was installed in her mud hut and began life in our community. Over the next few years I became accustomed to Nakato's smile and greeting. Sentongo taught her the English greeting and she would be so pleased with herself when she greeted me in English. Then I would return the greeting in Luganda. Since she had come to stay at the hospital village there had been a marked improvement in her general condition but she was painfully thin and had few reserves. When she contracted gastroenteritis we thought this was the end. She became quickly dehydrated and semi-comatose. We admitted her again to the hospital and the reports I was receiving were pessimistic. Late one evening I called to see her to find Margaret and Pulcheria sitting up with her. They were both off duty but had come to help. They were sitting by her bed, praying with her, holding her hand and giving her sips of oral re-hydration solution from a spoon. Nakato looked pathetic, she was emaciated, dehydrated and close to death and I knew the chances of survival were slim, but Margaret and Pulcheria persisted and she slowly turned the corner. I had no doubt that it was their efforts which kept her alive, the love they expressed to her, the re-hydration they administered and the prayers they offered. They truly practised their faith. They loved the unlovely and gave themselves to the helpless. I would often come into the ward in the evenings and find Pulcheria talking and praying quietly with an AIDS patient. Most of these people were in a critical condition and didn't know who to turn to. Pulcheria would quietly get alongside them to help and it was usually when she was off duty as she didn't have time on her own shift.

The nurses weren't always gentle and loving with the patients. They would have been super-human if they were. Sometimes the pressure and the work load got to everyone and tempers became short and nerves frayed. This happened particularly at busy clinics if the staff felt the community were not pulling their weight. We had been asked to start a clinic in the northern part of the Luweero district. The local member of Parliament had come to the hospital and pleaded with us to get involved. There were so many sick people in his area, he said, and virtually no medical facilities. We decided that before we committed ourselves we would first have a meeting with the local Chiefs and Elders. So we asked him to arrange a meeting. It was the custom for many public announcements to be made every day on the radio, so we were not surprised to hear the meeting announced, but it was not in the way that we had discussed it. The announcement said that the Kiwoko Medical Team were going to 'build' a hospital in the north of Luweero and all the community leaders should meet to discuss it. I was suddenly inundated by people remarking, 'I hear you are going to build another hospital!' Nothing could have been further from the truth or the original discussion with the MP. We had made it clear that we were committing ourselves to nothing as yet. But if the community wanted it and needed it we would consider coming once per week and holding a clinic. They were to provide the building, the necessary furniture and some food for us, while we were there that day. So it seemed there had been a certain amount of mis-communication to start with. Perhaps it was a not-so-subtle way for the MP to put pressure on us. Perhaps it was a genuine misunderstanding of terminology. On the appointed day, a delegation of our staff set out for the meeting. It took place under a tree and there was a fair representation of local community leaders. We patiently tried to explain the position. They should assess what the needs were and they should decide how they could best meet them. We could provide some medical expertise, but we could not and would not do everything for them.

'When are you starting to build the hospital?' was the response.

There was obviously still a gap in our perspective, so we tried over again. I told them how Kiwoko hospital had taken time to evolve and explained the role of the whole community. I went to great pains to explain how basic things had been at first, how everyone played their part and finished by saying that metaphorically 'we had to learn to crawl before we could walk'. I really thought I had succeeded in communicating this time. I felt the crowd was with me. They had understood my gifted oratory, my nuances of meaning, my metaphorical references. As I sat down congratulating myself on my communication and oratorical skills the Chairman of Resistance Committee (the local political committee) stood up. He was brief and to the point. He had obviously taken in all I had said.

'We are not interested in crawling,' he said. 'We want a hospital now, when are you starting it?'

My speech might have been well received but they had not understood a word I was trying to say. I had better leave the communication skills to the other staff. Perhaps I didn't have a gifting after all.

Our staff explained again and again that they were not going to come and do everything for their community. We could provide the medical skills but they needed to help themselves.

'You must organise yourselves to help your own community,' they concluded.

Finally the meeting accepted that we would only come once per week and decided that they would arrange premises and food for us. We would do vaccinations, antenatal examinations and see patients. We would bring the drugs and the necessary staff. They would help to organise the patients, the premises, the furniture and provide food.

The first day we arrived, patients were gathering but there was no sign of any community leaders. We knew which premises to use so we got on with the job. Finally in the afternoon when we had finished, the Health Assistant from the area arrived. He was full of apologies that no one had come to help us but promised it would be different next week. We weren't too impressed with the community leadership, but many patients had come, many babies had been vaccinated and we knew there was a definite need for medical help. The following week we arrived and there was slightly more co-operation. This time someone organised tea, but still no food. It was obvious that there was a lack of good local leadership. They wanted us to do everything for them. So what help they got wasn't sustainable.

221

During the clinic a young man arrived supporting his brother over his shoulder. His brother was almost unconscious. It didn't take much clinical acumen to know that, from the history and his present state of unconsciousness, he had meningitis. We laid him down on the floor and gave an injection of penicillin. As we treated the brother, the young man remarked that he didn't feel too well himself. Perhaps he would just rest a bit before going home. At the end of the clinic the two were lying unconscious side by side.

'We'd better give this one some penicillin too,' I commented, 'and we will need to take them both back to the hospital.'

It was ninety minutes drive back to Kiwoko. We had come with eleven staff in a small van plus all our drugs and equipment. We had no space. How were we going to fit in two more unconscious patients?

It was a situation where there was no alternative. If they had been any less ill we would have told them to find their own way down but we knew if we left them behind they would certainly die. So we laid one man along the floor under everyone's feet and squeezed the other onto a seat. In the state they were in they were past caring how they travelled. When we reached the hospital they were admitted and the penicillin treatment continued. I was away for about a week after that but when I returned there were two men in the ward asking for a lift back to the clinic in Northern Luweero. It was the two previously unconscious patients.

'No, we are already full,' I replied, 'now you are well enough to find your own way home.'

Experiences like this made us persist despite the lack of help from the local leaders. However one day Bosco took matters into his own hands. Bosco was a vital member of our staff at the hospital. He was a lay reader from a local church who was such a stalwart, reliable guy that he kept getting volunteered by others for more responsibility. When the staff wanted to set up a co-operative and buy food wholesale, Bosco was selected to run it. Bosco was the one, who with Robbie, did most of the counselling of AIDS patients. He was responsible for the supplies of food which we kept for needy AIDS patients or TB patients. On this occasion he was the person in charge of the clinic and apparently he gave the people a severe talking to, because they weren't pulling their weight. I couldn't understand why there were so few patients the following week, then someone suggested that perhaps the people thought we were not coming back again because of what Bosco had said. I never learned exactly what that was but things improved somewhat after that. Eventually we decided to reduce our involvement to once every two weeks. It was sad for the people as it was a very poor area which needed help but if the leaders, who represented them, didn't care enough to try and do something for themselves, then in the long run we could not do it for them.

Chapter 24

Elsa

The truck pulled up to the front of the hospital and a crowd immediately gathered, peering and exclaiming at the unusual cargo. On board, a large friesian cow looked back and continued chewing the cud. Elsa had arrived, flown out all the way from England. She weighed in at 500 kilos and had the usual black and white friesian markings. What excited the interest of the people was that they had never seen a cow like this before. All the local animals were fairly scrawny creatures with long horns and ribs sticking out, often only weighing 150 kilos. Elsa looked like a giant cow, especially as she was perched high on the back of the truck looking down regally on everyone.

Perhaps she did feel royal. Who knows what goes on in a cow's mind? She had indeed been treated right royally. She had started life on a farm in England, then was purchased by a group of farmers in an organisation with the unlikely name of 'Send a Cow'. She had been flown with other friesian cattle all the way to Uganda. Not many cows could claim to have made the journey from England to Uganda by air.

Some people wondered how exactly this was organised, never having seen a cow on an aeroplane. How many seats were allocated per cow? Or was there a special herbivore class? The answer was that 'Send a Cow' chartered a whole cargo aeroplane and brought a complete load of cows, something like a package charter deal for cows. The plane also had a few places for the farmers as well but one gathered that they were considerably less well catered for than the cows.

About a year earlier we had heard about this organisation which sent friesians to Uganda and approached their representative with a request for a cow for the hospital so that we could have milk for our malnourished children. It may have seemed an incredible amount of trouble to fly a cow from England to Kiwoko just to get some milk. However our motivation was not just to get the milk but to introduce a good breed of milking cows to the area. Luweero had been ranching country before the war with a number of huge ranches having thousands of cattle. They were the local longhorn variety bred for beef but they gave almost no milk, less than 2 litres per day. During the fighting all the cattle disappeared so that currently the area had few cattle and no good milking varieties. 'Send a Cow' recognised that many parts of Uganda had no milking breeds and by introducing stock from England they hoped to upgrade the level of breeding. So eventually we had received our cow. The first problem was to get it off the truck, which it was reluctant to do, as there was a three foot drop to the level of the hospital verandah. We had prepared a paddock for it behind the hospital, so with much coaxing and many volunteers to push and shoo the animal she eventually disembarked and made it to the paddock, where she became a star attraction for all visitors to the hospital. At all times of the day people could be seen hanging over the bars of the paddock discussing this unusual cow.

Elsa was 'zero grazed', that is – the food was brought to her. A boy went out with his sickle, chopped up the elephant grass and brought it back to her. She also had a taste for banana-skins which were abundant. When the local women prepared matoke – the steamed banana dish which was a staple food in Uganda – we asked them to keep the skins for Elsa who would devour them voraciously. One reason for zero grazing was that cattle introduced into the country, or 'exotic varieties', as they were called, had little or no resistance to the local diseases, especially those spread by ticks living in the grass. If Elsa grazed freely she would pick up ticks and succumb to tick borne fever, a killer disease. So she was carefully tended, served hand and foot, or hoof and foot, in this case, sprayed regularly, washed and fed. No cow could have wished for more loving attention.

On the first night after she arrived we discovered two things about Elsa. Number one – she had a wanderlust and number two – she could jump. In the dead of night I was awakened by a knock at the door and someone calling, 'Doctor, Doctor.' I arose thinking I was needed for a patient, to find Ando at the door telling me the cow had escaped and disappeared into the bush. I was most upset, after all we had only received the cow less than 24 hours ago. How was I going to explain to 'Send a Cow' that we had lost the animal they had given us within the first 24 hours? Ando assembled a search party, but it was pitch black so I thought their chances of success were slim. I spent a sleepless night imagining our cow lost in the bush, being attacked by wild animals, or being captured by cattle rustlers and transported to the north of the country. The next morning I was up at first light to get more people to look for the cow, but there she was, standing in the front of the hospital chewing the cud. Kassana our electrician had been the man who had found her. He had been searching all night and had found her in the next village about three miles away. When Elsa had seen Kassana she had followed him home, she must have been lonely. As we now realised that Elsa could clear the top paddock bars with impunity, another layer was added along with some barbed wire. I was relieved at not becoming the person with the shortest record in the history of 'Send a Cow' of keeping one of their cows.

Elsa was in calf and soon delivered her offspring. Unfortunately it was a bull, and we would have preferred another cow. Doctor Amos took great interest in the delivery, but really only had to act as a Consultant as the delivery was carried out successfully by the electrician Kassana, who knew something about cattle, as well as being an electrician, and was certainly eager to help.

Things went well for some time. Elsa's milk yield increased steadily until she was giving 25 litres per day, more than 12 times that of the local cattle. Then I had another call during the night. Elsa was sick. I wasn't sure what I was meant to do. I did really feel that veterinary medicine was outside my parameters, so I advised Kassana to call a vet in the morning. By the morning the cow seemed bad, lying on the ground looking as if it was about to die. It was a catastrophe for the hospital. This was our cow, looked after more lovingly than any human, giving gallons of milk for the children on the Nutrition Ward. She couldn't just die. All of the staff were really concerned, prayers were said for the cow and tremendous efforts were made to keep it alive. In fact it didn't die, at least not just then, it recovered, sat up, started to eat and even started to milk again, but it didn't stand up. It wouldn't get up, no matter how much coaxing, tail twisting, pushing or shoving went on. It looked contented, but didn't seem to have any power in its hind legs so since it was lying in one position all the time nursing measures were introduced. The cow was turned four hourly so as not to get bed sores, it was rubbed down to improve circulation and its bed of hay was changed frequently, but I was seriously concerned.

Since the local vets were not able to offer much help I finally went to Kampala for more advice. I came back with a winch and an intravenous infusion of calcium. The winch was to get it up, the infusion was to correct any calcium imbalance from milk fever. So a drip set was rigged up, the jugular vein was found and Elsa had an infusion. By this stage Kenneth, a native of the mountainous south west Uganda, where they had friesian cattle, was lending his expertise. It was a touching sight to see this big sad eyed cow lying on the ground while Kenneth held up the infusion which dripped in calcium.

227

Unfortunately the calcium had no magical effects as we had hoped. The animal didn't suddenly arise and walk and we decided to move on to plan B, the winch. It was one of the few days in Uganda which happened to be cold, wet and miserable. At first there was no shortage of volunteers. A beam was rigged up above the cow. The cow was rolled on to the canvas truck tarpaulin so that it formed a sling and it was winched up. At least that was the theory. In practice – everything that could go wrong, did go wrong. The ropes broke, the nails pulled out of the beam, the beam broke, the back end of the cow came up but the front stayed down, the front end came up while the back stayed on the ground. By this stage people's enthusiasm was noticeably waning and the number of volunteers had fallen off sharply. Most of the workers now anticipated a juicy steak being available by the next day, so why hinder the inevitable? Talk of slaughter of our cow was thick in the air. However Kenneth, Kassana and I couldn't give up yet; we had to do everything possible. If we could just get the cow on its feet perhaps it would survive, after all it was healthy otherwise. It still ate and gave milk, so we persisted all day through the rain. By the end of the day we were soaked, cold and bedraggled, but we had the cow up, at least on two feet. The cow was upright, supported in its canvas sling, but it wouldn't put any weight on its back legs. Even a three-legged cow could work I reasoned, though I had never seen one. A cow could stand on three good legs but two legs were just not enough.

We decided to leave her in the sling to see if she would try to use all four legs. So there she was, a pretty funny looking sight, suspended upright only standing on her two front legs. By the next day we knew we had to give up and face the inevitable, Elsa was still not using her back legs and would have to be slaughtered. So reluctantly she was lowered onto a trailer and taken away. The next day I asked Kenneth if he had got a steak. He looked at me sad-eyed and reproachfully, like Elsa, and said,

'Doctor, how could I eat a friend?'

After Elsa, we were somewhat disheartened, but still not prepared to give up. The hospital had acquired a piece of land for a farm and we wanted to clear it and commence a farming project to raise income for the medical work. Finances were always a problem, as we spent much more than we raised from fees or the sale of medicines. So long as donations kept coming in we would be OK, but we wanted to set some long term goals for generating income locally. Farming was a natural resource to choose as Luweero had lots of fertile land, but essentially no industry.

However first of all we needed the money to develop the farm itself. The land was cheap but a massive clearance job would need to be carried out to bring it into a fit state for cultivation and grazing. Not only was it covered in scrub and bush but ant hills or termite mounds were everywhere. Parts of it looked like a lunar surface. Some of the mounds were fifteen feet high by thirty feet in diameter. I was mulling over the problem while I was on a visit to Nairobi. I didn't often visit Nairobi, and certainly didn't expect to bump into an old friend from Ireland there, but having attended church one Sunday I walked around the corner to find Bill McAllister loitering after the service, as most good churchgoers do. Bill's family and my family had known each other for years. His parents had been missionaries in the Belgian Congo when the uprising took place in the '60s, and they had almost lost their lives. The last I had heard of Bill was that he was in Zaire. We looked at each other in surprise and after the initial exchanges I found he was working with an aid organisation called Compassion Canada.

He was the East Africa director with this Christian based development organisation. What was even more interesting was that they were looking out for worthwhile projects. Having the farm uppermost in my mind at the time, and not being backward about coming forward and asking for money, I immediately launched into a description of our project. As a result Bill made a visit and after some time Compassion Canada funded the development of the farm.

With the money available we purchased a tractor, trailer and plough, built barns and housing and cleared the land. Coming from a farming background I was in my element, but I soon discovered that farming in Africa was very different to farming in Ireland. Farming in Uganda was definite pioneering stuff, with problems I had not even thought of before. When we had 15 acres cleared we ploughed the land and planted corn. I took great pleasure in seeing the corn grow and the land produce something. The termites also took real pleasure in eating the corn. Termites usually ate wood or rotten vegetation, but on our farm they gnawed through the corn stems and then ate the cobs themselves. It was rather clever; these insects were able to harvest the corn before eating it. So a certain percentage of our crop was eaten by termites. As the corn grew I discovered another problem. The weeds grew with it, so a small army of workers were employed to keep the weeds down. Then when it came to harvesting I realised that it would also have to be done by hand as no harvester could negotiate all the termite mounds, and the corn hadn't been planted in straight lines. This was no surprise to the local people as, although they would plough the land when a tractor was available, all the other operations, such as sowing, weeding, harvesting and shelling were done by hand. However most of the villagers had less than an acre planted. We had started with 15 acres and could grow up to 80 acres. In the first few seasons the partially mechanised, partial hand cultivation went on, but as I did my sums I realised that profitability was low. Also, as this was a corporate enterprise, it was hard to get the productivity from the workers that they would have given to their own small holdings. Two things would have to happen if the farm project was to have long term viability. Number one, we would have to diversify from arable farming to something more profitable, such as milk production on a commercial scale. Number two, we would have to clear the land of termite mounds, if proper mechanisation was to be introduced. Therefore even though Elsa died we were determined to try to develop our farm as a dairy project. Our only problem was that we now had no cows.

Heather's father wrote to me sympathetically when the cow died. He had a farming background himself, so his letter was full of genuine concern for how I felt. 'What can one say,' he wrote 'to a budding farmer who has lost his only cow?' One could say – that was very careless of you or words to that effect, but Charlie would not have been so unkind. I didn't know quite what to say to 'Send a Cow' either. After all, they had donated the cow and we had let it die. In fact the farmers in 'Send a Cow' were very sympathetic. Not only were they understanding, but against all their rules, they decided to send us another cow. This was a great risk for them since we hadn't exactly built up a good track record. One could say we had so far had 100% failure in the dairy enterprise, when Hilda the heifer arrived. We were very excited to get our second friesian cow, but also a little apprehensive. Although Hilda was a friesian she was almost white. But she was another thoroughbred cow. This time we had prepared for her arrival elaborately and built a large cowshed at the farm. The cowshed wasn't just for her as we hoped to get more cattle later but at first she was the only occupant. Elsa had been big when she arrived, Hilda grew large after she arrived. She was a good sized cow by any standards, but massive by Ugandan standards. She also gave birth to a calf, also a bull; for some reason a high percentage of all the 'Send a Cow' cattle sent to Uganda, gave birth to bull calves.

Kabale in the mountainous south west of Uganda near the Rwanda border was the one area of the country which did have good milking cows. This was because it was high and the altitude suited the friesians. There was lush grass and less susceptibility to disease. Unfortunately for the farmers in Kabale, although they could produce abundant milk, they had a more limited market for it, being far away from Kampala. Thus milk prices were low. The opposite was true of any area such as Luweero which was within striking distance of Kampala. Here milking cattle were few, milk prices were good, but susceptibility to disease was high because of the different climatic conditions. We decided to make a trip to Kabale to see if any cows could be purchased there. At this stage we felt that friesian cross breeds would be more resistant to disease, and although the milk yields would be lower, the risk would be less from disease. Prices were also lower, considerably lower. Kabale was Kenneth's home territory, so one Christmas a delegation from Kiwoko arrived at his home prepared to buy cattle. I was surprised by the beauty of the place and the total scenic difference from Luweero. Our area was dominated by elephant grass and banana plants, there were few panoramic views as the hills were low and many parts of the district were covered in dense bush or swamp. Kabale had steep mountains, tiered for cultivation, sloping down to beautiful lakes and lush valleys. After a few days of tramping through the pastures and examining different cows, we bought some cattle. I don't think any of us were experts in cattle dealing or selecting a cow which displayed the traits of good milking but we picked out what we thought looked good and what was within our budget and returned to Kiwoko with a further eight friesian cross bred cows. Hilda now had company. A few months later Bate, the farm manager, returned to Kabale and bought a few more cows, so we were gradually building up our herd. The whole process was slow and we made mistakes in our selections but Bate was increasing his knowledge of friesians and progress towards a commercial dairy was being made.

There was still the problem of clearing the termite mounds. This could not be done by hand. Termites built hills to last, and they were much harder than the surrounding soil. This job would require a bulldozer. A bulldozer would also be useful to dig a valley dam where water would collect in the rainy season and keep the cattle supplied through the dry season. However hiring a bull-dozer was an expensive business and our finances were limited, so I did not pursue the matter too vigorously. We had been supplied with a generator through an engineering firm in Kampala run by some Turkish people. Although the owner was Turkish he had been born in Uganda and when expelled with the Asians at the time of Amin, he had returned from Canada at the first opportunity. He said he found life rather dull in Canada. He had now built up a successful business by buying, reconditioning and selling heavy industrial machinery. Mr Begani had two bulldozers in his yard which looked like they were for scrap but he assured me that he would soon have them in good working order.

'I might have some land clearing to do,' I said vaguely, not really believing that he would actually get the bull-dozers running. However within a few months they were fixed and he asked me about the land clearing that I had mentioned. He paid a visit to the farm and we looked at all the ant hills and the place for the valley dam. At the end of our inspection I admitted that we didn't have much money for the job.

'Tell me what you can afford and I will tell you what I can do for that,' he offered.

We had two million shillings, about £1,000, and Mr Begani agreed that he would do the whole job within our budget. So within a few days the bulldozers arrived at the farm. Then the complications began. Some of the termite mounds were much harder than had been anticipated and it could take hours to level just one large one. The drivers were not very experienced and first managed to get both bulldozers stuck in the dam, then to turn one over. I had never seen anyone turn over a bulldozer before, but Murphy's law was in full operation here. Then the bull-dozers began to leak oil. It hadn't been clearly stated who was responsible to pay for the oil but the bill was escalating daily and it seemed that the hospital would have to pay. The job had proved to be much more difficult than

Mr Begani had estimated and was taking much longer. In fact it seemed, at times, the only people who were happy were the villagers who were collecting the ants from the termite mounds as they were destroyed. These were full of protein and were a delicacy for the people. As soon as a bulldozer would expose the ants, people would swarm over the mound, eating the ants or collecting them for later, sometimes coming perilously close to the huge blade of the bulldozer. Eventually the job was finished and although I had been grumbling about the amount of oil that we had to purchase, I realised that the original hire charge had been very low. When I came to settle the account I was even more surprised when Mr Begani deducted another six hundred thousand shillings from the bill. He was giving us an extra discount, he said, because we were a charitable hospital and we were helping the poor. He also loved his country and was making his contribution to the needy in Uganda. The job had actually cost him a lot of money; I checked, and if we had used a Ministry of Agriculture bulldozer the price would have been at least four or five times as much. Once again I was surprised, this time because a Muslim businessman was helping a Christian hospital. There were times in Uganda when everyone helped everyone else, Hindus, Muslims, Christians, Black or White. It was at such times that it was good to work with such a community.

Chapter 25

Ando

Tears dripped silently on to his lap and I realised he was weeping. I moved closer and put my arm around him. He covered his face with his hand but the tears continued to fall. As he fumbled to dry his eyes with the corner of his shirt I offered him my handkerchief. There was nothing I could say. I was fighting to keep control myself. Ando said something which I couldn't pick up. I bent closer.

'I will be missing you,' he repeated.

It was so characteristic of the man and it rent my heart. It was my first experience of telling a close friend that he had AIDS. It wasn't a situation where I could detach myself from my own feelings and emotions for this person. I knew him, I loved him. He stood out as a person who had been the most faithful and helpful to us since we had come to Africa. He was a trustworthy friend. Our children loved him. As we had struggled to find our feet in Africa, he was always there to help when they had a need.

The reality of AIDS in Africa had come home to me in the most poignant way. This wasn't just a patient who was affected. This wasn't a situation where I could maintain a detached, impartial, professional attitude. Ando was like one of the family.

He wasn't very sick. He had only a few symptoms, but when he had found out there were some AIDS tests available he had insisted on being tested. Perhaps he had a deep rooted suspicion that he had AIDS as his previous wife had run a brewery business. Brewing in Uganda was often associated with promiscuity and Ando wasn't at all sure he had been her only partner. Besides, few people in Uganda could claim that they were not at risk.

When the tests were completed Ando showed up weakly positive. It can't be, I thought and repeated the test again. Again there was the same result. Finally I sent the blood sample off to a reference laboratory. The test was confirmed to be definitely positive. All this time he had been pressing me for his result.

'Wait, it's not back yet,' I told him, procrastinating and hoping against hope that the initial test would be proved wrong.

Finally I could procrastinate no longer. We sat in our house and I told him the result. Though I had been a doctor for over ten years I still didn't know of any formula to break the news to someone that he was dying. I simply said,

'The test is positive, Ando.'

At first he didn't seem to react. Then I noticed the silent tears.

He had been one of our first Community Health Workers and from the outset there had been something special about him. He wasn't very assertive, if anything he was quite shy and introverted. He didn't try to curry favour with anyone but there was an outstanding characteristic about him which ultimately shone through his introversion. It was his straightforwardness and integrity. He was a man of his word. Perhaps it was a combination of little things. If he said he would be there at a certain time, he was. If he promised to do something, he did it. If he knew he couldn't do something, he said so. He didn't try to ingratiate himself by making promises he couldn't fulfil. He was a man whose Yes meant Yes and his No meant No.

Ando had a talent for fixing things. If a pedal came off Sean's bicycle, he could fit it back on again. If Robbie needed something done in the house, she could always ask

him. Usually this was a last resort, after I had procrastinated for about a year, and she had got fed up with my
excuses, which usually ran something along the line of
'Yes dear, I will put it up tomorrow, but I'm tired tonight,
I saw a lot of patients today.'

She couldn't believe it when Ando did the tasks the very
day he was asked.

'Doesn't that make you feel ashamed?' she would chide
me. But despite Ando showing me up in my lack of
application to domestic tasks, I valued his friendship in so
many ways. If there was any little awkward task that
needed to be done at the hospital everyone asked Ando.

The previous Christmas we had conducted some evan-
gelistic and teaching seminars and many people made
commitments of faith in Jesus Christ through the ministry.
After the seminars, when Robbie was chatting to Ando,
he confided that he wanted to be a Christian, but he felt he
couldn't because he had some problems. He said he
needed to talk to me.

His problems concerned his first wife from whom he was
now estranged. Up to this point I had not even known he
had a wife. Apparently he had a wife and three children
but they had separated during the war.

When I probed more deeply he said that they had never
been officially married and she didn't want him now. She
had told him that he was a poor man and he couldn't
support her. She was a 'businesswoman' with her own
brewing business. So they had gone their separate ways.

Although Ando and the lady had never been 'officially'
married, like everyone else they had lived together as
husband and wife and had children. Then like many others
when they had a disagreement they had separated. Many
people in Uganda were not officially married as real marriage was a costly business. There was the bride price – at
least several cattle where they came from, the cost of the
wedding ceremonies, either traditional or as a church wedding, and the expected gifts for the relatives. It all added
up to a great deal of money. If there was talk of a real

marriage all the obligations had to be fulfilled, but if the couple simply moved in together, nothing was demanded. Conversely if disagreements arose there was nothing holding them together.

After the war Ando had gone to look for his mother who had been in the Luweero triangle during the war. He had found his mother and not had any further contact with his first wife. Since that time he had been living with another girl.

Now he was having pangs of conscience. He wanted to be a Christian but he thought that he couldn't until he sorted out the situation regarding his relationships. I admired his honesty. He wasn't trying to cover up his sin or turn away from his responsibility, but I explained to him that God didn't require us to be perfect before we could come to him. He accepts us as we are. That night Ando committed his life to God and found faith as a Christian. He also determined that he would make the long trip north to sort out the situation regarding his first relationship.

A few weeks later he returned from his trip. It had not been successful. The lady didn't want him back, but he had seen his children and when he had the means, he wanted to bring them to be with him. So Ando had made a Christian commitment some months before he discovered he had AIDS. As the estrangement from his first wife seemed complete he had also continued the relationship with the girl he had been living with at that time. Now when I informed Ando that he had AIDS he revealed that the girl was pregnant. He also knew, since he was a trained health worker that he was likely to have passed the virus to the girl and she in turn could pass it on to the child.

It was a mess, I felt, and yet I couldn't really blame anyone. This was just the way the society was. He had done nothing more than anyone else. He had moved in with a woman, they had lived together for some years, they had a disagreement, they parted, he had taken another wife, she had got pregnant. Then he had discovered he had AIDS. He could have got the AIDS through any of these relationships.

One difference in Ando's cycle was that in the midst of these events he had turned to faith in God. Having known Ando I couldn't bring myself to believe that his life was now meaningless, that he was just another victim, just another statistic in the cycle of AIDS.

'Ando, God has a purpose for your life,' I said, 'we are all sure of one thing. We will all die sooner or later. You know now that your life may be limited but God has a purpose for your life. Some of us waste our lives because we never really face the inevitability of death. You have faced death and you have placed your life in God's hands and God can use your life to His glory.'

Perhaps in the shock of hearing he had AIDS it was hard for Ando to take these words in, but at least they helped me to get a perspective. In the days that followed we watched him fight against his despair. He also had another advantage which I had noticed many people with AIDS didn't have. He had friends whom he could confide in. He shared with people and they cried with him. He talked to people and they listened. Gradually we saw him accept his diagnosis and realise that it wasn't the end. For the present he had his life, he wasn't sick, he had a job to do, he could place his life in God's hands and go on.

His first task was to tell Rose, his girlfriend, that he had AIDS. When he told her she agreed to have a test. We held our breath again knowing that it would probably be positive, but there was a small chance that it could be negative. The results came back. She was negative. They were one of those minority of couples where the virus is not passed on.

Ando then put his conclusion to her. As he was positive, and she was negative, they would have to separate so that she did not get the disease.

'But what else have I?' she responded, 'you are all I have, if I catch it, I catch it, I will take my chances with you.'

Rose's reaction was fairly typical of many village people. They would say, 'What have I to do? If I die, I die. If I am going to get it, it is beyond my control.'

Rose didn't have any family in the area and Ando cared for her. Her father had been chased from Luweero, accused of being a trouble-maker. It was a sad, pathetic story. It had been an unusually dry season. The rains had not come and the people were very worried that the weather patterns were changing. Rose's father wasn't of the local tribe and perhaps he didn't feel accepted, perhaps he became drunk and became spiteful or vindictive. However in an ill-judged moment of boasting he claimed that *he* had stopped the rains!

In an area where witch doctors are accepted as having wide ranging powers, his claim was taken seriously. However it didn't have the effect which he had intended, of bringing him respect in the community for his supernatural powers. Instead he was burned out of his house and sent on his way by a crowd of irate villagers. Rose was left with few choices. On the one hand she had a partner who cared for her, but who had AIDS, but on the other hand, she had no other family to turn to. She would be on her own. She was eighteen and pregnant. It wasn't surprising that she decided to throw in her lot with Ando.

He and Rose began planning a proper wedding. But first they decided that she should have the baby. As an Irish doctor I was familiar enough with the sequence of events of someone getting pregnant, then married, then having the baby. However in Uganda people didn't mind if they had the wedding after the baby. I knew it was a major step that Ando and Rose were taking to have a wedding at all. It was a witness to the community that they were doing this because they were Christians and this was not just a casual relationship.

Rose delivered a healthy baby girl, named Lauren after our daughter, and some months later the wedding took place. It was a particularly moving occasion for us. Not only did we know that Ando had AIDS but Rose was wearing Barbara's wedding dress which had been sent out. The bride looked beautiful and the groom solemn. I was asked to be Master of Ceremonies at the reception and as I looked at the couple I knew that neither Ando nor Rose could know what lay ahead of them, but they had a steadfastness and trust in God for the future.

By this time Ando had moved out of the health work because of the risk of him picking up infections from other patients. He had been put in charge of all the supplies and building materials for the clinic and he soon took on other responsibilities in supervising the building work. He earned the respect of the workers by working with them, instead of trying to be the boss. He would shovel cement alongside them, help with the carpentry or do any task which needed to be done. They respected him as one of them. However they had a problem if they tried to manipulate him or get him to collaborate in any illegal schemes.

He worked with us for three years. Even though he often had very little to say he made friends easily, probably because he inspired confidence by his deeds rather than his words. During that time his contribution in building the hospital was critical. He watched the supplies, he hired workers, he supervised construction. I grew to depend on him more and more. He believed in what we were doing and gave all that he had to see the hospital built.

We had some friends, Sam and Jill Rutherford, working in Tanzania with Tear Fund. Sam set up a school to train hospital technicians in servicing generators and hospital equipment. He offered our hospital a place on the course, and we decided that Ando would be the best man to send. He was delighted he had been chosen. He was keen to learn new things, and he had never been out of Uganda, so he was happy to see more of the world.

As the time drew near for the course to start, Ando became ill. He developed severe headaches and an almost catatonic state of withdrawal. His condition was poor and deteriorating quickly so I admitted him to the hospital and carried out a lumber puncture, taking a sample of fluid from his spine. The test showed that he had cryptococcal meningitis, a form of meningitis unique to AIDS patients and very difficult to treat.

We treated him with what we had and prayed. By the next day he had made a startling recovery. His headache had gone and he was back to his old self in personality. I knew enough about the progress of this form of meningitis to realise that it was unlikely that it had resolved completely, but the clinical improvement was amazing. I was now faced with a choice of whether to allow Ando to go to the course or to pull him out as the risk of recurrence was high. However I realised that going on the course was so important to him that the demoralisation he would suffer by cancellation at this late stage would be more harmful to him than going.

So he took the course and completed it. He wrote to us frequently while he was away. He was having some minor episodes of sickness and was finding the weather very hot but was enjoying the new things he was learning.

Late one evening, one of the nurses came rushing down to the house to tell us that Ando was back but he was very ill. We dashed up to find him on the ward but he was so weak he could hardly speak. We pieced together the story. He had been getting gradually weaker and Sam had decided to fly him back as far as Lake Victoria. He made the rest of the journey by steamer across the lake and then found someone who brought him by car to Kiwoko. It was a miracle that he had made it. He could not walk and he was barely able to speak but he had come back to us. Over the next few days as he regained strength he talked constantly to Robbie about his Tanzanian experiences. He had enjoyed the course and he was now ready to tackle fixing the hospital equipment. He was glad to be back home.

Over the next week his hearing deteriorated until he was almost completely deaf. I decided to repeat the lumber puncture and it showed a massive increase in the meningitis infection. I could tell that his days were numbered. Gradually his condition deteriorated. He developed pneumonia and I knew the end was near.

The children sat with him and all the hospital staff took turns to stay by his bedside.

One morning at 1.30 am I was called to do an emergency caesarian section. Robbie went up to be with Ando as we both sensed that he would die that night. As I got the theatre staff organised, he called for me. I went to visit him for what I knew would be the last time I would see him alive.

Ando died at the very moment I delivered the baby by caesarian section. At that moment life came into the world and life passed away. I knew that the Lord had given and the Lord had taken away.

The theatre staff all knew and loved Ando and were deeply affected by his death, but as he died, no one could pause in the busyness of helping to bring forth new life, not because they were uncaring about Ando but because their task was to care for the living. When the operation was finished I went to the ward to say a final farewell to my friend. He looked at peace, he had ceased to struggle. He had never been able to put into pratice what he had learned in Tanzania but he had accomplished far more in his short life than most of us would accomplish in our three score years and ten. He had worked steadily for three years to build a hospital and had witnessed the official opening before he died. Now he would be buried at the hospital he had worked to establish.

As I stood outside on the verandah I wept quietly for the true African friend I had lost. Everywhere around me was the mark of Ando's hand. He had mixed the concrete for the foundations. He had gone with me to collect the bricks. He had supervised the builders. He had helped with the painting, the electrics and the plumbing. Thousands of people had been helped through the work of his hands. He had never complained, never showed selfishness. He had always been ready with an encouraging word for me. I had known many people since I came to Uganda whom I loved and respected but never one like Ando. As I looked out at the lights of all the hospital buildings shining through the darkness, I thought, 'we did it together. Now you are gone and it can never be the same again.' I wept.

We buried him beside the hospital. There were hundreds of people at the funeral, paying their last respects to a man who had made a lasting impression on them all. The vicar asked me to say a few words.

'In Africa,' I said, 'you all have large families and many brothers, but where I come from we usually have few brothers. Back in Ireland I have one brother in the flesh, but today I have buried my dearly loved African brother.'

As I left the funeral a little old lady whom I had never seen before pressed money into my hand. Tony the medical assistant who was with me explained, 'Doctor, that is how we express sympathy for the relatives.'

At the end of each school term Ando would have had the children's bicycles serviced and ready for the holiday. That Christmas Sean's bicycle had a puncture for the whole holiday. Ando wasn't there and the rest of us just didn't have the heart to fix it. He was gone and although life would go on it could never be the same for any of us.

Chapter 26

The Hold Up

The gun was pointed at my head and someone was shouting,

'Shoot that one! Shoot that one!'

The thought flashed through my mind, 'Is this how it is all going to end?' I sat immobile, everything around me seemed to be going in slow motion and my mind was still trying to make an assessment of what was happening.

I had been driving along a road in Kampala looking for a particular house and when I had pulled up at the driveway two men had suddenly run up to the car brandishing guns. I just didn't know what was going on at first.

'Get out of the car, don't touch anything,' the man at my side was saying.

But I had refused to move, not because I was going to argue with a man holding a gun, but my body wasn't responding. The man repeated his instructions, and still I sat staring at him. 'It's the car,' I realised. 'They are going to take our lovely new Land Cruiser.'

By this time the man's partner was very agitated and having ejected my companions from the passenger side he was shouting, 'Shoot that one, shoot that one!'

At that point someone grabbed me, yanked me from the driver's seat and I was left standing on the road watching the Land Cruiser disappear over the hill. It had all happened within a few minutes but during that time I had come within a hair's breadth of my life being ended.

In order to appreciate a new vehicle it is best to suffer a little first with the old one. Then when the sparkling new car arrives you think it is the nicest, most comfortable automobile you have ever driven. This was how I was feeling when the new Toyota Land Cruiser arrived provided through Oxfam. We had been using the Suzuki for two years on the bumpiest most pot-holed roads imaginable. It had served us well, but either the roads were getting much worse or something was wrong with the springs. I think it was a combination of both. I could feel every stone we went over and my rear quarters were becoming sensitized to bad roads. When I knew we had to go to certain destinations I would groan and look for excuses not to go, already feeling the shaking, rattling and bumping we would have to endure. There was also no doubt that a Suzuki wasn't big enough to fit nine people, the number we usually took to our clinics. Changing from the Suzuki to the Land Cruiser was like going from a Mini to a Mercedes. We drove along roads where I had previously bounced and shaken and I couldn't feel a thing. The big wheels and springs of the Land Cruiser rode out bumps which had previously set my teeth rattling.

We had had the Land Cruiser for a few months when I was in Kampala one Wednesday collecting supplies. I had just filled the car with drugs and equipment when I remembered that I had to see the sister who was in charge of the Laboratory at the big Catholic hospital Nsambya. It was lunchtime and the laboratory staff told me to try the nun's house where she stayed, down a back road about half a mile away from the hospital. Edward, our own Laboratory Technician, and a young girl whom I was taking back to school in Kampala were with me. As I hadn't been to this house before, I was driving along looking at the plot numbers and house names. By the time I saw the one I was looking for I had overshot the driveway so I stopped and reversed. That was when the man pulled the gun on me.

During the whole incident I felt a sense of detachment

from the situation. I didn't feel fear, I felt numb. Something was being done to me which I had no control of. It was like being at the dentist – you just had to wait until it was over. It is said that when you are about to die your whole life flashes before you. That was not true in my case but I *was* thinking about feeling all the bumps and potholes again. As the car disappeared over the horizon I felt a real sense of loss. We had only had the use of the Land Cruiser for a few months. It had been nice while it lasted. When I started to come out of my daze I realised that the sisters had seen it all happen; they had been watching from a safe distance. In fact it is most probable that the thieves had been waiting near their gate to hijack their car. However I had happened to come along a few minutes before the sisters left and they had hijacked mine instead. They had made a good haul. The car had contained medicines, money, my passport, cheque book etc. That was the last we would see of the vehicle or any of those possessions. Car theft was rife in Uganda and most of the vehicles seemed to vanish into thin air. It is likely that many of them were taken to a neighbouring country such as Zaire. I ran up the drive way and one of the ladies asked me if I would like to phone the Police to report the theft.

'Is there a phone anywhere around?' I replied.

I was not used to having phones available and in my experience the phones in Kampala were often out of order.

'Ours was working this morning,' she replied.

'Does anyone have the number of Central Police Station or what number should I ring?' I asked.

'Why don't you try 999,' someone replied helpfully.

I would never have thought of ringing 999 in Uganda. However I suppose it was the obvious number since Uganda had been in the British sphere of influence. When I dialled, a voice answered, 'Central Police Station, Mobile Control Unit.'

I hadn't known that such a unit existed.

'I have just had my car stolen,' I informed the policeman, and went on to describe the vehicle and give the registration number.

'Just now?' asked the officer.

'Yes, within the past five minutes.'

'We will get back to you,' he said and hung up.

As the policeman hadn't taken much information I thought I had better go in person to the Police Station and fill out some kind of Official Report. One of the sisters offered us a lift and we were deposited at the Station in the centre of Kampala. Central Police Station was a large rambling building with lots of people coming and going and no obvious indications as to where I should go to make a report of a car theft. Someone downstairs advised me to try the top floor, so we made our way up the four flights of stairs. As we neared the top I could hear a radio crackle and a jubilant policeman came out of a radio control room.

'We've got them, we've got them!'

'You've got whom?' I asked.

'We've got the thieves who stole your car. You were the person who phoned in weren't you?' he replied.

I was flabbergasted. Barely thirty minutes had elapsed since the robbery had taken place. This bit of police work must have ranked as one of the fastest recoveries of a stolen vehicle in the history of the Ugandan Police. Then he told me the bad news.

'It appears your car was damaged in the chase.'

I was still too dazed by the series of events to be worried by the knowledge that the car had been damaged. To get a damaged vehicle back was better than no vehicle at all.

When I had phoned my 999 call it had gone straight through to a radio room with links to mobile patrols, motor cycles and pickups equipped with radio. One police motorcyclist had immediately spotted the car being driven through Kampala to the north. He had followed and radioed ahead to his colleagues who set up a road block. When the thieves saw the road block they rammed another car in an attempt to escape. The police opened fire and a gun battle ensued. The thieves then tried to make their escape on foot while firing at the police, but they ran out of ammunition. It became clear that they would have been shot dead in the course of the battle except that the policeman's gun jammed at the critical moment, so they were taken alive. Understandably the police in Uganda are not lenient in their treatment of gunmen. The thieves were brought back to the cells and the Land Cruiser was towed back to the police yard. It was now in a sorry state, with the whole front end stoved in, but all the drugs, the money etc were still there.

After filling out lengthy reports and making statements the Officer in charge said,

'Now I would like to go and inspect the scene of the crime.'

'Fine,' I said, 'let's go,' and we proceeded down to the police yard.

'Where is your vehicle?' he asked.

'That's it,' I said, pointing at the wrecked Land Cruiser.

'How are we going to travel?' he asked.

This question hadn't occurred to me. I had assumed a police vehicle would be available, but Third World countries can't provide vehicles for all their Police Officers. He was depending on me for transport.

'I have an idea,' I volunteered. 'If I hire a breakdown truck and we tow the Land Cruiser to Mengo hospital I can probably borrow a vehicle there.'

So we set out. I rode with the driver of the breakdown vehicle and the three policemen drove in the Land Cruiser suspended behind. They were quite comfortable and didn't seem to find anything in the least unusual about this form of transport for policemen.

Late that night I arrived back in Luweero. Robbie had been very worried because we were so late and was horrified when she heard the reason, but neither of us could help thinking that in Uganda this series of events was nothing short of miraculous. None of us had ever heard of such a recovery and such efficient police work before. By this stage I also had time to reflect that I had narrowly escaped death. The gunman would have just had to move his finger a fraction of an inch and my life was over.

Soon after the incident I was called by the police, along with Edward and Lydia to attend the identity parade. I didn't know what to expect, but I hoped there would be a one way mirror system whereby I could identify the criminals without being seen by them. I'm afraid such a sophisticated system had not yet been installed in Uganda. Eight or ten men were lined up in classic identity parade fashion and I was instructed,

'Walk around them, look at them, take your time. When you feel you have identified the man, step forward and put your hand on his shoulder.' I was not even to be allowed to identify the man privately by number to the police.

Africans are not easy for Whites to identify as Whites are not used to their distinctions in features. The same could be said in reverse. Fortunately the two men were quite distinctive and the image of the man with the gun was forever imprinted on my mind. When I stepped forward and identified the first man he gave me a steely look which said, 'If I get out, you are a dead man.' I think he must have given Edward the same visual signals as Edward failed to identify anyone correctly. However Lydia, the little girl, was not so easily intimidated and pointed them both out.

Proper identification by us was critical to the success of the case, as even though the police had, as it were, caught them 'red-handed' one of the men was claiming he was really an innocent bystander. What happened, he claimed, was that he had been given a lift. He knew nothing about any holdup. Then the police had opened fire and he was caught in the gun battle. It was all a terrible mistake. However his defence depended on us not being able to identify him so it didn't work.

Several months later we were asked to attend court and

after three false starts the case finally commenced. We then learned that the defendants had been using delaying tactics in the hope of being able to escape. They had almost succeeded, having managed to saw through the bars in their window after procuring a hacksaw blade from the workshop, but they were caught in the prison yard. The men knew that when they were sentenced by the court, security would be much tighter than when they were on remand, so they had done all they could to delay the court case.

The Judge in the case was a lady, Counsel for the Prosecution was a young female lawyer and Counsel for the Defence a middle aged man. The proceedings appeared to resemble a British Court, except that the judge made copious notes on everything in long-hand. I was called as the first witness. It was obvious that the case of the Defence revolved around trying to cast doubt on my ability to identify the thieves. What clothes were they wearing at the time? Could I describe them? How could I as a white man identify Africans, since whites were known to have difficulty with this? The questions went on and on. Eventually the lawyer came in for what he thought was 'the kill'.

'I put it to you,' he began, in classic Perry Mason style, 'that you were too frightened, too much in a state of shock, too unfamiliar with African features to possibly identify these two men correctly. I put it to you that you were so stricken with terror at the time that you could not possibly remember a thing. I put it to you that it all happened so quickly that you have only a fuzzy recollection.'

Finally exasperated, and somewhat angry at this trumped up bit of court room drama at my expense, I interjected.

'You can put to me whatever you like, but these men sitting in this Court room are the two men who held me up at gunpoint and stole my car.'

I was a little bit overheated and I was surprised when

sniggers broke out around the Court room. I was even more surprised when I noticed the lawyer himself give a hint of a smile, which he quickly suppressed. The next line of attack was on my statement.

'How is it,' he began, 'that today you have identified two men, but in your statement you didn't mention any second man, not once?' he said, his voice rising. 'Not once have you referred to a second man.'

'That's odd,' I thought, genuinely concerned. 'I had thought that I mentioned both men in the report.'

'May I have a look at the statement?' I asked and the lawyer handed it to me. There clearly at the top of page two I had written, 'a second man approached with a gun from the other side of the car.'

'But I *have* mentioned the second man,' I protested.

Now it was the lawyer's turn to be disconcerted. He grabbed the statement and scanned it. More suppressed sniggers were heard around the Court room, but the lawyer wasn't amused. After that he definitely had less enthusiasm for pursuing this line of questions and I was excused.

I didn't hear the outcome of the case until many months later when I met Bob. Bob was a market boy who often helped us with our shopping in Kampala. He had become caught up in some Muslim riots and been sent to jail. This was unfortunate as Bob was not really a trouble maker. After ten months he was released and was back at his duties.

'What was prison like?' we asked.

'Not bad,' came his reply, 'we had beds and blankets and we were well fed. We even did some studying. Oh, I met someone you know. He was the leader of our study group.'

Imagine my surprise when Bob's friend proved to be the man who had hijacked the car!

'Clever guy,' said Bob, 'good education, but he has been a thief all his life. He has been stealing cars for years.'

'What happened to him and his friend?' I asked.

'They got the death sentence,' replied Bob, 'they have been moved to Death Row.'

Armed robbery, especially when it involved shooting at the police, was a serious offence in Uganda carrying the death penalty. It is possible that the death penalty will never be carried out. Certainly the process of Appeals etc could take five years. But there is a high probability that these men will be executed some day in the future. It gave me an odd feeling to know that these men were awaiting the death penalty. I wondered if, when it came to their moment of facing death, they would be prepared for it. After the identity parade I had bought two Good News Bibles and asked the police to give them to the prisoners. I wondered if they had ever read them.

Chapter 27

Young Victims

She was sixteen when I first met her and she was in terrible pain. However as I looked into her eyes I saw something more than pain. I saw stark terror. When I asked that she remove her blouse I saw the reason for her pain and her fear. She had Herpes Zoster, a painful rash, a marker of AIDS in 95% of Africans infected. The rash was now blistered, angry and weeping, running in a broad band exactly half way around her chest. As I examined her I teased out the story as gently as possible. She was from the Luweero area but her father had been killed in the war and her mother had remarried, so she had been sent to a boarding school in Mbarara near her grandmother's home. A few months ago there had been a disco at another school and the girls from her school were invited to attend. After the disco she had been brutally raped, so brutally in fact that she had to be admitted to hospital for treatment. The man had apparently been caught and was still languishing in prison. However she had never told her family. In time she healed and hoped that would be the end of it. Then during the school holidays the pain had started and the rash appeared, so she came to the hospital. Instinctively she knew that this rash had something to do with the rape. She knew about AIDS. She knew that the man could have given her the disease but she had put the terrible thought to the back of her mind until she developed the searing pain.

'Would you like us to do an AIDS test?' I asked, knowing that the result would almost certainly be positive, but hoping that she might be one of the 5% who escaped.

'Yes,' she whispered, 'I would like to know the result.'

Since the rash was so painful and she was in distress we admitted the child, for she was no more than that, so that we could control her pain and calm her fears. Her test was positive, as we expected, so there was no good news to impart, but Grace the nurse could see that her main problem was not the result, but the fear of being rejected by her mother. Her mother knew nothing about the whole incident of rape, since it had happened far away, and as she had recovered, she had hidden it from her. Now that she had got AIDS she felt her mother would blame her, reject her, wash her hands completely of her and stop paying school fees. She would be an outcast and destitute and she would have no one to turn to. She needed love, at this time; especially she needed a mother's arms around her. She needed understanding and security but all she could feel was rejection.

'Would it help if I talked to your Mum?' I asked. 'I could talk to her first and explain that this was not your fault,' I continued, 'and I could explain about the disease, that it is not contagious and the rash will go away.'

I could see the relief in her eyes, she wanted our moral support. A message was sent to call her mother at the village and a few days later I sat down with the mum to explain about her daughter's illness. She wept, she was shocked, she was distressed. She had known nothing of all this. Then I explained that her daughter feared rejection more than anything else. She felt her family might turn their back on her if they knew the truth. She felt she would become an outcast. That was not her mother's reaction. The love of a mother was greater than any sense of condemnation or blame. She could not reject her own daughter, she could only comfort her and support her. She was outraged that we could think otherwise. So the two came together and mother comforted daughter in the midst of their suffering. In time the pain decreased and the rash resolved leaving only the tell tale scars of the infection. However the child still had the AIDS virus and later she would develop more signs of illness. She would need her mother's arms around her, she would need the whole-hearted support of her family.

Mama can you hold me?
I need your arms around me;
It's strangers that surround me,
And I'm lonely and afraid.

The pattern of disease and care was so different from what I had been used to. I had seen the children look after their ageing and sick parents. The children buried the parents and mourned for them. One generation passed on and the next wept for them. Now I was seeing the pattern change. Now the young were getting sick and the old were caring for them. The young were dying and the old were burying them. No longer were the beds taken up by the old and feeble, now the young were growing feeble and they needed the old to look after them. This child was by no means the youngest we saw who was infected by AIDS. An old man brought a child to the clinic, her head covered by a cloth. When we removed the cloth we saw the worst Herpes Zoster infection we had ever seen. One side of the child's face was blistered, black and raw. She must have been in excruciating pain. We asked the old man what age she was.

'Twelve as far as I know,' he replied.

The child never had an AIDS test carried out. It would have been opening a can of worms, but we asked ourselves if she was one of the 95% who had underlying AIDS. How had she got it? Was she one of the very few children in that age group who had got it at birth and yet showed no symptoms for years? We knew of a few cases in that category, but they were very few and we knew of none as old as twelve. Or had she been taken as 'the wife' of some older man? We knew of some instances of this where an old man took a very young relative and said she was to be his bride. Sometimes the family or community stood against him but sometimes no one knew or cared and these child brides were the virtual slave of the man.

For whatever reason this twelve year old was likely to have AIDS. We knew that the nature of the epidemic was that it would claim the young, leaving the old and the children, but we now were seeing the children become victims. It seemed that young girls were particularly at risk from becoming infected at the first sexual encounter, particularly if trauma was involved, as it inevitably was. The loss of virginity provided the ideal conditions in breaking down the natural defences for the virus to get into the blood stream. Hence the rate of infection of the young victims, (who might have had very few partners, compared to an older population), was high. The spectrum of disease was leaving a gap in the generations, but as younger and younger people were infected that gap became greater. AIDS education was carried out widely in schools and the experts rightly said that this needed to be geared to a young age group from ten years up, but education was no guarantee that behaviour would change. So many factors mitigated against fundamental change in behaviour, that a veneer of AIDS education would do little to halt the progress of the epidemic. Young girls were particularly at risk. They were seen by many men as 'safe'. The younger, the better, the reasoning went. They would have had less chance of contracting AIDS, so they would be 'clean' for the men. Businessmen with access to ready cash were said to be the worst culprits. They could offer inducements to the school girl, a few shillings to pay school fees, a new pair of shoes, a pretty dress. The peer pressures were strong. Contemporaries were coming back to school with new things, so what was the harm in having a wealthy boyfriend? The girls might have been free of AIDS but the men were not, so many of these teenagers picked up the virus. Most didn't get any signs for some time. Perhaps not until they were in early or mid twenties, but some did not even reach the third decade of their lives, for once they had AIDS their life expectancy went from a further thirty years or more to three years or less.

Sarah was little more than a school girl when we got to know her. She was eighteen, but she had a child, like so many other young girls around the village. We gave her a job as an auxiliary nurse and when our first maternity ward was opened she decided that her true vocation in life was to be a midwife. She worked with our midwives and her heart's desire was to do her midwifery certificate. She had a very vivacious personality, sometimes being outspoken in her views, which was unusual in young women in Uganda. However this very trait in her personality endeared her to everyone. She seemed so sure of herself, she knew what she wanted to do with her life. She had a strong faith in Jesus Christ and the world was her oyster. But it was not to be for Sarah. Her hopes and ambitions would never be realised. At first she had just a few skin signs but by the time she drew them to our attention she had visited a number of other dispensaries and hospitals and received numerous treatments with no effect. She had the early signs of AIDS. How did one tell an eighteen year old that she had AIDS, she had all the promise of life ahead, all her hope for the future, all her vision for getting a profession and doing good for her fellow man? How did one tell her that she had a life expectancy of perhaps three years? That she would never see her goals and ambitions fulfilled? That the promise of youth would wither and die? How could one tell a teenager, about to set out on the adventure of life, that it would be over before it began? I knew these things, but I couldn't tell her. I couldn't place the burden of my knowledge on her young shoulders. However I did have the responsibility, at least, to tell her she had the AIDS virus. I knew that if I told her that in the right way and counselled her properly, she would remain with a positive outlook on life. She had a strong faith. She told me that when she was a school girl she had a number of boyfriends but that had all finished since she got 'saved'. Now she trusted in God and lived out her faith. I was surprised by Sarah's strength of character, on hearing the news that she had AIDS. She appeared unmoved, she said she knew her destiny was in God's hands.

During the following year I saw no signs of her being depressed, anxious or fearful. She could be heard singing as she helped the other midwives and went about her duties. I knew she still cherished the hope of going on for further training as a midwife. She rarely complained but when she told Gudrun that she had a sore throat, Gudrun found that she had widespread oral thrush. She sang in the choir at Ando's wedding and even though she looked a little thin, she was in her usual cheery spirits. A few days later she developed a headache, and died within three weeks, of cryptococcal meningitis. It was only in the last few weeks that her family realised she had AIDS. Sarah had never told anyone; she had decided at the beginning that she wouldn't seek help from anyone else but just hold on to her faith in God. When I saw her dying she still looked beautiful and I thought of the morning glory which grew in profusion over our verandah. Her life was like one of those delicate flowers, beautiful but fragile, opening in the morning to show off all its colour and fragrance, but closing in the heat of the day and falling to the ground so quickly. Sarah had scarcely the morning of her life to show us her beauty but we had been warmed by the glow of her faith and courage. She didn't even have three years from when the diagnosis was made. She had only fifteen months, but I was glad I hadn't given her the message of doom and gloom. She knew she had AIDS but she had never given up hope, she had never lost her zest for living. She had so completely entrusted her life into God's hands that she genuinely didn't worry about the future and that is how she faced death – with complete trust in her Father, God. She was nineteen years old when she died.

Sarah is no more,
She has passed on from this life,
A brief fleeting visit,
A fragile flower.
She bloomed brilliantly,
Like the morning glory,
And we shared her fragrance.
Now she is gone,
And we have lost,
But she has gained.
Sarah we miss you,
But we would not call you back,
To this life of suffering.
Go and be a bright star,
In another place,
Where your light will never be extinguished.

Sarah's baby was healthy, he survived and was brought up by her sister. Sometimes a baby was the first to show signs of infection while the mother appeared completely well. Sometimes the first indication that a young mother had AIDS was given when her baby got sick. There was a ward in the hospital where we treated babies who had failed to thrive. It could be due to TB, Kwashiorkor, Marasmus or AIDS, among other things. The most hopeless to treat were the AIDS babies. These little mites didn't ever get a fair crack of life. They were born to die, babies of six or nine months who weighed two or three kilos and looked like they were tired of life. The skin hung off their limbs in folds like an old coat and no matter what good nutrition they were given there was no effect. Some had TB as well as AIDS and showed some improvement on anti-tuberculous drugs but they would eventually succumb. Other AIDS babies showed few signs but died after minor infections.

Dorothy * had a baby girl whom she looked after

---

* Not her real name.

lovingly. The child was fifteen months old and was doing well. She looked healthy and well nourished, she had been given all her vaccines and her general progress had been good. When she got measles no one was alarmed as the illness didn't seem serious. The child appeared to recover and went home only to be readmitted the following day with more worrying symptoms. The pattern of illness was somewhat unusual and an astute doctor took an AIDS test. The child died within the next twenty four hours. She had AIDS. I had to tell Dorothy that, not only had her baby died of AIDS, but that she was carrying the virus herself. She had no signs of the disease. Until the baby had become sick, life had appeared rosy, now her baby was dead and she knew she was an AIDS carrier. It was a hard situation for her to cope with but she took the news calmly, almost stoically. I knew Dorothy well and over the years I watched as she got on with her life. After all life goes on whether one is a carrier of AIDS or not. She was a fine example of somebody who lived 'positively with AIDS' as the publicity material from some organisations working with AIDS sufferers exhorted. Dorothy had a real faith which worked itself out in her morality and lifestyle. I found a graciousness of spirit in this girl at which I marvelled, as I was probably the only one who knew the burden that she was carrying. She wasn't one of those people who became bitter or swore that she would go and spread her disease to others. She did not deny to herself that she had the AIDS virus, but because she felt well, she just went on living, giving of herself in her work and community. No one really knows how long someone with no symptoms of AIDS, but infected with the virus, can live in Africa. I have met people who were infected for seven years and still were not sick. Since Dorothy had no symptoms she could have a longer life expectancy than someone who had early symptoms of the disease. I was blessed and encouraged to know someone who, even though she was a victim herself, didn't compound the problem, by spreading AIDS to others.

Tenderly she cared
This was her baby
Gurgling and cooing
Growing and laughing
Apparently well
Then suddenly sick
'My baby is dead, Doctor.'
'Your baby had AIDS, Dorothy.'

Young mothers who found out their baby was sick and dying of AIDS often responded with tears, sometimes crying and screaming. It was the hardest diagnosis for me to give. Not only was I telling the mum that there was no hope for the child, I was saying that she too was carrying the disease. Sometimes the mother had signs of AIDS, sometimes not, but it was difficult for them to take in the knowledge that the baby was dying of something they themselves were carrying. Most of these babies died within a few days or weeks and it was a tragic scene to see the mother take the little bundle, and the family collect the belongings and trudge home for the burial.

Not all the babies born to mothers with the AIDS virus were infected. The percentage was thought to be 30–50%. On the other hand sometimes the mother died and the baby lived. This pattern of transmission was confusing for everyone for there were no absolutes. Sometimes the baby was infected while the mother had no symptoms and appeared to be in the best of health. Sometimes the baby was well but the mother was sick. A husband usually passed it on to his wife and vice versa but not always. A husband and wife might both have AIDS but usually only one was sick. The exceptions to the rule made it more difficult to convince people of the risk. They didn't understand why some babies 'got it' and others didn't, why some wives were negative yet their husbands died of AIDS. They didn't understand the difference between being infected with no symptoms and being healthy and not infected. Both sets of people looked the same and felt the same yet they were told that one had AIDS infection and the other didn't. In many ways the exceptions made education and behaviour change even more difficult. It was a tremendous relief when one partner learned he or she didn't have AIDS though the spouse had. But this exception seemed to reinforce the belief that one could 'beat the system!' It was hard for people to realise in the face of conflicting evidence that the vast majority of people didn't get a second chance.

Sexually transmitted diseases had been around for a long time, probably as long as anyone could remember. People had realised for years that the price of their lust could be an uncomfortable discharge or rash or even extreme difficulty in passing water, but it was an acceptable price to pay to satisfy the sexual drive. Besides most of these things could be dealt with. Folks had become used to going to various hospitals and clinics with their slightly embarrassing problems and getting an injection or a course of pills. There were always plenty of private clinics and quack doctors who would give the customer what he wanted, so it was almost a way of life. One sinned, there was a price to pay but that was accepted, the private doctors got rich and the sinner got his injection. Whether the injection brought a cure or not was slightly irrelevant, the patient never died of the disease and everyone was happy. Why could AIDS not have the same scenario? Everyone knew it was transmitted by sex and these sexually transmitted diseases had been around for a long time. It was a risk one took. People tended to say – if it happens, it happens – not really believing it would happen to them, and if it did there would always be someone around to give them 'the cure'. At least that is what they told themselves.

Some of the victims of the epidemic whom we saw were completely without hope. There appeared to be no care or compassion available to them from their family or community. These were the true refuse of society, the people who had been dumped even by their relatives, or perhaps the relatives were so involved in the daily problems of disease, poverty and deprivation that they themselves had turned their backs on it, or retreated into their own world of unreality or into an alcoholic haze. One of the village health workers asked us to visit a man who had AIDS. He lived in a poorly constructed mud hut in the midst of a small community. I was invited to go inside and at first, could see nothing, but as my eyes adjusted to the darkness, I realised that there was a person inside. A man was squatting naked in the corner. The old lady, who was apparently his only relative, seemed to be living in a state of euphoria unrelated to the dreadful reality of the situation. The man, who could have been thirty or sixty, had diarrhoea all the time, so she had taken away his clothes. The man sat shivering in front of the dying embers of a fire, even though it was bright sunshine outside. The whole scene spoke of squalor and human degradation. This man was no longer treated as human, he had become a sick animal. We left food and blankets but we realised that he was almost beyond human contact and beyond hope. He died a few days later.

The girl on the filthy mattress stirred herself slowly. She couldn't walk, she could only crawl to the door of her house. She was probably in her thirties. Her mother and father moved around outside but paid little attention to her.

'They are well known drunks in this area,' confided the village health worker.

A child of eight or nine appeared. This was the daughter of the girl. She used to go to school, but now she stayed at home to look after her mother as the grandparents took no interest. The girl's condition was pathetic, she was emaciated and dirty and she had deep pressure sores. The child fetched water and some food, but most of it her mother couldn't eat. Most of the day she lay in the filth and darkness of her hut, while her parents drunk themselves into oblivion on the local brew. We berated the parents for their neglect of their own daughter but they didn't seem to care. These people were truly hardened. We said we would take the girl back to the hospital and tend to her sores, wash her and give her more nutritious food. They didn't care, we could do what we liked, but they didn't want the child to go because she fetched water for them. We took the girl to hospital and insisted on taking the child also. A week later the grandparents took the child away. I simply failed to understand how someone could be so callous about their own daughter. I felt so angry, but perhaps I was not in a position to judge. Perhaps poverty and misery had done their own special work and turned these people into creatures without feeling, humans whose emotional framework had been dismantled and discarded. They were no longer complete human beings. The sensitive parts of their souls had been ripped out, so that what was left could survive and all that was needed for the continued existence of these 'non-persons', was a plentiful supply of banana beer.

Chapter 28

Fred*

Fred was one of the local traders in the Kiwoko township. He was a friendly guy known to the staff. He developed some symptoms suggestive of AIDS – weight loss, diarrhoea and fever, so after some discussion with us, he decided to have an AIDS test carried out. It was positive and Fred was distraught. I talked to him about the result and my heart went out to him. After all here was someone who might face death within the next few months. However against the odds he didn't die and he improved considerably over the next few months. He looked a bit gaunt but he continued with his shop and seemed to have adjusted to the knowledge that he had AIDS. When we had counselled with him we explained that even if he felt well he was still carrying the virus and could spread it to someone else through sex. So Fred was well aware of his condition and the ways to avoid spread.

Eighteen months passed and he seemed to be in a stable condition with no further problems so I was happy that he was doing so well. Then one of our student nurses got pregnant. It was against the rules of the hospital for an unmarried student to get pregnant so she concealed the matter for as long as possible until she was six months pregnant and the bump was showing quite clearly. When she finally admitted that she was pregnant she told me that Fred was the father. I was horrified. This man knew that

---

* Not his real name.

he had AIDS, yet he had got a young nurse pregnant. She was only seventeen.

'Please, doctor, it was a mistake,' the nurse pleaded.

For this young nurse it was a moment of indiscretion but a moment that would cost her her life as a test revealed that she now had the AIDS virus.

What made Fred do it? He knew he had AIDS. Was he deliberately trying to infect someone else? It was possible. Some people said that a commonly held attitude among those who had AIDS was that they would not die alone. They would take other people with them. I would have liked to believe that this attitude did not exist in the community, but other Ugandans told me that this was a firmly held attitude among some. I would like to have believed that this was not true of Fred. It is hard to see someone as a deliberate murderer. It seems more likely that Fred simply denied the facts. When he felt sick he was prepared to believe he had AIDS, but when he was feeling better he told himself that they must have got it wrong. Now he had no diarrhoea, the fever had gone, they had made a mistake, there was nothing wrong with him. It seems that the person most easy to deceive is one's self. As Fred seduced the young girl, he probably had no problem whatsoever in telling himself that he was completely healthy. In the heat of the moment it was easy for his natural desires to overcome cold rationale. No matter what Fred told himself he was still HIV positive and he shared his disease with someone else. In fact he had probably shared it with two other people, as the baby had up to a 50% chance of getting it.

So what happened to the girl? She went back to her own village where she now has the status of being a 'mama' – in village terms a step up the social scale. Probably neither mother nor baby have any signs of ill health. Maybe the baby will escape, maybe it will suddenly die at the age of two or three and it will be said to have died of measles or malaria or just fever. As time goes by the girl will put to the back of her mind the information that she is HIV positive. Another man may come along who wants to marry her, and by that time she will have decided that she is in perfectly good health. After all, it was only a lab test and hasn't she been well for a few years now? Eventually the girl will get sick but not before she has given her disease to someone else. Her relatives will be told she had typhoid or dysentery when she dies, or some other vague diagnosis. The husband will be completely unaware of the legacy he has received from his wife and will remarry, so the story will go on. It all started with an 'accident' and a bit of self-deception for some physical pleasure and self-gratification.

So what of Fred? What will happen to him? No matter what he told himself he was guilty of spreading the disease. Could anything have been done to have stopped him? The answer is that in today's world there is really no way to stop someone spreading AIDS. The responsibility lies totally with the individual. It is a sad fact that the denial of that responsibility may result in the death of someone else who is innocent. If Fred carries on with the same attitude the best that one could hope for would be that he dies quickly before more innocent girls suffer. I talked to Fred again. I told him the consequences of his action but he denied he had AIDS. What can one do about someone who absolutely refuses to face the truth? Unfortunately his denial didn't make the AIDS go away. He could tell himself whatever he liked to believe but he was still spreading his disease to others.

Living in the community where I sometimes knew who was HIV positive could place me in an interesting and difficult position. Was my responsibility to the patient or to the person at risk of being infected? We had developed a well-defined system for AIDS testing. No one had a test done before they received counselling and gave their permission. This then prepared the ground for further counselling when the result came through. However, if an AIDS test was carried out with inadequate counselling, this led to complications.

One such case was Ruth .* Ruth , had a skin rash and some other early symptoms of AIDS. An AIDS test was done but then Ruth told the staff that if the test was positive she would go out and spread the disease. As she was obviously not prepared to handle a result responsibly she should not have had a test done in the first place. She was one of those people who said she would not die alone. Her test was positive and the staff involved decided not to give her the result but informed me of what was happening. This left me in a very difficult position. I procrastinated. I had a dilemma. If she was told, she was likely to have a bad reaction and possibly try to infect other people. I knew that she had a very stubborn personality. Conversely, if she was counselled properly, she could be faced with her responsibilities before God and to her fellow man. She would also be told how to handle the diagnosis and what life expectancy she might expect, since she had only a few indications of infection. She could be counselled to have a positive outlook on her life and also consider the spiritual aspect. One always wants to believe that proper counselling and support will bring about a good response, but as we had learned in Fred's case it might appear to have no real effect.

After some time I was informed that Ruth was pregnant. She was not married. The information which followed was even more devastating. The father of her child was someone I knew fairly well, someone whose wife was attending the ante-natal clinic and was soon to give birth to her own baby. I was devastated. This man had a lovely young wife and every prospect of a long and happy life. I was on friendly terms with Harold * and decided to have a chat with him. What I had heard was second-hand information and I wanted to confirm it for myself. He admitted immediately that he was responsible for Ruth's pregnancy. He hung his head and said that he was deeply ashamed.

---

* Real name has been changed.

'Harold, you understand that AIDS is widespread in this community,' I told him.

He nodded.

'When you have casual sex like this, you have a high chance of getting AIDS.'

'Yes,' he said he understood that too.

'If you get it yourself you can then pass it on to your wife,' I continued.

It seemed that Harold was aware of all this. At this point I couldn't tell him that Ruth was an AIDS carrier but as a result of our conversation, he decided to have an AIDS test himself. Unfortunately Harold was not one of the lucky ones. His test was also positive.

Harold and I got together for another chat. He had no symptoms whatsoever. His life expectancy could be many years. He was carrying the virus and could spread it, but otherwise his life would be no different. The big question was, had he already infected his wife?

I advised him that his wife should be tested but he refused. He didn't want to tell her. The whole situation raised too many difficulties which he couldn't face. He wanted to go on with his life as if nothing had happened. While I could advise someone, I couldn't force them to take a certain course of action. In theory I knew that his wife might still be negative, therefore if they used condoms she could be protected. The best course of action was for her to be tested. If she was positive there was nothing more to be done. They could live together as a married couple with no change in lifestyle and provided they remained faithful to each other they would not spread the disease. She should also be advised not to get pregnant again as pregnancy would hasten the progress of her disease. However it was unlikely that they would heed that advice. On the other hand if she was negative, it was a whole new situation, she should be protected from infection. This would mean Harold using condoms, or simply that they should split up. Both options were difficult. The men did not like using condoms. They said that it was like

eating a banana with the skin on, that is, it severely inter-
fered with their pleasurable sensation. The more sophisticated African men were getting over this difficulty in the
interests of staying alive. All these things presented themselves as more immediate difficulties than the risk of getting AIDS.

I think Harold realised all the implications of his wife
having a test, the most important being that she would
then know the whole sordid story of his involvement with
the other girl, which he preferred to hide. In his mind it
was better that life would just go on as normal without
anyone rocking the boat. There was a small chance that his
wife wasn't infected but it was likely that she too had the
virus now so they could go on living together as before.
Harold was prepared to gamble with someone else's life –
the life of his own wife, rather than to stir up trouble.

In some ways this was a natural response given the
human and cultural factors involved. First of all, did he
really believe us when he was told he was carrying the
AIDS virus? After all he wasn't ill, there were other
traditional beliefs which found equal credibility in his
thinking. In communicating with a patient there were difficulties because of their concept of disease. When a person had few symptoms or was the partner of an AIDS
sufferer it was often very difficult for them to accept the
medical scientific diagnosis even though they had heard it
time and again. They were being told that they had been
infected by an invisible virus which had given them an
invisible disease which they would pass on through sex. It
all seemed like a plot to curb their enjoyment of life ...

Sometimes the scientific explanation and the conse-
quent rational action were apparently in direct contradiction to the traditional culture and beliefs which prevailed.
To a people with their roots firmly planted in the culture of
traditional healers, witch doctors and herbal remedies, it
seemed at least as likely that they should believe someone
had put a curse on them and they should turn to their local
witch doctor for healing. Of course there was also a tradition of Christianity going back over one hundred years;

271

but for many, Christianity had been grafted onto the other traditions, so they went hand in hand. Every villager knew, that despite what the doctor said, there was a definite chance that their symptoms could have been caused by bewitching. Someone had put a curse on someone else and that is why he was fading away. They were not denying the scientific explanation, but they were not denying the traditional explanation either. They were just joining the two together without any apparent contradiction, in a way that the western mind could no longer do. Also the traditional healers were there to offer help; bring a goat or a few chickens and he or she would give the patient the remedy. In many ways AIDS was the ideal disease for a witch doctor to treat. Its course fluctuated, the person got sick and then improved, only to get sick again and eventually finally die. So, often the patient improved after he had had the herbal remedy or whatever had been given by the local healer. When he started to deteriorate he got sent off to the hospital to die. It was therefore obvious that the traditional witch doctor could at least do as well as any modern doctor.

It must be said that not everyone believed in the traditional healers, but it was part of the culture and the hope of a cure by any method was natural. People suffering from a terminal disease would clutch at straws. Some time ago a lady living in the Masaka area claimed that her daughter had been cured of AIDS through eating the soil from their garden. The soil was made into a suspension and swallowed. Obviously this soil had supernatural qualities.

Somehow the news of this unlikely cure spread all around Uganda. One would think that this news would have been greeted with scorn and derision and hoots of laughter. Not so, people travelled from miles around to eat this soil. Special buses were laid on from Kampala to take people to the lady's garden. Queues of people formed to get this mixture of soil until eventually the government put a stop to it. In a society where large numbers of people are dying from AIDS, it is not surprising that they are prepared to believe in traditional remedies of unknown composition to bring a cure. Indeed, in Ireland in recent years we have had thousands of people flock to Knock after claims were made of statues with supernatural powers which moved. In both Ireland and Uganda there is an underlying tradition of superstition. However in the villages of Uganda this belief is more overt than in present day Ireland. So the villager is not about to discard his traditions simply because a doctor has given him a scientific explanation.

Another factor in shaping the Ugandan's outlook was the history of the country over the past twenty five years. During that time they had lived through regimes of oppressive brutality, where people literally didn't know if they would survive to the next day. They learned to live one day at a time, to keep their heads down and not question things. At times they learned not even to think, just to get on with the routine of living and perhaps the evil would pass. They saw their friends and relatives killed; many people simply disappeared and those left didn't ask questions. Eventually those who survived saw their formula for life had worked, ie they got on with their lives, kept their head down and hoped the problem would go away, and it did. One day the soldiers were gone, people weren't being abducted and killed any more and people could move about freely. It all obviously went to prove that if you ignore the problem, it will go away. So, in 'Harold's' case, all his instincts told him to ignore the problem and go on living as if nothing had happened. He felt no sickness, his wife was well. He had been told he had a virus, that was what 'they' said. He had no evidence. He would do nothing. If something happened in the future he would face it when it came.

The problem of not wanting to tell the spouse or partner was widespread. Sometimes it was through fear. One girl was brought into the ward by her husband who was an Army Officer. The rate of AIDS infection in the army was tragically high. Although the husband seemed fit and healthy his wife had terminal AIDS. As we talked to her and told her the diagnosis, we advised her that she should tell her husband. She was distraught.

'I couldn't tell him,' she said, 'he would throw me out of the house.'

The thought of her husband knowing, worried her more than the actual diagnosis. This posed another ethical dilemma for me, but I had to honour the patient's wishes. These situations raised an interesting question on medical ethics. Was my responsibility to my patients wishes only, or did I have a wider responsibility to the community, to the innocent victims who would be affected? In this case my first responsibility was to my patient but I knew that when she died some other innocent person would probably be infected.

Chapter 29

Musoke*

While AIDS in Uganda was normally spread through heterosexual means, there was also a small percentage of people who had contracted it through blood transfusions, before blood was routinely screened in the country. That problem has now been largely overcome by the National Blood Bank which screens blood for the hospitals. Of course there was still the window period during which a person, who had very recently been infected, had a negative AIDS test. The risk that someone could be given HIV positive blood was now well under 1%. However because of this slight risk, blood transfusions were limited to those patients who would otherwise die. Surgery would be performed in an emergency on patients with blood levels which were much lower than would be acceptable in a western hospital without a blood transfusion. It was a question of balancing the risk of AIDS against the risks of blood loss.

One of our commonest causes of admission of babies to the hospital was severe anaemia due to malaria. The malaria parasite destroyed the blood cells until the baby became so anaemic that he would die of heart failure. The level of the blood was measured by the haemoglobin which in an infant should be 11 grams or more, but blood transfusion was not done unless the haemoglobin level had

---

* Not his real name.

fallen to less than 3–4 grams, i.e. 36% of the normal level. When it had reached such low levels there was usually no option but to transfuse, otherwise the baby would die. Unfortunately an efficient system of screening blood did not always exist in Uganda and some people were transfused before the risk of AIDS through transfusion was so well known. One such case was Jane*, Musoke's wife.

Musoke was a local carpenter. He was a good man with a wife and five daughters – one of the local Parish leaders who was respected by everyone. He had been one of the first people to return to the area after the war and was working hard to see his village redeveloped again. He had a small coffee plantation which was now overgrown and almost wild, and one would find him in the plantation early in the mornings struggling to pick coffee from the high straggling branches, or hoeing vigorously in his garden. Later in the day he would be making furniture for the orphanage where he was employed. I was always encouraged by Musoke. Here was a local man who was setting a good example to the community. He had one wife, he was a community leader and he was giving a lead in rural development, and rehabiting his small farm after the destruction of the war. He was also an excellent carpenter and when we started building the clinic, he made all the window frames and door frames. Late at night I would find him with a tilly lamp hung outside his house, sawing and planing. I was very grateful to him for his hard work as there was no other skilled carpenter in the area at that time who could do the job. He was also a devout churchgoer and I would sometimes visit his house and find him reading his Bible. He was a serious, intense kind of person whom it was easy to respect.

My belief in Musoke was almost shattered after I had known him for about three years, when I learned he was to take a second wife. His wife Jane was now in her forties and they had five daughters. To me they had always been a

---

* Not her real name.

model family. Why had he suddenly decided he needed a second wife? He wasn't a Moslem, he was a staunch member of his local Church of Uganda. I also knew his brother well and we talked about this decision of Musoke's to get another wife.

'You see, Doctor, we have our African traditions,' his brother explained. 'Musoke only has daughters and his wife is too old to bear him any more children. If he dies without a son he will have no heir. His property will go to his brothers and their family and there will be no one to follow him.'

'What about his daughters?' I asked. 'Can his line not be passed on through them?'

It appeared that they didn't really count. He needed sons. In some ways I couldn't argue with them. Many cultures through the ages have seen sons as important, including biblical cultures. Modern values have changed and most people from the First World don't care if they have sons or daughters. However it was obviously very important for Musoke to have sons.

However I felt sorry for his wife who had been his faithful partner for twenty five years. Now a new young bride was to be introduced into the house hardly older than his own eldest daughter. Although I couldn't accept Musoke's values, I could understand them and I realised that he saw this as his only alternative. There was also a tradition of polygamy in his family. His father had three wives, and his brother had three wives. As his brother said to me,

'Doctor, I like to think that we are good men. We are honest, we are upright, we work for the good of our community, but we are also African men and it is our tradition that we can have more than one wife. Musoke has no male heirs and it is essential for him to have a son. I hope you do not now think that he is a bad man because he has taken another wife.'

He was right, I couldn't judge Musoke because of the step that he had taken, though I still wondered how his

first wife felt about it. Later when Musoke talked to us
himself, it emerged that Jane, like Sarah in the Bible, had
urged him to take another wife to bear him sons.

Some time after the marriage, Jane was brought to the
hospital. Since I had known her she had always been thin,
but that was not so unusual in itself. She now had intermittent fever and had lost even more weight. She also had
oral thrush, usually a tell-tale sign. Jane had AIDS. At
first Musoke didn't accept the diagnosis. It was impossible.
Until he took his new wife he and Jane had been together
for over twenty years and they had been entirely faithful to
each other. I had often found that, on questioning people
who said they had been faithful to their wife, they then
admitted to a few other casual relationships, but discounted them as irrelevant. Musoke was adamant he had
been absolutely faithful and he was sure the same thing
could have been said of Jane.

'Has Jane ever had a blood transfusion?' I asked as a
routine question. The answer was usually no.

'Yes,' said Musoke, 'she had a blood transfusion seven
years ago.'

Seven years ago she would have received unscreened
blood. She had almost certainly got the AIDS from the
blood that she was given.

Jane's sickness fluctuated for months but she gradually
deteriorated. Eventually Musoke accepted the diagnosis
but he was completely distraught. He had an AIDS test
carried out himself which showed that he was also positive
but at that stage it hardly seemed to matter to him any-
more. He was totally preoccupied with Jane. Robbie and I
saw him often and he expressed how he felt to us.

'I can't live without her,' he said, 'she is my right arm.'

He looked into the distance with that intense expression
of his and repeated, 'She is my right arm, she is part of me,
we have always been together, everywhere I have gone
she has been with me, we have never been separated. How
can I live without her?'

Robbie and I could hardly hold back the tears as we felt
his pain.

Musoke would go to any lengths to get treatment for her. We had a few tablets for treating the oral thrush which was causing her great discomfort, but they were very expensive and of limited availability. When our supplies ran out, he went to Kampala and bought them from a private pharmacy, paying thousands of shillings. He virtually stopped his work so that he could look after her. I wondered how the other wife fitted into all this. She was still around but very much in the background.

Jane's condition fluctuated for many months, sometimes feeling a little better, often being in acute discomfort. We often visited her and prayed with her. We would find Musoke sitting by the bed with his Bible open. I had seen few men so devoted to their wives. As she became weaker Musoke fed her, bathed her, took her to the toilet, lifted her and carried her. He was heartbroken. One day he talked to Robbie about the future. He had now watched Jane slowly dying over many months. He had been her nurse and attendant all through that period. He knew that he too had the AIDS virus.

'When Jane dies, who will look after me?' he confided. 'When I get sick who will feed me, bathe me and take me to the toilet when I am helpless? I have seen people with AIDS here and their family treated them like dogs.'

Musoke had a good family and it was unlikely that he would ever be treated in that way, but sadly, it was sometimes the case that some families neglected their sick relatives with AIDS, treating them worse than animals. He was a man burdened by sadness and grief.

As we continued to visit Jane she became more skeletal in form until she eventually faded away. Musoke had looked after her every need until the moment she died. The following day we went to the funeral and as we expressed our sympathy and shook hands with him, we realised how frail and tired he had become. The following week he came up to the hospital complaining of pain on his right side. He was seen by a doctor and an ultrasound scan was carried out. It showed cancer of the liver which is fatal – inoperable. There was nothing medically which could be done. Musoke went home to die. However none of us thought he would die so quickly. Within four weeks of Jane passing away Musoke was dead.

Perhaps he died from the combination of AIDS and cancer but more likely, he just had no will to live. He had lost the one who was his right arm, he had probably used up all his resources looking after Jane and watching her dying slowly. I think when he was told that he himself had cancer he let go his grasp on life. He had feared the possibility of a long lingering death from AIDS; at least he was spared that and he did not have to go on living without his beloved Jane. Perhaps the combination of circum stances and the timing of his own sickness dealt him a mortal blow.

Musoke had always said to me, 'you are my true friend. He had shared with us about his hopes and fears for his life at a deep level. He had a large family, with many brothers and sisters and cousins, but I think that he felt there were certain things which were not appropriate to share with them. Although he had the AIDS virus I had not expected him to die. I had wanted him to live, because he was a good man and a good friend. I wanted to talk to him again to hear his views and opinions. I respected him as an African. He had seen a lot of life. He had been through a lot, he had survived so much, yet now he was struck down

Perhaps I wanted him to live for selfish reasons. I didn' want to lose another friend. I valued the relationship, valued his advice. I didn't want to see all the good people die.

But I think life had thrown too much at Musoke. He had seen Jane pass away. He was tired, he was sick himself and he had no reason to go on fighting for life.

He let go and died.

Chapter 30

The Unwanted

Going to funerals in Uganda was almost a way of life as more and more people died of AIDS. I was usually able to go only to those of our closest friends like Musoke and Ando but although I wouldn't have considered the person being buried to have been a very close friend, this was a special occasion.

This funeral was a bit different. As I stood watching them lower the corpse into the grave I thought about all the other victims of this dreadful epidemic. Uganda had seen thousands die through war and civil strife, but AIDS would claim millions. Normally when someone died in the village everyone went to the funeral, even though they may not have known the person very well. Part of the reason was that they might not be well thought of by the relatives if they didn't go. People could even say that the person didn't go because he was happy that the other person died. It was expected that everyone would go to the funeral. Of course the relatives were expected to put on elaborate arrangements for the funeral. As people would arrive the previous evening and sleep overnight, food and shelter had to be provided. The mourners showed that they were grieving with the family by setting up loud wailing. New waves of wailing would arise with each successive influx of mourners. As all the relatives and friends were expected to attend, they had to leave their work and responsibilities to go to the funerals. Therefore attending funerals had become a regular pastime, so that other responsibilities to the living fell by the wayside.

Being Irish and knowing that the Irish wake had always been an important part of the culture, I had some sympathy with my Ugandan friends regarding their attitude to funerals, but when duties to the dead outweighed responsibilities to the living I drew the line. As Jesus said, 'Let the dead bury their own dead.' So I didn't usually have time to attend funerals.

However this case was slightly different to the norm. In this case there were no other mourners, except the grave diggers, the church lay reader and myself. There were no relatives or other friends, there was no wailing, none of the usual show usually seen on such occasions. Christine had no one left to mourn her. I suppose we at the hospital had become her only family. As I watched the soil being shovelled into the grave I thought of how we came into the world with nothing and left with nothing. 'Earth to earth, dust to dust, ashes to ashes,' the layreader intoned. But even so there was usually some evidence at the burial service of our life that had been. Usually our family were gathered there, our friends, those whom we had influenced in some ways. We didn't take any possessions with us, but we left some things to those that we loved and we left behind those in whom we would live on as a memory.

What of Christine? Who did she leave behind to love her memory? Which loved one did she give her worldly possessions to? She didn't have any. She had nothing to give, no loved one to entrust her memory to. She vanished into the ground, the only thing to remember her by was a patch of new-dug earth. How many others I asked myself, will die like Christine, before this AIDS plague is over? None of us wants to die with no one grieving for us.

In retrospect we had the tremendous privilege of showing Christine love while she was alive. One day, about one year previously, she showed up at the Out-Patients Department. She had weight loss, diarrhoea, skin rash and all the symptoms of AIDS. She was forty four. We counselled with her and gave her medicine. Heather was the one to see her and she finally told Heather that she didn't have any family or money. She was dirty, she smelled and her clothes were ragged and torn. She really wasn't someone that you would want to get too close to, but Heather reached out to her. She talked to her, prayed with her, gave her money and gave her one of her own dresses. She even gave her perfume. Christine had been told that she had AIDS, she had reason to be downcast, but the joy that she had over her new friendship with Heather, and being given the clothes and perfume, cancelled out everything else. Obviously no one had reached out to her and shown her love for a long time. She kept the money that she had been given, so that she could use it for transport to come back and see Heather again, and she became a regular visitor. She kept in contact with Heather for about a year until Heather had to go back to Ireland. Then one day I discovered her sleeping on the verandah of the hospital.

'What are you doing there?' I asked. 'Why don't you go home?'

'There is no one at home and I am too weak to dig my shamba (garden). There is no point in me going back to my village. I want to stay here, let me stay here and I will work at the hospital.'

She had no surviving relatives. They had all been killed during the war. Looking at her, I could see that she was emaciated, she was tired, and I knew she was in no fit state to work but I also knew that she was destitute and she had no one to go home to. So I made an arrangement whereby Christine would cook for another old lady who was crippled. They both stayed in a mud hut beside the TB Ward. Over the next few weeks I saw both of them frequently and I knew they were happy by the big smiles I was greeted with daily. But Christine's happiness was to be short lived. After only a few months her condition suddenly deteriorated and she died.

Although there were not many people to mourn for Christine, I grieved for her as she represented all those victims who had died, and would die anonymously of

AIDS. It was very unusual for anyone to die in Uganda without the support of their family. The extended family group consisted not just of father, mother, and children, but grandparents, aunts and uncles, half brothers and sisters. Indeed the term cousin or half brother was very rarely used. A relative was your brother or your sister or your father or mother. This used to cause tremendous confusion for me as it appeared that people had more than one father or mother. When I heard someone say he is my 'small father', that confused me even more, until I realised that 'small father' was their real father's brother, but because he was a brother to their father, he was considered a father to them. To call him anything less would have been disrespectful and indicated a lack of closeness in the family. The extended family had so many good aspects. For example if a relative arrived to stay he would never be turned away. He would be given a place to sleep and he could stay as long as he wanted. If a man's brother or sister died leaving children, they would be taken in without any fuss. Even children of distant relatives would be accepted. Therefore, although there were hundreds and thousands of orphans in Uganda, not many of them were completely homeless and not many were in institutions as they got taken in by the extended family. However the extended family also had its limitations. Children of the relative might not be sent to school if there were financial problems. They might be put to work in the garden or as water carriers or as minders of other children. This was not because the head of the family was being cruel, but because he didn't have the resources to look after any more children. With the extra demands placed on it through the AIDS epidemic, the extended family system was creaking at the seams.

Another problem was that of people like Christine who had no relatives. Her whole family had been killed during the war and she knew of absolutely no living relative. In certain parts of Uganda AIDS had wiped out all the adults leaving only children. Everyone tried to find homes for orphans and not to institutionalise them, but sometimes there was no other option and on occasions we ended up taking in orphans by default, because no one else would care for them. One such case was Moses.

A mother gave birth on the way to the hospital. I didn't hear the whole story, but the baby lived and the mother died, so the father arrived at the hospital with the new-born baby. He asked if we would look after the baby until he saw to the burial arrangements. A new-born baby in Uganda, without a mother, is in a precarious position. Usually they become malnourished, get infections and die within a short period. I told the father that we couldn't look after the baby for a long time, but we would keep him for a few weeks until he could organise something. It was a tragic situation for this father and this was the least that we could do. He returned a few weeks later to say he hadn't been able to make any arrangements and could we keep the baby a little longer? That was the last that was ever seen of him. Perhaps it was because the baby had club feet and he didn't want a disabled child. Perhaps he had decided the hospital was the best place for him. We will never know, but he didn't come back to collect his child. The baby had been born along a stretch of road which ran through a papyrus swamp so the midwives named him 'Moses' (the baby who was found among the bulrushes) and Moses grew up in the Maternity Ward. At first he stayed in a cot in the delivery room. I don't suppose he would remember it, but Moses must have been present during more deliveries than any other baby on record and one of the first words that he learnt to say was 'push!' From the moment he arrived, the midwives treated him as though he were their own son. Moses didn't have any natural mother to look after him, but he had at least six other substitute mothers, all loving him, caring for him, changing his nappy, bathing him, feeding him and talking to him. I have read about babies who were brought up in institutions and really lacked emotional stimulation. Moses certainly did not suffer from this problem as he had so much attention from so many people. These girls loved him and he thrived under their care. When Michael, our son, came back during school holidays the first person he wanted to see was Moses. He would bring him down to our house, feed him and even change his nappy if necessary. This baby was experiencing a truly cosmopolitan upbringing. The club feet were a problem. It was a severe deformity of both feet that needed surgery but the skill required were beyond our expertise at the hospital. Finally we were able to make arrangements to send him to Mulago hospital, the major teaching hospital in Kampala where there was an Orthopaedic Unit. The Professor of Orthopaedic Surgery operated on his feet and straightened them. He was sent back to us in plaster, which he then proceeded to get absolutely filthy. He obviously didn't like these things on his legs and somehow realised that a mixture of food, urine or any other liquid would make them soft. Eventually he succeeded. More plasters were applied. Now that he had got the idea the second lot were easier, so within a matter of days he had them sufficiently soft, smelly and disgusting that they had to be removed. A third plaster was applied and I was surprised to see Moses a few days later minus any plaster whatsoever.

'What happened to the plaster?' I asked the nurse.

'Oh, Moses removed it,' she replied.

Moses had obviously become completely fed up by the whole business by this stage so he apparently managed to chew and eat parts of it and the rest he had unwound. Despite Moses' determination to remove all plasters his feet were improving and he was now standing. He was a beautiful child who was healthy and normal in every way. I don't know what the future holds for him. Perhaps one of his substitute mothers will adopt him. Maybe like his biblical predecessor who was found among the bulrushes and led his society, Moses will become a leader of his own society. I think it is easy to believe that God has a purpose for the life of this little babe who was rescued from the swamp.

Moses was not the only orphan we had at the hospital. We had commenced a community health training programme at Namsale, about fifteen miles south of Kiwoko, where some twenty community health workers were receiving training. After one training session, Gudrun was approached by one of the village health workers about a family in his village. When Gudrun visited this family she found a number of children who appeared to be looking after themselves. It seemed that their mother had died and there was no father around. There was one older brother who was taking responsibility for the others and the older children were coping fairly well. However there were younger twins, the youngest of whom was in a worrying condition. In Uganda male twins are named Kato and Waswa, Kato being the first twin and Waswa the second. In this case Waswa was definitely the runt of the litter. While Kato was doing reasonably well, given the circumstances, Waswa looked like a famine victim. He was five years old but looked as if he was two or three; he was emaciated and miserable, and there was no doubt that if he wasn't given help urgently he would die.

Recognising that the other children were not in such dire straights and that they could continue to live in the community, with help from the neighbours and friends, Gudrun took Waswa back to the hospital for intensive nutrition therapy. At this time we didn't have a specialised nutrition unit at the hospital and Gudrun soon discovered that Waswa couldn't be properly treated in the general ward. He refused to eat and the nurses had difficulty looking after him as he had no attendant. So she took him to her house and kept him with her, where he could be fed under her constant supervision. Children who are severely malnourished usually have no appetite and unless they are fed small amounts, often they will not eat voluntarily. With perseverance, cajoling and threats Gudrun was able to make Waswa eat. Another characteristic which is common in severely malnourished children is that they are totally miserable. They never smile and they always seem

287

bad tempered. Waswa was no exception, he was a pathetic miserable little kid who looked awful. He was certainly not one of those lovable little African children who melts everyone's heart.

However Gudrun persisted with him and gradually he improved. Slowly he gained weight until the skeletal frame was covered with some flesh and he began to look more human. He would always be small, as his growth had been retarded at a critical time in his life, but at least he was beginning to look like a normal child. Then one day he smiled and we knew the battle was being won – Waswa would survive. By this time Gudrun had become very attached to Waswa, as had everyone else who was involved in looking after him, but she realised that she couldn't look after him in the long term and that she would have to make a more permanent arrangement for his future. Hence she contacted the orphanage, run by our friends Jay and Vicki Dangers, which was only a few miles down the road and asked if they could accommodate him. In that way he would still be in his own district but would be assured of a good education in a Christian family atmosphere. Over the next few years we saw Waswa frequently when we visited the orphanage, and each time he had a broad smile on his face. He was certainly a very different little boy from when we had first seen him. Perhaps it was because of Gudrun's strong maternal instincts, but she seemed to attract destitute children. Waswa was the first, but then there was Timothy and Juliette.

As the hospital grew we developed a small nutrition unit. However it was necessary for the children to have someone to look after them while they were there, in order to see that they were being fed regularly, washed and generally cared for. One day a very old man appeared with a very small miserable baby. At first we assumed that the baby was his grandchild, but it soon transpired that the child was actually the old man's daughter. This was a case where a very old man had taken a young bride who had borne him a child. The mother of the child had then died leaving the old man with a baby. Juliette, as we found she was called, was now between one and two years old. She weighed about five to six kilos and she cried all the time. We were told by the village health worker that the old man was a hunter and that when he went out on his hunting expeditions he left Juliette at home in the mud hut with some food and the dog to keep guard. However the dog ate the food.

This old man could hardly be blamed for poor treatment of the baby, he looked about seventy years old and obviously had no idea of how to look after a young child. It was surprising that the child was alive at all. When he brought her to the nutrition unit he wouldn't stay to look after her, the hospital was all too strange to him and he wanted to get back to his hunting. However Juliette needed someone to look after her almost twenty four hours a day, so Gudrun took her in. When she was busy at the hospital she employed a nanny, or jaja as they were called in Uganda, to look after her.

Around the same time Timothy arrived. He also had no mother and his father was having great difficulty looking after him. Timothy was under one year old and was severely malnourished. After his father had left him at the hospital he was never seen again. Timothy had been abandoned. Gudrun probably felt that since she was already looking after one child that she might as well look after two, so she also took in Timothy. Both Timothy and Juliette were hard to cope with, requiring to be fed by nasogastric tube at first. There was no easy road to their rehabilitation, they needed months of persistent nursing care and attention. However Gudrun did persist and they gradually improved. There is no doubt that without this, they would both have died. Timothy and Juliette stayed with Gudrun for the next year and during that time they were transformed from bad tempered miserable children who were very malnourished, to normal happy children who were thriving. Over the period they had become a brother and sister and Gudrun was keen to find a Ugandan family who would adopt them both. Since almost every family in Uganda is looking after the children of other relatives who have died through AIDS, war, or some other disaster, it is not easy to find a family who can take in extra children to whom they are not obligated. However Gudrun started asking around among churches and friends until she heard of a family in Kampala who were interested in adopting Timothy and Juliette. The old man who was the father of Juliette was contacted and was very happy with the proposal, so the children were installed in their new family. Once again it was hard for Gudrun as Timothy and Juliette had become her children, but there was no doubt that this was the best course of action for their future. They would be brought up in a family where they would be loved and cared for.

Christine, Moses, Waswa, Timothy and Juliette were the unwanted in their society, perhaps because all their relatives had died as in Christine's case, or their mothers had died as with all the others. These were the unwanted, not just of their own society, but of the whole world. Third world countries do not have any welfare state, so when someone falls off the rungs of the community's ladder there is no safety net to catch them; they end up on the bottom of the pile. People such as Gudrun were able to rescue some, but the majority who ended on the bottom of life's heap just lay there, until they were relieved from their sufferings by death. In today's age of instant technological communication, the plight of the victims who are at the bottom of life's heap is beamed into our living rooms daily. However most people are left not knowing quite how to respond. They can give some money, but they are still left with a vague uneasy feeling that something more needs to be done. It was certainly easier for me to meet these challenges head on, than to watch from afar, and be unable to do anything about it. On the other hand, constantly being on the raw edge of life was a draining process. One was continually assaulted by the grim realities of life for the 'have nots', those whose only sin was to be born into a society with few material resources. As we read through the gospel of Matthew at prayers with the staff in the mornings, we came to the story of the rich man and Lazarus. The rich man had everything in the world and Lazarus had nothing. Lazarus was definitely one of those at the bottom of the pile. However when they died their situations were reversed. Lazarus enjoyed the delights of paradise while the rich man scorched in hell. The teaching of the story indicated that the rich man didn't go to hell just because he was rich, but because he ignored the needs of Lazarus while he was on the earth and had the opportunity to do something about it. Perhaps it was easier for people like Gudrun and me who could get involved in the nitty gritty of the situation than for others somewhat removed from it. There was one thing for sure, we could certainly not ignore the harsh realities around us and we were glad that Jesus showed us a way of reaching out to people. The gospel we believed in, did bring a message of hope and care to the people on the bottom of life's pile and it wasn't one which consisted merely of words but which got involved with them where they were at, showed them love and gave them hope. None of us could measure what it meant to someone like Christine to be loved in the last few months of her life when she had no one left to love her.

Chapter 31

Partings and Disappointments

It seemed that our children were exposed to partings and death more than most children, because of the lifestyle we had chosen.

When we left Northern Ireland Sean had to leave his dog 'Lady' behind. Lady was a Cavalier King Charles Spaniel with big sad eyes and droopy ears. Sean was ten at the time and the decision to leave her behind was a real wrench for him. It was made a little easier, as the family who were going to look after Lady had a small handicapped child. As Sean parted from his friend, he consoled himself with the thought that at least Lady would bring some joy to that little child's life. Sean regarded Lady as being 'on loan' and felt his separation from her to be purely temporary. About a year after we left, a letter arrived. Lady had run in front of a car and been killed. As I read the letter I dreaded breaking the news to Sean. Lady might not have been a person but she had a personality. Sean hadn't seen Lady for a year, but in his mind he saw her scampering around, and he was looking forward to seeing her some time again in the flesh. When I broke the news as gently as I could, Sean looked at me for a moment and then his face crumpled and the tears flowed. The death of Lady illustrated the children's feelings about so many of their partings. Sean articulated it well:

'I could bear to be separated from her when I knew I

would see her again. Now I will never see her, never ever again. It's worse than if it were a person because I could see them in heaven, but I don't think I will ever see Lady again.'

Sean had a heavy heart.

'Mum, will there be dogs in heaven?'

Robbie had obviously not thought about that before and she wasn't sure that the Bible had much to say about it, so she was gentle but non-committal.

'Why don't you ask your Uncle Barney Coombs when we see him?' she suggested, knowing that he was visiting Uganda at the time, and feeling that Barney would have a greater theological knowledge of these matters.

It so happened that just a few days later, we were having lunch in a restaurant in Kampala when Barney unexpectedly arrived. Robbie had not had time to prime him, but this seemed like a good opportunity for Sean to ask his question. Sean was in good spirits and seemed to have accepted the death of his pet, so without any preamble Sean launched in.

'Uncle Barney, are there dogs in heaven?'

Without much thought Barney replied, 'No, I don't think so.'

The reply was disastrous for Sean. I can still feel his pain. He dissolved into tears. It was the dreadful finality of the separation that he found hard to accept. Barney immediately recognised the seriousness of the situation and called Sean over to his table where he and Sean had a private tête-a-tête. Sean may only have been eleven and Lady may only have been a dog but this was literally a life and death issue. He emerged from his session with Barney, smiling through the tears, but I don't think he ever got his question satisfactorily answered.

The reality of heaven sustained the kids through many experiences of the death of loved ones. When Barbara died, the whole family grieved together. We clung together and wept out our sense of loss and isolation. We comforted the children and wiped away their tears but the children comforted us.

'Don't cry, Mummy. We shall see Auntie Barbara in heaven.'

It seemed so simple and straightforward to the children. Barbara had died but she had simply gone to another place where we would one day meet again. In the same way that we had left Ireland and gone to Africa, Barbara had left earth and gone to heaven. We were parted but we would all meet up again one day.

One of Lauren's hardest experiences was being told of the death of her Uncle John. Uncle John was a Ballymena farmer. John and Lizzie had no children of their own so consequently they lavished all their love on the next generation of relatives' children. Every Sunday the extended family would gather at Uncle John's farmhouse. Aunts, uncles, nephews, nieces, brothers, sisters and, of course, the Great Grandma in her hard chair in the corner. Uncle John, who had now retired from farming would sit in his recliner with Lauren on his lap and the family around him, while Aunt Lizzie plied everyone with more tea and fresh home made cakes.

'Go on, Ian, have another, you must be starving,' and this barely an hour after we had feasted on a four course Sunday lunch at Nana Swann's house. Lauren formed a bond with her Uncle John, he represented kindness and security for her. I can't imagine what they talked about, but Uncle John was always special to Lauren. Then a few weeks after we had received the news of Barbara's death, Uncle John also died. Another of Lauren's links with the past had been cut. Gone was the experience of sitting on his lap, gone was that feeling of warmth and security she had had when the extended family met together. There would be no more such gatherings.

Death seemed to be a constant feature of life in Africa but one never got used to it. Christmas sometimes seemed to be an especially bad period when we were aware of more deaths in the hospital. One Christmas when we had just opened the General Ward of the hospital, I got malaria. Uganda is almost always hot but suddenly I was putting on a pullover and asking people if they didn't feel the chill. Robbie looked at me and instructed me.

'You had better get to bed and take some 'Fansidar'' (the treatment for malaria). So the day I should have been feeling a sense of achievement and satisfaction at having got another ward opened, I felt rotten. What was compounding my depression was the news from the nurses on the ward. Many sick babies had been admitted and too many of them were dying. When patients died I sometimes became introspective. 'Are we helping or hindering?' I would ask myself. 'I am sure there is more that we could have done, maybe we missed something.' People kept stealing in and out of my bedroom asking questions, 'shall we put this child on such and such?' 'the result of that patient's blood test is back.' But I was cheered up by one visitor. Ando crept quietly into the bedroom, and stood about two feet away from the bed.

'Sorry you are sick,' he commiserated, 'I would like to pray for you,' and without further ado he stretched his hand out over me and prayed for me to be healed. A few days later I was back on my feet and feeling much more positive about life. What encouraged me about Ando's prayer was its simplicity. None of us had ever instructed him how to pray or told him that it was the correct thing to do if someone was sick. He just heard I was sick and figured he could help by praying for me, so he appeared by my bed.

The toughest Christmas was the Christmas when Ando himself died. Robbie and I had known that he had AIDS for about three years but the children hadn't known. We felt it would be too hard on them to be told because he was so special to them. However when we picked them up from school for the Christmas holidays he was very ill, and we knew we had to prepare them for his death. But how do you tell your three children that one of their most beloved friends is going to die? We all sat in our hotel room on the way back from Kenya.

'You know that Ando has been sick recently,' I opened.

'Well your Mum and I have known for a long time that he has not been very well, in fact we have known for some time that he has AIDS.'

If Sean, Michael and Lauren had lived in Northern Ireland all their lives where AIDS was uncommon, they would have been shocked by this disclosure. As it was, their reaction wasn't one of shock but deep sadness for their friend. It was a reflection of having lived in Ugandan society for four years that the news of their friend dying of AIDS didn't arouse any questions such as 'how did he get it?' or, 'why?' but only a terrible heavy heartedness and sorrow because their friend had an incurable disease.

When we reached home the children went to sit by Ando's bed and held his hand. He could barely communicate with them by this stage, but he knew they were there. Ando's condition deteriorated quickly and he died within a few days. He passed away during the night and when I awoke Sean with the news the next morning, he said,

'Why do all the good people have to die?' and wept silently.

The holiday was made doubly distressing when another of our friends died. Lauren had a little Ugandan friend named Justine who was eleven and the oldest in a family of four. Her mother Joyce, was a teacher in the local school. Joyce had a lovely spirit despite the fact that she had a hard life. She had been abused by men, deserted by her 'husband'. Now she was bringing up four small children on her own. Despite all this, Joyce was one of those people who wanted to go deep in her knowledge of God. Every holiday Justine would come to our house to play with Lauren. She was a beautiful child and would also frequently bring little gifts. That Christmas Justine had an injured toe, so I had found some new shoes for her to wear. By way of thanks Justine's mum had sent us a present of a large bag of potatoes. A few days later Joyce was admitted to the hospital. She had been seen first by the medical assistant and appeared to be simply dehydrated from gastroenteritis. However as the day progressed Joyce's condition rapidly deteriorated and she died in the afternoon. Joyce died so suddenly that we were all shocked. Her four children had come to visit her and were waiting on the hospital verandah when she died. Robbie and I had been with Joyce and had watched aghast as she deteriorated and died within a few minutes. So Robbie had to take the children aside and tell them that their mother had just died. Lauren, as a child of eleven found herself in the position of having to comfort her friend Justine, who had just lost her Mum. Justine was crying and soothing the youngest brother who was still a baby. Lauren did what most adults would have done, she took them down to our house and offered them food and a drink – biscuits and coke in this case. They sat in a row on the settee and stared ahead of them – four little orphans who had no idea what the future held for them – and Lauren tried to comfort them.

If we had stayed within the UK our children would not have been exposed to so much sickness and death, but the experience was not all bad for them. Even at a young age they had learned not to take life for granted, they had experienced death at close quarters and it made them appreciate the gift of life. It had also deepened their own faith and trust in God. We had never force-fed the kids on our beliefs, but during many of these experiences I had seen them find a source of stability and confidence in their own faith in God. Sometimes when I said 'Good-bye' to the children for yet another school term I felt that their lives were full of partings. Saying 'Good-bye' to their grandmothers when they left Ireland, saying 'Good-bye' to friends at school who were leaving Africa, final partings from friends who had died and the regular partings from their parents. Often it wasn't easy for us, but one thing I noticed as a result of these partings, we all appreciated the relationships with one another far more deeply.

Perhaps all the partings the kids endured prepared them for the time when I got sick myself and had to immediately fly back to Ireland. The decision was taken so suddenly, that it must have been a terrible shock for the children.

However they all urged that Robbie should go back with me to Ireland immediately, leaving them to follow later. That particular parting was the most difficult I have ever experienced. There were no certainties for the future any more, everything had changed and none of us knew what the next day held, or if we would have a future together. Could life ever be the same again as we had known it? As we hugged the children and held them in our arms, our emotions were too deep for words – very little was said, except a few 'I love you's', then we were on our way waving at the little group who were a part of us.

The children joined us later in Ireland when I was undergoing treatment. They had expected to be back at school among their friends at Turi but instead found themselves adjusting to new schools and a different life in Ireland. It was a big upheaval for everyone, but it was going to mean a complete disruption for Sean, as he was in the final year of his International GCSE course. If he was to change courses at this stage he would probably lose a year's schooling, perhaps he should go back to school in Kenya. Sean was torn, he wanted to be with me but he also wanted to pass his GCSEs. In some ways his motivation was just to please me, he knew I wanted him to study well and pass his examinations, but he also wanted to be with me. After a lot of thought, we finally decided that Sean should travel back to boarding school in Kenya. All of us felt more peace about this decision; we didn't want to be parted at this critical time, but we knew that no matter what happened to me, life must go on for Sean.

It was not an easy process for Sean to go through. There were many conflicting interests and emotions at work. He wanted to be with me, he wanted to continue his course, above all he wanted me to get better and I wasn't showing much sign of that. It all spilled over on the night before he left. The night before, when I had been going to bed, I had been very sick as I went up the stairs. It was a loud and uncomfortable retching which went on for quite some time. I didn't know that Sean was awake, but he was and he heard it all. The next night as we talked a few things over before Sean left, he mentioned that he had heard me being sick the previous night.

'Dad, I prayed that the sickness would stop,' he said, 'but it just went on and on. I got so mad at God. Why didn't he stop it? He could have, but He didn't.'

Sean was in tears, he wanted his prayers to be effective and he wanted me to be healed. How did one answer the heartbreak of one's son? Sean was speaking out a deep struggle of faith which would not be answered by any stock answer. It always helps in these situations if you have been through the same heartsearchings and questions yourself. I had struggled with the same question many times before. As I stood beside the bed of someone who was suffering and cried 'God, do something', it was never an academic matter for me. I wanted God to change situations right there and then because I was asking him, because I couldn't bear to see the person suffer any longer.

'Sometimes, Sean,' I said, 'I have stood at the end of the bed of a patient and prayed the same prayer, and usually I have been disappointed, because I didn't see the patient healed instantly. Often I cried like you – "God do something" – but the heavens were silent. Then I would look around at what had been done, I would see the hospital which had been built, I would see all the patients who had been healed and I would compare it with what was there before and I would know that God had not been deaf to my prayers. I would know that He did care about these people in their need. Sometimes, Sean, we do not see our prayers answered immediately but we have to look at the bigger picture. As I look back over my life, I see so much that was beyond my control, so many "coincidences" working together to allow things to happen. In 1986 I prayed, "Lord, put me somewhere where I am needed." At that time I had never heard of the Luweero Triangle. I didn't know that they desperately needed doctors there. But that is where I ended up. I believe that is where God put me, as an answer to my prayers. I don't think it is any coincidence that things worked out so that we were able to build the hospital, I don't think all the things which have happened to us over the past five years were coincidences, I see the fingerprints of God on what has happened.'

The next day Sean flew back to Kenya to continue his course at St Andrew Turi. He wrote to us regularly while he was away and his letters were upbeat. However we knew from other people that he was going through struggles because he was worried about me, yet he was separated from us by thousands of miles. Michael and Lauren had also suffered tremendous dislocation by being suddenly thrust back into a different society, but they adapted readily. Lauren seemed to have adjusted well to the new situation, she had a good group of new friends and she was enjoying school. Then one day we were sent a video from Kiwoko of the staff and friends there. When Lauren had seen the video she said softly to me,

'Dad, I want to go home.'

'But you are home,' I replied.

'No, I want to go home to Uganda and Kenya. I want to be with my friends in Uganda and Kenya again, I want to see Justine. I want to see people like that who are simple and straightforward.'

Lauren's heart was still in Africa.

Through all these situations the children increased their depth and experience of life, they had seen people die. They had said good-bye so many times and in many different places in the world, but they had also made friends and known so many people. They were still just children, but their journey through life had given them a far greater depth of experience and insight than many adults. We were not sorry that we had exposed them to life's traumas, there was no way that we could have shielded them even if we had tried. We hoped that when their time came, they would be ready to face the world for themselves without fear, yet with a real understanding of what life is all about. We hoped that they in turn could bring compassion and understanding to others who were in need or without hope.

Chapter 32

Cancer

I hadn't realised how my life could be changed in a moment.

Before that moment I had been going about life in the usual busyness of the hospital and making plans for the future. After that moment everything changed, including any plans I had made. The moment came when I saw the picture of my own chest X-ray. As I stood gazing at it outside the X-ray room, all the other key people from the hospital arrived as if sensing by instinct that something momentous was about to happen.

'Are you sure that is my X-ray?' I asked Isaac the Radiographer.

'Yes, Doctor,' he replied. 'I have just developed it.'

The lower two thirds of the picture were covered in small round blotches. I knew what they were. Doctor Richard knew what they were, Isaac knew what they were, but no one was prepared to say. Finally I said,

'They look like secondaries from cancer.'

'Yes, secondaries.' Isaac complied a little too eagerly, relieved that someone else had said it first.

So the moment had arrived. I knew I had cancer with secondaries in the lungs. Everything in my life was about to change.

For a number of months I had been having backache, but then with the bumpy roads and the amount of driving I did, I regarded my problem as fairly normal. Lots of people got backache. However, despite advice from a physiotherapist, bed rest and pain killers, my backache wouldn't go away. I even had to admit that it was getting worse. Sometimes I would start a ward round determined to carry on as normal, only to have to abandon it half way through. I knew that I was causing confusion and consternation to the nurses when I suddenly walked out in the middle of the round, but I found I could not carry on, I needed to sit down or lie down. Then the next day I would try again. Sometimes I would be a little more successful and make it to coffee time, so that it did not look so obvious that I had abandoned things in the middle. I wasn't a worrying type of person, I figured that everyone had backache at some time or other and it would ultimately go away. I just felt somewhat guilty about not getting on with my work properly.

I had just passed my fortieth birthday and I noticed that I was becoming more tired, but I felt my fatigue could be accounted for by the frenetic pace we kept up, and after all I was getting old! At forty I was over the hill. I confided to our friends, the Brownlees, that I had periods of exhaustion and I wondered if I was no longer up to the pace of life in Africa. However the exhaustion would pass and I would carry on as normal. There were always things to be done, responsibilities to be taken care of. The pace of life carried on and the demands of it carried me on as a flood carries a piece of driftwood. Usually I didn't have to make the decision to get up and go, the pull of the different demands on me just kept me going, that was until I was just too exhausted to carry on, or the backache was too excruciating to allow me to continue. However, after some rest and some pain killers I would be ready to go again. I noticed that my weight was slowly falling, but the decline was slow and unremarkable. Robbie would comment that I looked haggard and gaunt, but that was, after all, not so different from many other colleagues who worked in tropical conditions. The weight loss was accelerated by a couple of uncomfortable bouts of dysentery which left me drained. I had to admit that I seemed to be going through a period of poor health, but all the symptoms seemed unrelated and didn't add up to a unified clinical picture. Backache and tiredness were exactly the sort of symptoms that patients commonly complained of, but were difficult to pin down as a specific disease process. Patients were usually treated with pain killers and advice on posture and rest. If the backache persisted, an X-ray would be carried out. This was exactly the agenda I had for myself and when the X-ray of the back was carried out it showed nothing abnormal.

By this time much of the routine clinical work had been taken over by Richard, a CMS doctor who had arrived with his wife and family six months earlier. I was very glad that my poor health had occurred when there were other doctors available and not when I had been running the hospital alone, as in the previous six months. As my health continued to deteriorate, Richard was concerned and suggested further investigations. So a block of blood tests was taken. All were normal except one, the ESR, which was grossly elevated. It should have been at a level of ten or below, but my reading was over one hundred. Unfortunately, while this test indicated that something was wrong, it was a very non-specific indicator of disease. I had just suffered an episode of bacilliary dysentery followed by amoebic dysentery, so the raised ESR could have been caused by any of those. Nevertheless I was surprised to find this abnormal result. That night the back pain was so severe that I had to have an injection of pethidine. Richard was now seriously concerned. He suggested that I should have some more tests such as an AIDS test and a chest X-ray.

I had had an AIDS test several months before which had been negative, so I didn't think the chances of me having contracted AIDS in the intervening period were very high, but I was happy to go along with the suggestion and have another test. AIDS had been a very definite possibility to account for my tiredness and weight loss.

Robbie and I had considered it some months earlier. Sometimes at night as we lay in bed Robbie would question me.

'Do you think you *could* have AIDS Ian?'

As I pondered the question, I had to admit there was a definite possibility. I had carried out a lot of surgery over the last two years, a spot of blood in the eye, a minor puncture wound or a splash of blood on broken skin, was all but impossible to avoid. However I reminded myself that the statistics on the incidences of AIDS through medical contamination were very low.

'No, I don't think I have AIDS,' I would reassure Robbie.

But just to be sure I had a test carried out. The chest X-ray was also a routine screening measure. I had no chest symptoms, but in the normal manner of doctors looking for a diagnosis, which was not immediately apparent, it was routine to order a whole batch of investigations in the hope that something abnormal would show up, which would lead to a specific diagnosis. So purely as a matter of routine a chest X-ray was ordered. I confidently expected it to be normal, as I had absolutely no problems with my chest. So when the X-ray was carried out I was sublimely oblivious to what lay in store for me.

As I stood in shock at seeing the X-ray I commented, more to myself than anyone else, 'That's a terrible X-ray.'

Robbie had heard enough, she ran down to the house to be with the children. Sean, now aged fifteen, immediately sensed that something was terribly wrong and within a few minutes he extracted from his Mum the information that his Dad probably had cancer. He held his Mum in his arms and comforted her. By this stage my mind was whirling, what should I do? We had now carried out all the investigations our hospital had to offer. It was now a matter of urgency that I go back to Ireland for more tests. What about the kids? Perhaps they could stay here until I got a definite diagnosis, for although the X-ray looked like secondary cancer there was a slight possibility the changes might be due to TB or some other obscure tropical chest disease. Also if it was cancer, where was the primary site? Getting a specific diagnosis would tell me what the prognosis or the outlook was, in a word, how long I could expect to live. I felt that if I went back to Ireland immediately and got the answers to all these questions, then the children could join me and we could plan for the future – if there was a future. Robbie was torn.

'I can travel on my own,' I said. 'You stay and look after the kids.'

However I was in poor physical condition and the children were adamant that she go with me.

'We have lots of friends here. You need to go back and look after Daddy.'

It was true they would be in good hands. Heather who had worked at Kiwoko had since been married, and she and her husband Andrew were visiting again. They could take care of the kids. Later that afternoon, having thrown a few things into a suitcase, we left for Kampala. Saying goodbye to our children was hard. They were such a spunky little lot, they had seen so many changes and been in so many different circumstances without any complaints, but this was different. Their Dad was very ill and they didn't know exactly when they would see him, or what the results of the tests would show. We waved goodbye to the forlorn little group and I waved goodbye to Kiwoko. I hadn't the strength or the emotional stamina to collect the staff together to say a formal goodbye. Anyway there wasn't time. So we left, not knowing if we would ever see the place or the people again. Kiwoko had been my life, I loved the people, it was my home. It had grown up from nothing to a fully equipped hospital. I just couldn't have faced a final goodbye. I handed the responsibility over to Richard and we drove away. The following day as we walked across the tarmac of Entebbe airport to catch our flight to Nairobi and on to Ireland, Richard and Heather were there with their children to see us off.

'We love you Clarkes,' they called out to us as we left.

I was too choked up to respond. Indeed we felt their love for us as we felt the love of all our friends at Kiwoko. Richard and Heather had come out to Africa to run a hospital in Zaire. Only a few months after arrival the political and security situation in Zaire became very unstable and they had to leave. They were in a state of confusion and disillusionment because of this, as Richard had given up his job in England to take on this work, and then they had to flee the country after only a few months in the job. It was at that point that we met them in Kampala and suggested that they come to Kiwoko to help us. This they had agreed to, but only for an interim period until they sorted out their own future. Now suddenly I was departing and the whole responsibility for the medical oversight of the hospital was descending on Richard. Unknown to either of us, over the previous six months, Richard had been prepared for a future as Medical Superintendent of Kiwoko.

I was glad that Robbie was travelling with me. My condition was deteriorating so quickly that it was doubtful I could have coped with the rigours of the flight on my own. Robbie was my ministering angel and she willingly continued that role during all the time that I was sick and in need. The flight took us from Entebbe to Nairobi, to Paris, London and finally Belfast. We had a stopover in Paris for three hours and as we sat in the airport departure lounge awaiting our onward connection, we were at last able to articulate some of our thoughts. As we looked ahead both of us were close to tears. Although there was the vague hope that the chest X-ray picture represented some inflammatory disease, I was almost certain it was cancer. The widespread extent of the disease also convinced me that it was too late for a cure.

'I am so glad that we have had the last five years in Kiwoko,' I murmured. 'It has all been worthwhile, I wouldn't change any of it.'

But as we looked ahead to a future apart we could hardly bear to think about it. We didn't regret the past, and we didn't fear the future, but a tremendous sadness had descended upon us as we looked ahead.

On arrival back in Ireland I immediately made an appointment with a chest physician. We put the X-rays on the viewing box.

'What do you think?' I asked, hoping that he would talk about the possibility of atypical TB or some other rare inflammatory disease.

'Well, I have to say that it looks like cancer,' he responded. 'Do you see how well defined those blotches are? That is typical of cancer.'

I had been almost certain that the chest X-ray showed cancer, but there had still been a small ray of hope in the back of my mind that the chest physician would suggest other less sinister possibilities. These hopes were dashed when he pointed out that these particular forms of shadows were very typical of cancer. However we still hadn't established a specific diagnosis. We knew the cancer in the lung hadn't originated there, but had spread from somewhere else within the body. Then there was my back pain to be explained, more persistent and more acute than ever. The consultant suggested having a CT scan carried out, and doing a needle biopsy of the lungs, under scan control. In that way we would get a definite answer from the scan and from the pathological result of the biopsy. Unfortunately a scan was not available until Friday, five days later. We would still be in a state of suspense for another five days. As Robbie and I drove home a cloud of despondency settled on us. We were now facing the fact squarely that I had cancer and that the outlook was likely to be poor. I knew as a doctor that most cancers, which had secondary spread as far as the lungs, were incurable. By that time the cancer would be established throughout the body and usually there was little which could be done to eradicate it.

However our despondency wasn't despair. We had to face whatever the future held for us. We had to talk about things and make preparations. I couldn't just turn my back to the wall and die. I had to communicate with my wife about what was best for her and the family. We needed to say things to each other, even if the tears sometimes flowed. If this was the end, many things needed to be said and done while I was in a fit state. I phoned up my financial agents to check on life insurance and make sure that policies and details would be easily available. We did our sums on how much the family would have to live on, whether it would be better to buy a smaller house, what schools we would like to send the children to. Above all we talked to one another about how we felt. I saw a wall up ahead, as if I had been driving down the avenue of life, turned the corner and suddenly found that the avenue which I had expected to be on for many years still, had become a dead end. Someone had built a wall across my road. I realised how many of my hopes in life were tied up with an expectation of a future, a future to see the children grow up, a future swopping jokes with Sean and Michael, talking things over with the family, sampling Lauren's cooking, a future to see them reach the profession they desired, get married and have kids themselves. Now I had no future. I was cut off from the land of the living and when I realised I would be cut off from my family for the future I was filled with deep sadness – a depth of sadness which I have never known before. When Robbie and I looked back over our life together we were glad we had good memories, we thanked God for all the experiences we had walked through together. We had been married for nineteen years and had always been close. Robbie was not only my wife she was my best friend. Both of us were especially thankful that we had been able to work in Kiwoko for the past five years.

'You know,' I confided in Robbie, 'God's timing in this is good. If this had happened five years ago I would have been so frustrated. I wanted to serve God at that time but couldn't see how my life style was really doing that. Now we have had the unique opportunity to serve Him in Kiwoko. At least if I have to go now I can look back on the past five years and know it was the best thing I have ever done in my life.'

Robbie also looked ahead to see what life would be like without me.

'I just can't see myself as a single person again,' she confided. 'I have been your wife, part of a married couple for so long that I can't imagine life on my own. I will find it so difficult to relate to other married couples.'

When we talked about these things and prayed together we had no sense of rebellion against God. We did not go through the questioning 'why me?' because we had already seen so much suffering. Death and suffering seemed to be a part of life at Kiwoko. Robbie had sat by Ando's bed only that Christmas as he died. We had witnessed the emaciation, diarrhoea, and so many other painful and uncomfortable symptoms of patients dying of AIDS. Many of these were young people. We realised that in a large part of the world people could not automatically expect their three score years and ten. Indeed our attitude had changed through all this from, 'why me?' to 'why not me?' We didn't see God as responsible for all the pain and suffering. God had even sent Jesus to be with people in their suffering. We understood that suffering, sickness and death came through Satan and evil, not from God. There was good and evil at work in the world. We were committed to the good but, we were not immune from the effects of the evil. I didn't want to die, I loved living but if I died I had no regrets. I was committed to God's hands, Robbie and the children were in God's hands, we could trust our future to Him. In that sense, although we were going through a cloud we were not despairing. We might not be able to put our hope in a future together but we could put our hope in God. I saw then how much we naturally do put our hope in the future, a future which could be taken away from us, but I also realised that beneath that, we had a firm hope which couldn't be taken away, our hope in God. I could not deny the immense sadness which I felt, but it was not a sadness of gloom or filled with regrets, it was the sadness of parting from all that I loved. I loved Robbie and I loved Sean, Michael and Lauren. I loved the people I had worked with in Kiwoko. We had shared the same vision, we had suffered together, we had done something good together in this world. It struck me how irrelevant material things were at this point. We could make such an investment of our time in material things but from my perspective, now they suddenly had no value. When about to go through the door of death the currency had changed and materialism no longer had a value.

Before I had left Uganda Christina suggested testicular cancer as a possible diagnosis for the primary site of my cancer. However I had no lumps or bumps or swellings and I understood that if the primary site was testicular I would have some objective signs. That form of cancer gave a better prognosis than most, but I had discounted the possibility because of the lack of physical signs. So when the CT scan was carried out I did not know what diagnosis to expect. The scan took pictures of slices, or cross sections, of the body. The radiologist moved me through the tube taking pictures of the lungs and then the abdomen. After taking the pictures of the abdomen he stopped the process.

'From what I have seen so far,' he explained, 'the pattern I am finding all points to carcinoma of the testis. It may not be necessary to do the biopsy to get a definite result. We can do an ultrasound-scan which will give us the answer.'

The ultra-sound confirmed the radiologist's suspicions. The right testis was almost totally invaded by a tumour which had not caused any irregularity or change in shape that had been noticed by me. The cancer had then spread rapidly to the lymph nodes of the back and to the chest. That explained the back pain, the nodes were pressing on the nerves and causing pain.

Within the last few years a regime of chemotherapy had been developed for testicular cancer which was giving very promising results. The chemotherapy regime itself was very harsh but the results were good. The doctor carrying out the ultra-sound must have wondered why I was so happy to hear I had cancer. The fact was that I already knew I had cancer but I hadn't dared to hope that it would be this particular form of cancer which could perhaps be dealt with. I felt like Hezekiah in the Old Testament who was given another fifteen years of life. I didn't know how many years of life I would be given, but life and hope for the future had opened up for me again. I thought again of the verse from Jeremiah 29:11 which one of the staff at Kiwoko had sent me.

> *'For I know the plans I have for you, declares the Lord, plans to prosper you and not to harm you. Plans to give you a hope and a future.'* (RSV)

It was as if God was saying to us that He still had plans for *us* and he was giving *us* back a hope and a future. Our work here was not yet finished.

By the time the chemotherapy started we had been reunited with our kids who had travelled back with Heather and Andrew. On meeting them at the airport I could see how anxious they were about me. Lauren wanted to hold my hand and be near me and tell me that she loved me. Michael's face was puckered up, trying to control the tears and Sean hugged me. He was getting big now and it felt like a manly hug.

'How are you, Dad?' he enquired with concern in his eyes.

I couldn't honestly say that I was fine which would have been the usual reply in Uganda. Even if a person was dying he would reply 'fine'. Unfortunately I was definitely not fine. Just before commencing the treatment I remarked to Robbie that I was glad treatment was starting, as I felt I was slipping away.

Every day I was becoming weaker and losing more weight. The back pain had become increasingly severe to the point where it was only relieved by morphine. I knew that without treatment my days were numbered. Unfortunately the drugs I was about to get were indiscriminate in their action. They killed cancer cells but they also took a heavy toll on the rest of the body. Chemotherapy drugs are essentially poisons. The poison kills rapidly multiplying cells, therefore cancer cells are vulnerable. It also kills other rapidly multiplying cells in the body. Consequently the hair falls out, the gut and kidneys can be affected, the bone marrow suppressed, so that resistance to infection falls etc. Just how poisonous the drugs were, was demonstrated by the fact that the nurses used goggles and gloves to change the drip, in case they got a splash on the skin or the eye. I was at a low point when the treatment was commenced – I was dehydrated, emaciated and still suffering the after-effects of the bouts of dysentery that I had in Uganda. Whatever the reason I was one of those people who had every side-effect in the book from the chemotherapy and a few others which weren't in the book. The treatment regime for this form of cancer, involved being admitted to hospital for five days, during which time I was on intravenous fluids or chemotherapy twenty four hours a day. After the hospital treatment, I was discharged for two weeks. Then the whole process was repeated again. The regime could be carried out four to eight times depending on response. The first day passed reasonably uneventfully and I began to hope that I would escape the worst side-effects. However during the second night I began vomiting profusely. It felt as if my guts were trying to turn themselves inside out. Then came the diarrhoea and the nausea. The pattern continued for the next five days. Visitors who came were turned away as I was too sick to see them. It was a truly awful period during which I could think of nothing beyond my own nausea, sickness and diarrhoea. My world narrowed to a bed, a toilet and a sink. This change in my role from doctor to patient was very hard, but it taught me valuable lessons. I would not advocate that doctors should be put through symptoms such as I had, just so that they could empathise with their patients. However since I had been dealing with seriously ill patients and in particular with AIDS sufferers, my own illness allowed me to understand subjectively what many of them went through.

One thing which became clear to me was that if a person had a symptom which was severe, everything else in life would become secondary to that symptom. The person's life would narrow to a preoccupation with his particular problem. It could be an AIDS patient with severe diarrhoea, or mouth ulcers, or profound weakness or nausea. It could be a cancer patient being severely nauseated from chemotherapy. This was a time when the person might appreciate prayer, but to be active in their own faith was beyond them. I realised that there was a time in someone's illness when it was inappropriate to expect them to do anything apart from get through their suffering. It was not a time for preaching, but for words of encouragement or prayer.

During this time many people prayed for us. In fact we were overwhelmed by the number of people who contacted us to say they were praying and the number of letters we received from all over the world. We were constantly hearing of churches, individuals and prayer groups, many of whom we had no previous contact with, who were praying for us. One church, a large Pentecostal church in Belfast, which had not previously known me had 700–1,000 people meeting weekly at their prayer meeting. When they heard about my illness they not only prayed for me at every prayer meeting but raised several thousand pounds for the hospital. These were people who had never seen my face and never heard of Kiwoko hospital before. The spectrum of Christian denominations which got involved in praying was amazing. Baptists, Pentecostals, Catholics, Reformed Presbyterians, Anglicans, Fellowship churches, Presbyterians, Methodists. The prayers and love which they reflected were like a net stretched out below me. Without that support I might have slipped away and fallen into the abyss of despair. I was weak but other people were holding me up. I had never been in such a position of weakness before and I discovered what it was like to be totally dependent on other people. Of course the chief among those upon whom I depended was Robbie. She became more than my right arm, in my complete weakness she was my link with the outside world.

When I was discharged from hospital after five days of treatment I thought that I would now climb back to recovery. Unfortunately this was not to be, and my condition continued to deteriorate. By this stage I looked like a skeleton. My weight had fallen to eight stone (or 112 pounds). My muscles were severely wasted and bones protruded where before there had been flesh to cover them, I looked like an advert for famine victims. My hair was falling out and when I looked at myself in a mirror, a skull with sunken eye sockets leered back at me. I felt that sometime during the illness someone had stolen my own body and given me this leering half dead, famine victim's body. This body just didn't seem to fit me any more and bore no resemblance to the person I had once been. My clothes hung off, I couldn't eat, I vomited persistently and the diarrhoea continued. I couldn't lie on a normal mattress or sit on a chair as my bones protruded and it was too painful. Robbie bathed me, fed me, changed my clothes, helped me walk, encouraged me and loved me through it all. Friends from the church brought food every day, the Elders from the church anointed me with oil and prayed over me. Gradually I started to improve, every day I was a little better, the nausea stopped and the diarrhoea lessened. I regained my appetite and for a time I even had a craving for food.

The treatments still continued and were a time to be endured with much nausea and vomiting. However the severe debility was gone. If I could endure the side effects I could see I was definitely improving. Being immobilised by being connected to a drip for a week, becoming more and more familiar with the sink and the toilet, feeling nausea rise within me until a certain point when I would then 'throw up'. All these were not very pleasant to deal with and I could only have endured them because I knew the treatment was helping and I was looking forward to the end each time. I didn't feel a strong faith or a depth of trust in God as I went through these episodes, I just tried to get through them, but many people prayed on my behalf.

Over a period of five months I was in hospital seven times. I had numerous X-rays and scans. I had surgery, chemotherapy and biopsies. As a doctor, I got the best insights possible into how different hospitals, wards, consultants and nurses worked. Sometimes I didn't care what happened to me. I was too weak, or too sick to be bothered. Sometimes I didn't want to be treated as a 'patient', I wanted to get out of my wheelchair, or bed, and say 'I am a human being too, I am not just a patient.'

Sometimes I refused to play the part of the patient which I realised that everyone wanted me to assume. Hospital wards could not run if everyone did not assume their appropriate role. Doctors wore white coats and carried stethoscopes, nurses wore uniforms and patients wore pyjamas. There was a hierarchy. Nurses did what doctors told them and patients did what nurses told them. Most of the time, I was too sick with the chemotherapy to notice. However I did appreciate the care I got from the nurses. Often there was little they could do, but just sitting with me, or expressing their concern was enough. Some nurses unconsciously adopted a maternal attitude. They would even use a simpler grammar, or insert endearing terms. These were automatic little mannerisms that some nurses adopted to express to the patient that they cared for them. However they also conveyed the other message – you are helpless, you are childlike, you are a patient.

At one point in my treatment I was admitted to the thoracic unit to have a lung biopsy carried out. All the preliminary investigations had been done by the late afternoon but I had to spend the evening and night in the ward,

317

as I was listed for theatre first thing the next day. However I knew there would be no further tests and I wanted to spend the evening productively in the hospital library. It was rather thoughtless of me not to tell someone where I was going, but I didn't think anyone would miss me for a few hours. This was definitely not the case. Sister spied me leaving with my coat on and was sure I was absconding. Messages were passed to security and the higher echelons of the hospital. By the time I returned a few hours later I was confronted by a very cross little staff nurse who wanted to know just where exactly I had been off to, and did I know there was a security alert out for me? I was suitably contrite, as I had indeed caused worry and concern. The nurses were obviously not used to patients wandering off to the medical library to spend the evening – so that was the reason they sent the patients' clothes home!

Between treatments I was now beginning to enjoy life again, I appreciated the simple things – the fresh sea air, the view along the coast line, having a meal with old friends, being part of a worship service. Life was flowing back to me and many sensations were heightened. As I looked at my children I was overawed. These were my flesh and blood, each so individual, such unique personalities and I still had a part to play in their lives. I could still take them in my arms and love them. Michael and I could shed a tear together because we had each other. Lauren could still bury her face in my neck and whisper 'I love you.' Sean could give me a hug. I looked on in awe and wonder, I was still alive to enjoy them and to see them grow up. Robbie had a verse from the psalms for me *'May you see your children's children.'* Even now I hardly hope that this might be true but for however long, in whatever terms, God had given me back life. Sometimes Robbie and I just stared into each other's eyes searching each other, wanting to possess the other, because we were still here for one another.

As I slowly began to reorientate and look towards a future again I realised that things could never be the same again. As far as I was concerned life had almost come to an end, then it had been given back to me. What would I do with this new life? When we had faced death we didn't rebel against God. We knew that God wasn't being unfair to us, but that we were part of the circle of living and dying which we saw all around us. Every day we saw people die of AIDS, or sickness, or strife. This was not God's plan but the result of Satan's influence in the world. Our place was to bring love and hope in the midst of a sick despairing world. If in the process I too got sick I could not rebel against it. I couldn't say I was a better person than another who was suffering and therefore it was unfair that I should be afflicted. There wasn't an opt-out clause from suffering for Christians. Instead of saying 'Why me?' we could as legitimately ask 'Why not me?' No one was exempt. Now that I had been given back the hope of life I could ask the question the other way round 'Why me?' 'Why have I been given the unique gift of life again. What purpose is there in it?' Joseph's words came again to my ears from the Old Testament:

> *'You intended to harm me, but God intended it for good.'* (RSV)

Joseph nearly rotted in a jail, but he was brought out and given new life so that he could save his people from hunger and famine. Now I could say that I had almost died of cancer but I had been given back life. I couldn't presume to know how long that life might be for. But every extra day that I had was God's gift to me. What was the purpose of that life to be? Perhaps it was completely presumptuous to think that my life should be meaningful?

Then I remembered my friend Ando. He had ony three years of life after he got the diagnosis of AIDS. Three years is a very short span of life. Ando was just an African man living in the village. How could a mere three years of his life be significant? He was thirty three when he died. During the last three years of his life he helped to build a hospital. He was my right hand man and he was often the person who held things together. He gave the last three years of his life to build a hospital to help the poor and sick of his community and in the process he bore witness to much of the meaning of life. It was too easy for any of us to say 'Why me? My life is not significant, I am just getting on with living, I am a cog in a wheel, I have not been put here for any purpose.' It is too easy to be part of the crowd but when we truly realise the value of our lives, we will say 'Why not me? My life can have a purpose too.'

As I looked back over the past five years and saw those who had laid down their lives for a purpose, I was filled with awe. Barbara, Sarah, Ando. They were all close friends and their death meant a lot of pain and suffering, but their lives were filled with purpose. They laid down their lives in the service of their God and they left behind them a legacy of good for others to see and partake of. The example of Barbara's love and godliness inspired many of us to keep on. It was from her love for the people of Luweero that the very hospital itself came into being. Ando was a unique individual who came to faith and lived that faith out consistently and steadfastly as he served God and built the hospital. Sarah was like a ray of sunshine to us all. She lived her faith, spoke her faith, sang her faith, ministered to the sick and encouraged everyone around her. These were three people whose lives and deaths were intricately bound up with the birth and development of the hospital. They gave their lives to God and now, even though they are dead, others have received new life through them. It can be said of their lives as it was said of Abel in Hebrews *and by it, he being dead yet speaketh.*'

For further information contact:
   'Friends of Kiwoko Hospital'
   Holy Trinity Church, Amersham Road
   Hazlemere, High Wycombe
   Bucks HP15 7PZ
   England